W9-CKP-803

The New York Times

Practical Traveler Handbook

The New York Times
Practical Traveler
Handbook

An A–Z Guide to

Getting There

and Back

Betsy Wade

TIMES BOOKS

RANDOM HOUSE

Copyright © 1994 by Betsy Wade

All rights reserved under International and Pan-American Copyright Conventions. Published in the United States by Times Books, a division of Random House, Inc., New York, and simultaneously in Canada by Random House of Canada, Limited, Toronto.

The W.P.A. Guidebook entry originally appeared in a slightly different form in *The New York Times.*

Library of Congress Cataloging-in-Publication Data

Wade, Betsy.
   The New York times practical traveler handbook / by Betsy Wade. —
1st ed.
     p.   cm.
   ISBN 0-8129-2189-5
   1. Travel.   I. Title.
  G151.W33   1994
  910′.2′02—dc20   93-37259

Manufactured in the United States of America
9 8 7 6 5 4 3 2
First Edition
Book design by Janet Odgis & Company Inc.

For six teachers
Ellen, Jim, Joan, John, Rebecca and Ursula

And six students
Anne, Carol, Christopher, Jennifer, Leah and Mark

 **Introduction**

Next to falling in love or having grandchildren, travel should provide the most satisfying, exhilarating times of your life. And travel has never given greater rewards than now. A hundred years ago, only the elite could take the Grand Tour, but today, while a foreign trip may still represent a big investment, hundreds of thousands of us can feast at the major wells of civilization, catch our breath on entering the Piazza San Marco at twilight, see the motion and smell the aromas of Hong Kong.

We can reach places that in former times were visited only by daredevils and empire builders. Everyday Americans—climbers, trekkers, photographers, students, just plain walkers—can see remote interiors, secret harbors, high peaks, islands with no telephone wires. If you have $24,000 on hand, you can ride a Russian icebreaker over the North Pole and partake of no activity more strenuous than a cookout on the ice.

The range of possibilities is wider because much of the world now speaks America's language. Tours can be bought that will do everything for you but lift food to your mouth. At the other end of the bank account, a courier ticket might get you to your goal for nothing.

Air transport is a basically wretched experience, but as Paul Theroux points out, it *is* magic. "Anyone with the price of a ticket," he writes, "can conjure up the castled crag of Drachenfels or the Lake Isle of Innisfree simply by using the right escalator at, say, Logan Airport in Boston." It is also magic because using a plane means you need not take three months off the job to reach the Orient and get a good look around.

It's no wonder that since World War II travel has become a

major factor in the world's economy. At home, travel is so important that it is the biggest employer for an increasing number of states—12 when I last looked. The traffic flow to America's most popular tourist city, Orlando, has become a gauge of dozens of economic factors. In 1992, 30.2 million people visited Disney World.

With so many people in motion, and so many merchants in the market—travel is really a bunch of related industries —the choices are giddying. However, this book, intended for the pleasure traveler, the vacationer, will not suggest places to go. That is for you to learn from whatever authorities you consult. I know some hot springs you would probably enjoy, and I once traveled to Louisiana to see a house called the Shadows on the Teche because I was in love with the name. But directing you to happiness is not my purpose. My purpose is to safeguard you while you seek happiness.

As the writer of the Practical Traveler column for more than six years—it's a job where disengagement is impossible, akin to the one Nathanael West described in the novel *Miss Lonelyhearts*—I get discouraging and angry feedback about the world of travel out there. Perplexed letters ask legal, medical and financial questions that would have been incomprehensible a few years ago: resistant malaria, tour operator default, automatic teller machines, buying from a consolidator, lost tickets and passports, thefts in the street.

The expedients in this book will not cope with every problem, but they will help you in many cases. I want to provide basic tools to help you make good independent decisions, stay healthy and safe and know where to find further help: These are essentials for enjoying travel.

Broken into bite-sized pieces, this is a vade mecum, a go-with-me on the most important matters that will face you as a traveler. Because no one wants to carry an encyclopedia, and I do not want to write one, I have worked hardest to tell you places to get further essential information in a time of changing laws and economics. A basic example: Are you aware that the shot you need most before going abroad is a tetanus booster? Given the rate of traffic accidents, when tetanus protection is essential, that fact won't change much. On the other hand, the areas where you will need malaria protection are subject to change, as are the optimum forms of protection as resistant malaria spreads. So this book will also tell you where to call to learn which shots are important for your itinerary.

Lots of guidebooks will give you a rudimentary phrase list for each language: "please," "thanks" and "the check, please." I provide a few pages of international symbols that you can point to in an emergency whatever the language: toilet, doctor, hotel room, automatic teller machine.

If you have general questions—how to get a passport, where to get health protection help, what does a consolidator do, how to travel as a courier—I hope I have put these matters under logical entries. Cross-references may guide you. There are some longer considerations of major problems in the travel industries—tour operator defaults, hotel advertising jargon, responsibilities of a travel agent. These may prove helpful reading. Some odds and ends are just there for you to stumble on. Some oldies but goodies, some new, bad things, like diphtheria.

Because I could not bear to have you think that travel always involves losing your passport, your hotel or your wits, I have tucked in a couple meditations from my life as an amateur traveler, including one on my family's fondness for the W.P.A. Guides. Underlying entries both serious and frivolous is my realization that while time's wingèd chariot is not a scheduled airline, it is nonetheless on its way.

The New York Times

Practical Traveler Handbook

Advertising, How to Translate

Reading hotel ads and even hotel brochures is similar to reading a classified ad for an apartment: The phrases and abbreviations are terms of art—stylized and well understood by sophisticates, obscure to the uninitiated. There is no real need to worry, so long as you have the courage to keep asking questions until you are sure. If you feel that you are getting the brush-off, or are being given the feeling that you are imposing on your travel agent or the hotel staff by asking what the hotel means by the phrases given below, you should perhaps find another travel agent or hotel.

Oceanfront. This means that there should not be anything—another hotel, a highway, an oil derrick—between you and the salt water.

Oceanview is something else. It may mean you can see the ocean from a spot behind the headboard of the bed, or if you stand on the toilet seat. Check the variation in prices between oceanfront and oceanview; the margin should confirm the difference. Once a friend and I got an oceanview room on, approximately, the west coast of Barbados, and the palm trees were so thick on that side of the hotel we could barely spot the water. The place was not doing much business, so we asked the owner if she wouldn't like to have an oceanfront room occupied instead, for appearances' sake. She agreed and we had a lovely stay.

Double room. Ask if this means twin beds or a double bed. In the United States, it usually means a room with one bed accommodating two people; in Europe, it usually means a room with two single beds, which might be called a twin room in the United States. In American motels where children often stay free in rooms with parents, the double will probably mean two double beds, sometimes also known as a double double.

After I wrote about these definitions on the basis of research in a book published for the hotel trade, *Glossary of Hospitality Management Terms* by Andrew Schwarz and David C. Dorf, I got "you fool" letters saying that I had it all backward. This shows that it is important to be sure what the place in question intends the term to mean. If you are traveling with a friend who is not, in *Time* magazine's old code phrase for lover, "a great and good friend," ask about the beds first or you may spend a wakeful night with an about to be former friend who is a snorer or a thrasher.

In double occupancy. This means that the price specified is what you are going to pay, and the other person in the room is going to pay that amount, too. Every so often, for instance on weekend specials in the United States, the price given is for the room, whether one, two or three people occupy it, but since weekends are big promotional events for hotels that are customarily business hotels it is usually specified in splashy type.

European plan, or E.P. In the United States, this means you just get the room in a hotel or resort. In Europe, it usually means you get a breakfast, too. If the breakfast consists of bread and coffee, it is probably called Continental plan. To confuse the matter further, in the United States this may be called the B & B plan, sometimes found at seasonal resorts after the staff has gone back to school. I have been on tours where the specification was for Continental breakfast, but I ate everything in sight and nothing was added to my bill. Mario Perillo says that he always specifies Continental breakfasts on his trips to Italy, but that some of the hotels provide the full cholesterol load. When occupants of different hotels on the same tour get together, he says, the crust-and-coffee crowd is angry about what they have missed, but at least he can point to the brochure and say they were not promised more.

American plan, or A.P. This includes room and three meals a day. If the resort has a menu, the selections for the A.P. guests are normally restricted. If the selections are not restricted, the hotel or resort may advertise "full American plan" or some other phrase to indicate that you can choose anything off the menu, even steak or shrimp. The most common is the modified American plan, or M.A.P., which means breakfast and dinner. It's confusing, so mercifully the kind of place I go spells it out for the newcomers: "M.A.P., with hot breakfast and family-style dinners; lunch boxes may be ordered for $5." This tells everyone where they're at.

Rack rate is not a phrase you will see in any ad intended for you and me. It's rather sneering hotel jargon for the regular rate for the room. It makes me feel as if I were going to be hung up on those motel racks that do the work of a closet: "Poor Betsy, she got the rack rate." No one will tell me where it sprang from—perhaps from "off-the-rack," as mass-manufactured clothes were once called "off-the-peg," or perhaps from the prices listed on the brochure in the display rack—but the hotel pros who devised it clearly believe that only the gullible pay it. So take their hint. Ask for the corporate rate, the weekend rate, the senior rate, the A.A.A. rate, the A.A.R.P. rate, the ski season rate, the postseason rate. Anything. See what the reply is.

AIDS

A number of countries are now requiring that visitors, usually long-term ones, or applicants for residence or jobs be tested for the human immunodeficiency virus, or HIV, before entry. This opens up possibilities for frightful abuses of human rights and that is exactly what is happening. For example, Greece says it requires a test for "performing artists working in Greece." When I talked to a spokesman at the Greek embassy about the requirement in 1989, he was scathing. "We don't mean ballet dancers," he said. "We mean prostitutes who say they are dancers."

The first list of countries I saw was prepared by a human rights organization in London, and it was based on ad-hoc research. It troubled many at the travel health conference in Zurich in 1988 because experts pointed out half a dozen reasons why requiring such a test would do nothing to reduce the spread of AIDS in the host country while it would certainly provide another opportunity for xenophobia and discrimination. It is indeed unequally applied, as the Greek spokesman made clear: Moscow correspondents said they always worried if they would be asked for a test report when they returned from home leave, and they never were.

The State Department's initial list in 1989 contained the names of 29 countries with some requirement. The December 1992 list, still based on inquiries sent to the countries by the department's Citizens Emergency Center, contained 44 countries.

This list, "HIV Testing Requirements," which is updated periodically, is available from the State Department fax and phone information service. (See **survival overseas**.) The nub of the issue is whether a test given in the United States will satisfy the authorities. The list gives answers to this question: "no," "yes" or "yes under certain conditions." The conditions should be ascertained. As of 1992, only one country required a test for anyone staying less than 30 days, so the problem does not affect most tourists. The exception is Iraq, where anyone staying more than five days must have the test at a cost of $330, or pay a fine of $1,600.

It was Iraq's requirement that provoked the creation of the State Department list; business travelers, faced with large fines, asked why they had not been warned.

An organization in London called FACTS, the Foundation for Aids Counseling, Treatment and Support, has been collecting useful information for travelers who test positive for HIV; the address is 23-25 Weston Park, Crouch End, London N8 9SY.

In the United States, *Out and About*, a gay travel newsletter, has published information on the same subject. Subscriptions are $49 for 10 issues a year; back issues are $5: 542 Chapel Street, New Haven, Conn. 06511; 800-929-2268.

Airline Code Sharing

This is among the most impenetrable of the airlines' rotten tricks on the consumer. Two airlines agree to "share" a code —the flight number for a long trip from point A to point C, with one airline flying from A to B and the other from B to C. The result is called a "direct" flight and is sold to the prospective passenger as such. In these days of shaky airline finances, languid United States government regulation and Byzantine pooling/leasing arrangements, almost any passenger can end up on a plane with an unexpected name and crew.

I discovered this practice through a couple who had bought two first class Lufthansa tickets from New York to Mauritius, in the Indian Ocean. They paid $6,300 each for the round-trip

tickets; only when they got to Frankfurt did they discover
they were making the remaining 12-hour leg not with Lufthansa but Air Mauritius. The way the flight was listed in the
travel agent's computer and in other reference works con-
cealed the fact that this was a connecting flight using two
airlines rather than a true direct flight with a stop in Frankfurt. The first class cabin on Air Mauritius was not clean, the
New York couple said, and worse, there were only two rows
of first class seats in the 767 plane, and the first class smoking row was right behind the couple's nonsmoking seats, and
the husband was very sensitive to smoke. In essence, the
couple said, they paid for Lufthansa first class service and did
not get it.

Code sharing began in the 1960s, when Allegheny Airlines
began putting its code, AL, in front of the flight numbers for
its connections on smaller regional airlines. In the early 80s,
other big airlines followed suit for their feeder lines. A ticket
might show Delta Airlines as the carrier all the way to Albany, Georgia, but the Atlanta-to-Albany leg would be on a
24-passenger plane operated by Atlantic Southeast Airlines,
"the Delta connection." Opponents of this practice, including
two biggies, American and United, said it was deceptive. In
1984, a spokesman for United said: "It misrepresents two airlines with different levels of service which are indicated as
one airline. We think it misleads the public. It's like buying
an Oldsmobile with a Chevy engine."

In those days, it was fairly easy for the traveler to spot the
shift. For one thing, only the commuter lines used four-digit
flight numbers, so travel agents and alert travelers knew
right away that a leg would be on a smaller plane. But since
each flight number is distinct and not duplicated by another
airline, the airlines ran out of three-digit numbers, so four-

digit numbers came into use for main-line as well as commuter flights. Code sharing was accepted by Federal regulators and the practice moved into the international field, with major lines coordinating arrival and departure times and using each other's terminals. Sometimes one airline would fly the outbound trip and another the inbound. Airlines in Europe were thus able to advertise that they served Houston as well as New York, and domestic airlines were able to offer cities they did not really fly to. Even American and United joined the herd.

The computer sales aspect locked in code sharing. Two airlines sharing a code may list a flight in the computer as a "direct" flight, which some travelers, not surprisingly, may still believe is a flight where you do not change planes. But you do change planes, and airlines to boot. These faux direct flights appear on the computer screen before connecting flights, and the agent is thus more likely to find a code-shared flight before a connecting flight or, probably more to the point, before the exact same flights are revealed, further down in the computer, as merely connections.

A Department of Transportation policy requires airlines in "any direct oral communication" to alert consumers about what line they will be flying. The policy makes no reference to the duty of a travel agent, but a spokesman for the department has said that in this context a travel agent is acting as an agent for the airline and shares this obligation.

In the case of the couple going to Mauritius, their travel agent claimed not to know that a trip on Lufthansa 405/6474 would be mostly aboard Air Mauritius 6474 because the computer entry for the "direct" flight was widely separated from the separate entry for the Air Mauritius flight, which would have been a giveaway.

These days, travelers almost always have to deal with someone using a computer. If that person is an employee of the airline, the customer should ask specifically, "Will this be a United Airlines plane and crew all the way?" And the employee is obliged to answer. If it is a travel agent, the agent may have to call up the airline and ask the same question. Travel agents do not always want to do this. If you are left with doubts, or are embarrassed to press this hard, you can call the airline yourself and ask the question.

Alas, the burden is on the traveler.

Airline Regulation

Since 1978, when the U.S. government stopped regulating fares and most other aspects of the commercial airline industry, unhappy passengers may shout but the law will not do much. Other than safety rules such as the use of seat belts, and a ban on fireworks and the like in luggage, the areas where the government retains some control are overbooking, which may involve **denied boarding compensation**; a limit on **carry-on baggage**; and smoking, which is banned on all flights of six hours or less in the United States, whether you are aboard a U.S. airliner or a foreign one.

It is a delusion to think that the airline must put you up for the night if it strands you far from home (see **stuck at the airport**) or that the airline will replace your stolen ticket on the spot if you present a police report of the theft. There are other beliefs just as common and just as delusionary.

A Ralph Nader group called the Aviation Consumer Action Project marched into this swamp of confusion, publishing a 22-page commonsense pamphlet called "Facts and Advice for Airline Passengers." I have relied on it a lot and wish sometimes I was as concise. The pamphlet was revised annually until 1992, and it may be again. It costs $2, and is available from Aviation Consumer Action Project, Box 19029, Washington, D.C. 20036.

The Department of Transportation has published a similar book, but without the advice, called "Fly-Rights, a Guide to Air Travel in the U.S." It is 32 pages long, and includes some ungovernmentally unruly sketches. This costs $1, and is available from the Consumer Information Center, Department 131Z, Pueblo, Colo. 81009.

Both of these books include the government address to write to with complaints or to get advice about airlines:

Consumer Affairs Division
Room 10405
Office of Community and Consumer Affairs
U.S. Department of Transportation
400 7th Street S.W.
Washington, D.C. 20590
202-366-2220.

This, of course, is also the address to use to request a single copy of the "Air Travel Consumer Report" for the current month. If you have filed a complaint with the department, you will become a blip on the report's radar for a later month. This fascinating report is described under **bumping rates.**

Air Passenger Safety

See **safety in the air.**

Airport Carts

Airport carts, for my money, can join potholes, sagging mattresses, windows that don't open and loud air conditioners in the perdition I have reserved for destroyers of the joys of travel. I would a million times rather have some designated person pick up my battle-scarred luggage, put it on a big wagon and wheel it ahead of me. And I would pay, happily. But airports are more and more going to the do-it-yourself mode.

The carts with the one-handed handle, you will quickly discover, cannot be steered ahead of you and must be pulled behind, exposing your belongings to instability and pilferage. If there are two of you, one can pull and one follow and keep watch. Inevitably, there is a place where you can take the cart no further and you are reduced to what is colloquially called schlepping—toting unwieldy burdens as your arms increase in length by the minute. Even if this is the end of the return trip, you begin to rue the whole enterprise.

Overseas these carts are usually free, but in the United States they are offered for rent at 80 airports for $1 or $1.50 by the Smarte Carte company. You are supposed to get a quarter back when you slide the cart back into the lockup, but I have never figured out how to return the cart and guard my luggage at the same time so I just abandon it and watch someone else hustle it back to get my quarter.

The Smarte Carte company does offer one aid to people like me who find their dollar bills too wrinkled to work and usually get into a wrestling match with such vending devices. It sells a plastic card that offers up to 20 rentals for $1 per rental. My bet is that a couple should buy two cards with 10 punches each, to reduce the damage in the event of loss. With a credit card, they may be ordered by phone, 800-328-9006; by mail: Smarte Carte, 4455 White Bear Parkway, St. Paul, Minn. 55110. Personal checks are accepted for mail orders, and there is a handling charge of $1 for each order. The same company is now testing electronic mechanisms that release a cart when you swipe a credit card through. These may ultimately take over from the debit cards, but you pay the full fee each time, not $1.

The pay-ahead cards are nice gifts for people vacationing by air; small and practical.

Airport to City

Through its many annual editions, *How to Get from the Airport to the City All Around the World* rated as one of my favorite travel books. As is now clear, I am an advocate of public transit, mainly because the old and the young must have it, and a civilization is measured by how it provides for the vulnerable.

This compact book, originated by an engineer named Norman Crampton, passed through several sets of new hands when he decided to go on to other things. The 12th edition in 1993 is called *Airport Transit Guide* and is sold for $6.95, postage included, by Salk International Travel Premiums, Box 1388, Sunset Beach, Calif. 90742; 714-893-0812. It lists the transport choices for 400 airports, with a price tag on each: car rental, taxi, shuttle van, scheduled bus, hired limo, light-rail, subway. It includes phone numbers for information about cities from Aberdeen to Zurich. The type is pretty small, but it does fit into the carry-on weightlessly.

I hope this book, now really intended to be a premium for travel agents to give in lieu of a calendar at Christmas, lives forever. In most of our traffic-choked cities, a taxi is not only the most expensive way to get downtown but is also an environmental scourge and keeps the traveler isolated from the priceless experience of entering a new place. Besides, passengers who are strangers to a city may get ripped off by an

unlicensed cabby or by a legitimate one who takes them the
long way around.

Consider the alternatives. One of the high spots of an otherwise overpriced trip to Paris in 1993 was buying a ticket
for about $8 at Orly Airport to ride the charming, airy little
Orlyval light-rail train to a connection with the RER suburban line and the Metro subway, which stopped virtually at
our hotel doorstep. We relished our joy at popping up in the
middle of a spring day in the Latin Quarter, and knowing we
had done it on our own also gave us a boost. All such excellent transit tips are listed in the little guide, and it is worth
checking them out.

On an international trip, the airline seat pocket may contain
a leaflet of information published by the country of your destination. Take it with you. Most port or airport authorities
publish a leaflet about ground transportation from the airport, complete with charts. Orly and De Gaulle in Paris do.
Massport in Boston publishes a Logan guide, which is how I
learned about the network of bus lines serving much of New
England from the airport; the Port Authority of New York
and New Jersey publishes guides for all three of its airports,
including connections. San Francisco has a guide, and New
Orleans has a wonderful street map with tourist bus routes
in different colors.

If you are going overseas, ask the airline or a U.S. branch
of the tourist office to send you a leaflet. If you are making a
domestic trip and the travel agent cannot help, call the city's
convention and visitors' bureau and ask for assistance.

If you are going straight to a hotel or resort in a smaller
place, the hotel may have a pickup service. Ask where you
should go to call for it or wait for it when you make your
reservation. And do not buy a round-trip ticket until you find

out what the schedule for return trips is; a group of us lost
$9 each when we bought round-trip van tickets to Teton Vil-
lage from the airport in Jackson Hole, Wyoming, and then
found that the van made only three return trips on a Sunday,
and none of them matched our flights.

Like Crampton, the current proprietors of *Airport Transit
Guide* also like feedback, so if you find something new, or
amiss, let them know at the address above.

All-Inclusive Resort

This phrase should mean a resort where your sports, food,
room and internal transportation are included in the price
quoted—like a cruise, only land-bound. But it may not always
mean exactly that. When you are shopping, take care to understand what "all" means in "all-inclusive": I mean, don't be
intimidated, ask about specifics that matter to you.

Club Med really is all-inclusive, and it is credited with in-
venting the concept; it asks only that you buy beads to trade
for drinks. In some of the Caribbean resorts, that "all" may
mean drinks, too. But when you look at other resorts' small
type, you can see that the phrase is interpreted freely: use of
a sailboard may be free, but instruction may not be; skis, but
not instruction or lift tickets. A certain number of hours of
tennis or golf may be included, but not anytime you want to
play.

It's obvious, but when you are shopping for a resort see if
you are getting free the things you will really use—a fully
equipped 24-hour gym, not six hours of mambo lessons, for
example. Otherwise, price out a place that is not all-inclusive
and see what the extras will cost you.

Some of the all-inclusive places have a "dine around" provision that gives you a certain number of meals at other re-

sorts in the area as part of the price. Operators say this is a popular provision, but it again all depends on whether you would just as soon eat from a familiar menu or crave looking at something else. Of course, the food may be better elsewhere.

Early in 1992, some of the first all-inclusive resorts began to feel that the concept was being eroded. The SuperClubs in the Caribbean began to call themselves "super-inclusive," and the next year the Sandals Caribbean resorts began to describe their 11 properties as "ultra-inclusive." Whatever the term is, be sure to ask what it means.

Alumni Tours

You do not have to be alumni to participate in these tours bearing the imprimatur of a college. Usually, the brochures refer to "alumni and friends," but anyone wanting to join who can pay the charge is going to be welcome.

Alumni tours, tours operated by continuing education programs, organizations like New York's 92d Street Y and other organizations with bona fide educational or other nonprofit charters usually provide something that sets them apart from regular commercial trips, however similar the itineraries.

A Barnard College flier offers a trip to China with John Meskill, professor emeritus of Oriental studies, "who was the dynamic lecturer for our 1988 trip to China." The brochure also says, "Special events will be arranged with our alumnae in Hong Kong," and such projects usually involve entrée to places not open to group tours—specifically, people's homes, a lure that never fails. U.C.L.A. Extension offers a trip to Madagascar with Dr. Mildred Mathias, the botanist after whom the U.C.L.A. botanical gardens are named. A friend recently sent a postcard from a Smith College tour saying:

"All the names in gardening: Chris Lloyd, Penelope Hobhouse, Rosemary Verey, but a highlight had to be the Duchess of Beaufort showing us Badminton and watching Wimbledon on her telly as we passed through the great rooms of history."

It is probably not the ties to dear old U, which by now may be worn rather thin through fund appeals, but the idea of getting a special trip, with someone to answer questions and provide insights, that makes these tours successful. In the area of art, museums, history and architecture, we all want the insights that specialists can provide, specialists to whom we feel we have a particular tie. I noted no real difference between the work of a docent provided by the National Gallery in Washington for my journalism alumni tour and the work of a lecturer who went to my college, but both had a tie to our group and really seemed to get into the material more. Alex Haley, the author of *Roots*, was in 1990 a speaker aboard a *Delta Queen* trip sponsored by the Center for the Study of Southern Culture in Mississippi. He gave a talk about helping others along in which he referred to "a turtle atop a fence post," saying you knew a turtle could not get there alone. He became friends with the kitchen staff on the *Delta Queen* and, typically, donated his lecture fee for scholarships. After his death, "A Turtle Atop a Fence Post" was widely reprinted, but I wish I had been there when he spoke. That is the involvement I want. That's what travel is about.

I have never received a letter complaining about an alumni tour, although some tours operated by nonprofit groups with wider nets—museums, for instance—sometimes generate complaints, probably because the museum is not so closely involved.

Nonprofit groups' trips are usually costly and I have never

seen one cheaper than a commercial version. Sometimes, I am told by the companies that make the actual travel arrangements, the school or organization gets a percentage of the charge for travel, but these organizations would never tell me who or how much. In addition, there is usually a contribution to the school included in the fee; the government, in a recent tax case, ruled such add-ons to be voluntary. Barnard words it this way: "We ask you also to support (the organization) . . . by including a tax-deductible gift of $100 in a separate check"; and, on the coupon: "Please note that your tax-deductible contributions . . . should be included. . . ." The Metropolitan Museum of Art was still taking a hard line for its Red Sea Passage in 1993: "Rates include . . . $400 per person gift to the Metropolitan Museum of Art." Can you skip the gift and take the trip? I'm sure. Cheesy? You bet. I think of Bernard Shaw, as a drama critic, emerging from a theater and staring coldly at a beggar's extended palm: "Press," G.B.S. said. You may be an alumnus, but the school is running the tour to raise money as well as build solidarity.

But even without donations on top, these are top-drawer tours with a small number of participants because colleges do not want to send out alumni in a unair-conditioned school bus and then ask them to contribute to quality education. If there is one lecturer, there will certainly not be more than a bus full of travelers, say, 40 people. How many people can gather around a lecturer and still hear in a museum? If the group is traveling in Jeeps, only one vehicle will hear the running commentary of the expert. Capacity of vessels, size of dinner tables, access to the tour leader, all tend to limit the number of participants, and hence keep the prices up. Of course, something like a tour for Smithsonian members or some other vast organization is likely to be the size of a commercial tour.

In recent years, the National Tour Association, which groups companies that operate tours in North America, has signed up some three dozen coalitions of organizations and gone on the warpath against "nonprofit tours." They say a "halo effect" allows churches, universities and museums to trade on "public assumption of a lofty purpose." Meantime, the commercial operators say, the nonprofit groups get to use volunteer workers, nonprofit postage rates and headquarters that are not carried on the local real-estate tax rolls and thus can undersell the commercial operators on an unlevel playing field. Some of the complaining groups have nothing to do with travel; they sell computers, for example, in competition with universities. But the tour association is the moving force in this war.

Some points of their argument are troublesome, beyond the fact that the high price on the nonprofit organizations' trips makes one doubt that they undersell anybody. Major nonprofit organizations and universities almost always use commercial tour operators to put the trips together: The Barnard China trip mentioned above was organized by Academic Arrangements Abroad, a New York company; the Metropolitan Museum trip by Raymond & Whitcomb in New York; and so forth. Batia Plotch of the 92d Street Y in New York said that all her overseas tours were packaged by professional tour companies. So tour operators are seldom losing and are probably gaining through the increased role of educational groups in travel.

Bryan DeLeo of the National Trust for Historic Preservation said it was ironic that the coalition criticized nonprofit groups' "high-quality educational travel programs rather than endeavor to provide tours of comparable quality themselves."

What's going on here? People in the National Tour Association coalition gave an explanation they did not always want attributed to them: The real targets of the coalition's tourism sector are church groups and senior citizen centers, which do not use commercial operators, but book the bus and the motels themselves, dialing from the telephone on the Formica table in the clubroom. One angry travel agent said that a church in his area organized a trip to a religious shrine with a stopover at—where else?—Atlantic City. Thomas R. Frenkel of Presley Tours in Makanda, Illinois, former head of the National Tour Association, said: "A church in my town operates tours that look like mine." Senior citizens pile onto buses for trips to discount malls, shopping centers and the beach after the seniors themselves round up the participants and an employee rents the bus at the rate used for nonprofit groups.

No coalition of three dozen trade associations with names like United States Chamber of Commerce, National Association of Retail Druggists, National Tour Association and American Society of Travel Agents wants to tell its state and national legislators that it is out to zap churches and senior citizen centers. So in the coalition's battle, the big nonprofits take the heat for the real targets. Whatever you hear, the battle does not have much to do with a college's $5,275 trip to China.

Amenities

No one can explain why a hotel will give you a basket containing shampoo, hair conditioner and shoeshine cloth but not a toothbrush, the one thing you really miss if you did not pack one. Probably because a toothbrush costs $3.99 in La Amnésie Gifte Shoppe. However, hotels with two-star couth do have toothbrushes for you, and you should call and ask for one. Female sanitary supplies are another essential that hotels cannot always provide, but they are getting better about this and should be encouraged with firm words.

A recent survey of what travelers wanted in amenities indicated that none of the above was a front-runner. Safety, a clean room ready on arrival and a decent reading lamp ranked high, which probably tells the hotel industry what it needs to do. Budget-level motels have deplored "amenity creep," implying that those la-di-da soaps increase the room rate, but French-milled soaps are a minor factor compared with paying off the mortgage on a fancy hotel in the high-rent district.

The word "amenities," like "all-inclusive," is getting mushy at the edges. Almost anything is now termed an amenity, from an extra pillow to a coupon for a future stay. I don't collect soaps, but I do collect telephone pads, to use in the car. My amenity project for my sunset years is to count the number of pages in the pad and see if there is a correlation with the room price.

A.T.M., or Automatic Teller Machine

This device has altered our relations with banks radically, and even more so when traveling. If you can find out if A.T.M.s are plentiful in the area you are traveling to, you can reduce your currency hassle to almost nothing. You do not have to worry about other countries' unexpected holidays, and you do not need to fret a lot about the foreign language: Most machines give you a choice of languages now. At the least you can read the numbers.

But be aware that the entry of A.T.M.s into foreign markets has been spotty, and you need to get a clear picture of what is available in the area you will visit.

To get into your own bank account while traveling, your home bank needs to be a part of a larger network, of which the most extensive are Cirrus and Plus. Domestically, outlets often serve both, and regional networks as well. The use of an 800 number will guide you to the nearest machine. (For Cirrus, the number is 800-424-7787; for Plus, 800-843-7587.)

Overseas, both have grown rapidly in different parts of the world. Cirrus, which is owned by MasterCard International, said that in 1991 it had 66,000 A.T.M.s available in 23 countries; in 1992, 90,000 in 37 countries. In 1993, it was extending into Bolivia and Iceland. Plus, linked to Visa, announced in 1993 that its 100,000th A.T.M. had opened, in Harrods department store in London no less. Plus machines operate in 34 countries, and recorded a growth of 40 percent in 1992.

Two steps are essential before you plan to lean heavily on your A.T.M. card for walking-around money overseas. First, get the bank that backs your card to provide an up-to-date directory. These are thickish books about the size of a business envelope, and often enough the local branch clerk looks blankly at you when you ask. Ask again, and early. After you look at the minuscule type in these directories, you may want to enlarge the crucial pages to carry along.

When we last went to Paris, we assumed that our Cirrus card would be as easy to use as it had been in Marseilles the year before, but the cooperating French bank, Crédit Mutuel, did not have a really convenient branch, so we were stuck with using our credit cards, which cost us a small surcharge.

The second essential step is to be sure that your ID, or

Personal Identification Number (PIN), is four digits. If you have a longer one, you will have to get another. If you have an ID number that incorporates letters, be sure you know how to render it in numbers on a keypad. European phones and keypads often have numbers only; my sister had memorized my phone number as a word and was unable to reach us while she was in England until she called a friend in the States and asked her to read the matching numbers off the keypad.

Read all the instructions on the machine before you try it. I once ignored a pasted-down notice in France, "no foreign cards," and the machine digested my card. I did get it back, thanks to a rational and patient woman at the bank in Marseilles, but I aged a lot in that moment.

You will get a pretty good exchange rate, the bank-to-bank rate for the day the transaction is recorded, and you will not be stymied by unfamiliar bank hours.

Auto Liability Insurance

If you own an auto, you have this coverage, which should pay the bills if you injure someone accidentally or damage someone else's property. Each state has a minimum requirement, and you certainly carry that, and probably more if you have been watching liability settlements rise past the $100,000–$300,000 levels.

In addition, you can get still further coverage that starts where your home liability insurance or auto coverage leaves off, something called an "umbrella policy." For a million dollars in coverage, this may cost $200 to $300. Once you've paid the other premiums, the price seems almost trivial and you will probably be covered while driving overseas, where your auto liability policy may not work.

Auto rental companies, like people, are required to carry the minimum liability insurance for the state involved, but in the middle of 1993 these companies began to say that their insurance would provide only a backup for an auto owner's insurance, and although the company's coverage might remain in first place—"primary" is the term used—for a renter with no insurance of his or her own, the company might still make a claim against the renter in the event of a liability suit. But guess what, the rental companies, for $8 or so a day, will sell you liability coverage, just as they sell the collision damage waiver.

Assuming that all the auto rental companies follow the big five—Alamo, Avis, Budget, Hertz and National—in this shift of liability, frequent renters who do not own autos should get themselves some freestanding coverage from their insurance broker, because you can probably do better paying an annual premium than you will paying $8 a day for frequent rentals. Chubb offers their client homeowners and condo owners an add-on of $1 million in liability for a premium of $80 to $100 a year, according to my broker. Other companies offer something called "named nonowner vehicle" insurance that might cost $300 a year for $300,000 in coverage.

If you do not own a car and have no liability insurance, call your broker and see what you can buy for the duration of your trip. It may not cost much more to get it for even longer.

On the question of damage to the rental car you are driving, see **collision damage waiver**.

Auto Rentals

This is almost always a stressful process, whether it's your first rental or your ninetieth. Good travel wisdom is never to make a schedule that involves getting away from the airport in a hurry because you will overlook some crucial point in the deal that can cost you a lot of money—the price of a brand-new car for starters. Similarly, never get back to the airport so close to flight time that you have nothing to spare for hitches on the auto return. I know people who missed a flight from Italy that way, and it was expensive.

Car rental companies' statistics show that most rental-car accidents take place on the way out of the airport, while people are groping for the right roads. Do not be ashamed or worried about the people behind you when you ask the rental agent to mark the map for you. Relying on signs is a rotten plan in a period when most airports are undergoing expansion; "turn left at the bulldozer" is no help.

As for costs, I have tried, and a half dozen others have also tried, to create a nice chart on how to find the best deal for renting an automobile, pointing to days of the weeks, locales and companies. The minute it is printed, it is wrong. Here are my best general suggestions for getting a good deal, and, more important, for not getting stung:

First, if price is the overriding concern, put the proposition to a travel agent. When four of us were going to a meeting in Santa Fe on a budget the size of a taco shell, our agent found us an off-airport company with a wonderful rate. We called from the Albuquerque airport, they picked us up and drove us into an area of the city richly ornamented with cyclone fence that looked like the New York City stolen-auto compound. I was alarmed, and when we saw that the place was operated by four 16-year-olds strumming a couple of giant computers I wondered if I should call the travel agent and change our minds. It was fine. Getting away was slow, because the kids who answered the phone also apparently emptied the ashtrays, but those young people were sharp. When we returned the car in the evening, they hopped in their van and took us to our motel and waited to be sure that our reservation was okay. No, we did not get express check-in or next-to-the-carousel counters, or any fancy stuff, but we got price, which was what we asked for.

Can you find a little company with hustle without a travel agent? Yes, but it is time-consuming because you have to use the yellow pages and try all the small companies; the travel agent can read them on a computer. The smaller company may not have an 800 number and you may have to make a batch of phone calls. But my friends really get a boost out of finding a good deal; maybe you do, too.

Second, the question of whether the price will be lower or higher for a weekend depends on the place and what the travel patterns are. Where a city without public transit survives by business travel and wilts on the weekend—say Costa Mesa, California—you will get a good weekend package, probably starting Thursday noon. And vice versa. Also, events you are unaware of may affect a rental: a big sports event, particularly a postseason playoff, will cut the available car supply and raise costs. If you have a reservation in advance, it should be honored against all these pressures but no law governs this and if your reservation is not honored, you do not have a legal recourse. If the next couple of counters down the line are likewise sold out, look in a phone directory for an off-airport company, or call your travel agent's 800 number and have the agent shop for you while you have a cup of coffee and collect yourself.

Third, check to make sure there are no hidden hitches with the rental; for example, that you will not be able to drive into Mexico or Canada or even merely another state, or that someone under 30 will not be permitted to take the wheel. If you don't know the questions, just ask the reservations clerk if there are any restrictions. In some cities where crime using rental cars has been booming, a form of redlining has been practiced: local people are not allowed to buy collision damage waivers and must have their own auto insurance. If you are renting in the city where you live, find out how this works with the company you plan to use, or pick a suburban rental location, one near a rail or bus stop. You should be told about this when you give your name and address. If you do not have auto insurance, ask your broker about getting some just for rentals; the cost for six months or so will be less than the C.D.W.s anyway.

Damage waivers are seldom available for luxury cars, sports cars or off-the-road vehicles, so ask about this if you want such a rental. When you get to the crunch, saying that you were not told about a restriction will not save you.

Is the little company always the best deal? Not always. If your organization has a negotiated basic rate with a particular major rental company, it probably encourages you to rent from that company and to use the business rate because it enhances your organization's bargaining power every time a rental shows up under that account number. You may get a better deal this way, but some of the value will erode if your company has a good deal for two-door cars—the rental standard—and you want four doors. There may also be a price war going on and the big company may be trying to beat out the little ones.

If it is a rental at an airport, tell the rental company what flight you are arriving on, and if it is an evening flight be sure that the counter will be open until the flight arrives, not just until it is due. If an evening rental may be completed only downtown, find out if the rental company will pick you up and drive you there. Sometimes, when I have gotten stuck this way, I have found it easier to take a jitney to an airport motel and return to the auto rental counter when it opens in the morning. What you save on the extra hours' rental gives you some help on the motel room.

When a reservation is made, ask about all the extras. There may be a fee (ridiculous to my mind) for a **second driver**, for driving out of the state, for dropoff elsewhere, for a child-safety seat, for a cellular phone. Be sure you have it straight about the collision damage waiver. (See **collision damage waiver**.)

Get a reservation confirmation number. The travel agent will print this on your itinerary.

Bags and Bundles

And coats that you are carrying and all that impedimenta: Count them at every turn when you are on the road. I once walked off without my purse because I had received a shopping bag at one stage and had not revised my total. Probably the most frequent error occurs when you take your camera out of your suitcase and neglect to add it to the count.

B & B Guides

This will be short and sour. Because of a great deal of subtly keyed advertising, a bed-and-breakfast sounds to many people like a 1790 mansion with a four-poster bed, a fireplace in the bedroom and a waterfall in the flower garden. Most B & B's, at least the ones that will save you money, are not that but are simply homes adapted to accommodate strangers instead of the now-grown children. Ironically, most B & B's do not want children as guests because of all those little china things on the sideboard. At the other end of the age question, elevators are not likely except in big-city places, so people who have trouble climbing stairs should skip B & B's.

At one point, there were 50 bed-and-breakfast guidebooks published in the United States. Most of them were not worth the Cape Cod lighter fuel to burn them. Some consisted of entries by the innkeepers that were collated by an editor who charged a set fee for an entry, perhaps more for a picture. Some represented the membership of an organization. Some were cottage industry products compiled on a computer from others' listings. Some were published simply as promotional listings for a particular tourist area. The writing is heavy on gush, and the color pictures on the cover as often as not show rooms from inns, as opposed to B & B's. Some perfectly respectable publishers issue these things. One recent volume had a favorable quotation from the *New York Times* on the cover, but research showed that the laurel was many years old and referred to another book in the series. The *Times*'s lawyers wrote the publisher and the quotation will be removed from later printings if the *Times*'s lawyers keep their eyes open.

How to find a good B & B? A friend's recommendation is the best step because there are a million intangibles, from water pressure in the shower to cats in the living room. One guidebook does rate B & B's on the basis of inspection. This is "Inspected, Rated & Approved Bed & Breakfasts & Country Inns," published by the American Bed & Breakfast Association. There are 450 listings of members of the group, which charges $250 for an annual membership, outside inspection included. Most small one- and two-bedroom places cannot afford this fee, so the listed places are mostly larger. The ratings run from four crowns, the top, down to one crown, which is "acceptable." If the place does not like the ranking it wins after inspection, it can drop out and get a refund of $100 of the membership fee.

This book, in paperback, costs $16.95 in bookstores. By mail, it is $3 more, from American Bed & Breakfast Association, 10800 Midlothian Turnpike, Suite 254, Richmond, Va. 23235, 800-769-2468.

Many B & B associations do not give addresses but only phone numbers for a reservation service, of which there are now 400, or the like. The reason is that often zoning does not permit commercial establishments in residential areas and the B & B's operate quietly, and without signs out front. None of this reassures me much.

Some B & B's, particularly where the owner operates several, are staffed by nonresidents who cut up the fruit in the morning and prepare the coffee but don't mingle with the guests. At the other end of the spectrum are the places where the owner is oppressively cozy and wants to involve you with the most intimate details of the family and town. If you have never stayed in a B & B, you will not have any trouble learning what the protocols are on arrival.

I do not think that price or location drives the B & B business. I think B & B's are like olives: You like 'em or you don't. You know where I stand, but don't take it personally.

Beach First Aid

As a beach nut, I avoid talking about sea creatures that sting, but being stung can spoil a vacation.

These days, there are water shoes available for children and adults with gridded rubber soles and porous fabric tops with elastic edges. These come in brilliant colors and do not impede swimming or walking in water, which is more than can be said for the old flip-flops or worn-out sneakers. These are under $10 for children and under $20 for adults, and they are probably better investments than a whole medical kit when it comes to safeguarding the soles of the feet from splinters, glass shards and hookworm.

But if your destination is a beach, particularly in the tropics or on an inconvenient island, adapt your first aid kit accordingly. If you have children with you, ask the travel clinic or the family doctor for ointments and salves for bites and stings since the children's smaller systems may not be able to handle medications that you use.

In addition, include these items:

Polysporin, Bacitracin or Neosporin ointment and 0.5 percent hydrocortisone cream, depending on what your family tolerates.

An antihistamine in 4-milligram tablets such as Chlor-Trimeton, whose generic name is chlorpheniramine maleate. Don't take these pills with liquor, and don't drive after taking them.

A small bottle of rubbing alcohol and a small bottle of calamine lotion, each wrapped in socks and possibly tucked inside shoes to prevent breakage.

A bottle of papaya-based meat tenderizer (Adolph's is one), which can help in the treatment of stings.

A pack of plastic bandages, preferably waterproof, plastic swabs and a few wrapped gauze pads.

Good, expensive pointed tweezers and a pack of sewing needles.

Dr. J. E. Jelinek, a New York University Medical School professor who has served as a spokesman for the American Academy of Dermatology, points out that water is not the only hazard at the beach. He opposes walking barefoot on any beach frequented by dogs and cats because of the danger of hookworm.

As for the waterborne hazards, Dr. Jelinek says the most important thing is to identify the cause because the treatment for sea urchin spines is the worst thing for jellyfish stings. If you didn't see what got you, ask local people, who almost always know what frequents what part of the beach.

Sea urchins live on the seafloor and have toxic spines to defend themselves if you step on them, and the spines can go through water-shoe soles and flippers to boot. There is usually a burning pain, redness and swelling. There may be an infection, but this may possibly be delayed. For immediate treatment, if you are confident it was a sea urchin, wash with soap and hot water. If a spine is visible, pull it out with sterilized tweezers or a needle. Hot water compresses and antibiotic ointments may help. If you have a foot full of spines, they should be removed by someone with the right skills: This might be a doctor, but it might also be someone who is a professional fisherman in the area. I have heard of extracting spines with drops of hot wax from a candle, but this is not for the amateur.

Ammonia is the local treatment of choice for urchin spines in many parts of the world, and this means urine, so do not be taken aback if this is proposed.

Jellyfish, sea anemones and related creatures can attack while your feet are not on the bottom, and this may help you identify the sting. The jellyfish bite causes mild stinging and burning or hives and, in severe cases, shock. Only 10 percent of all jellyfish cause serious problems for humans, Dr. Jelinek said. Jellyfish stings are usually indicated by long streaks on the legs that are geometric and linear. If you think it is a jellyfish or sea anemone that got you, do not wash in fresh water or rub the spot. The toxin must be deactivated, Dr. Jelinek says, and the first choice is rubbing alcohol or the meat tenderizer. Witch hazel is the next choice, then perfume or anything mildly acid.

Five minutes after the alcohol or acid, a paste of talcum powder or baking soda with salt water may be applied. This can be scraped off when it dries. Any anesthetic ointment may help later. If there is a severe reaction or signs of shock, get professional help.

Try to avoid stepping on rocks, where the urchins live, or coral, which creates problems of its own. In all cases, if you are visiting places not familiar to you ask for local counsel about what to do, meaning the people who live on or next to the beach.

Birthplace on Passport

For some Americans, this is a touchy business. People born in Israel, for instance, have found it difficult to get visas for a number of countries so long as "Israel" was shown as their birthplace, and in periods of terrorist threats this notation can cause other anxieties. The legal requirement to state the place of birth on a passport appears in Section 101(a)(30) of the Immigration and Nationality Act of 1952, although an expert at the State Department said that a country name had been used on passports since 1921 and had been required since 1928.

Whatever its implications of discrimination between native and immigrant American citizens, there are no exceptions to the requirement that a birthplace be shown. Passport offices will at least enter a city rather than a country if the traveler prefers. Jerusalem might be an adequately ambiguous choice, as Berlin would certainly be. Anyone can replace a valid passport at any time, for payment of the appropriate fee. You have to appear in person at a passport office to do so.

Boarding Passes

It's better than a 50-50 chance that you already have your boarding pass when you leave for the airport. If you are a business traveler, or always use a travel agent, it's almost 100 percent likely. The hairy question is whether this guarantees you the seat marked on the pass.

Unfortunately, it does not. The answer depends on how crowded the flight is, when you arrive at the gate and if you have somehow alerted the airline to your arrival. Since the question of denying boarding to a passenger with a ticket and a reservation is still under government regulation, I put the issue to a Department of Transportation spokesman, who replied with a definite maybe.

"If the airline provides a boarding pass, does that represent a right to the seat?" said Hoyte B. Decker, Jr. "Well, it's a step in that direction."

Adherence to a few precautionary steps can ward off problems. If it is a flight you fly often, and you know it is always busy, get to the airport well before the airline's deadline for checking in, which may be 10 minutes or two hours. Check in at the gate and get your boarding pass scribbled on, put into a new folder or reissued, or whatever ritual is followed. You now hold most of the cards in any dispute, unless you are unaccountably absent at the last boarding call. You had your reservation, you were accounted for on time, the seat is yours and if the airline now cannot get you to your destination within an hour of the scheduled time—delays caused by safety problems don't count—it owes you what is called "**de-**

nied boarding compensation," which may be half the price of your round-trip ticket, or the whole price.

However, many travelers, executives in particular, dislike checking in at the airport counter, saying that they ordered boarding passes in advance to be able to stay on the airport phone or in the membership lounge until the last minute and walk right on. If the flight is not crowded, this works fine. The gate attendants may even make a loudspeaker announcement: "If you have your ticket and boarding pass, you need not check at the podium. Please wait for the boarding call."

But if this executive stays too long on the phone before a flight that is overbooked, woe betide. The gate agents have no way of knowing if the passenger is at the airport or not, and if the passenger has not registered his or her presence by 10 minutes before flight time the agents will joyfully give the seat to someone else. If the executive then goes and stands at the end of the boarding line, there is little to prove that he or she was on deck on time.

To confess a truth, sometimes by the time I get to the airport I am so cranky about the bus, the weather, the telephone busy signals that I am just spoiling for an argument with the counter clerk. If said clerk has had a similar day, we are an explosion waiting to be set off. I am sure others feel the same way and that such emotional minefields give rise to many angry letters I get.

If you want to get where you are going on a crowded flight even more than you want to bite the head off an airline agent, take your boarding pass, check in on time and keep your eye on the ball.

Budget Motels

The motel field has been dividing into narrower markets
in the last 10 years, and about the only part that has been
thriving is the budget—or, more particularly, what is called
the "minimum-service segment." Some, like the new Sleep
Inns, one of the brands offered by the Choice chain, have
built a low per-night price into the design, eliminating lobbies
and providing smaller rooms, *2001*-style bathrooms with fi-
berglass stall showers and minimal furnishings. Part of the
budget segment consists of some older name-brand motels
that have been renamed and offered at lower prices—HoJo
Inn and Holiday Inn Express, for example—although some of
these are newly built. Choice, which owns Econo Lodge, has
used the Econo Lodge chain as a "soft landing spot" for a
motel that can no longer meet the requirements of its original line, Quality. Some motels have been changing names as
often as bedspreads, and you may call a number you've used
for years and have a new name answer.

What's the best way to use budget motels? Here are some
guidelines.

Safety first, as always. See **hotel safety.**

If you have stayed in one town in a brand-name motel you
like, you may want to try it elsewhere, although sales and
franchise switching may mean the place has little resem-
blance to the one you like. Ask the 800-number operator if
the motel has the features you prefer—pool, in-room coffee
machine, balcony or, probably most important for families, a
readily accessible breakfast.

Many minimum-service motels are built near fast-food
places, but others spread the lobby with a big buffet breakfast, usually not involving cooking. The Hampton Inns, which
have a free-breakfast policy, willingly let our grandchildren
eat up the year's profits when their Portland, Maine, airport

motel laid out breakfast: cereals, toaster tarts, fruit, juice, milk. The real key, as traveling parents know, is the children did not have to sit down in one place and squirm while someone fetched cereal. They could serve themselves and take it to a table and eat. This is where the no-restaurant budget place may be a real plus from the standpoint of money, speed and stress reduction on the road.

Ask about the maximum age for children to stay in the room with you free. This age can vary and it will make a difference in what the visit costs. Sometimes, a second, adjoining, room is available at half the price of the first, which may be a more restful deal, providing the children with their own television. Ask about the bed configuration, although two doubles is the usual.

Some of these chains, like the Sleep Inns, Hampton Inns and Budgetels, are built new to basic plans. But I cannot rank the chains for you because the shifting of franchises and buying up of chains means that not all motels in some chains are standardized. When you reserve, you can ask when the motel was built or most recently renovated and that may tell you something.

Thin towels and thin walls—meaning noise—go with the territory. Dim lightbulbs may, too, and I know people who travel with a 100-watt bulb so they are able to read at bedtime. Dirt and bad mattresses are not part of the deal, so ask for a better room on either score.

Bumped

When you get to the airport early and a horde of backpackers is camped around your departure gate, your flight is probably going to be a scene for the bumping game. That is, passengers who hold confirmed tickets for that flight expect it to be overbooked, and are prepared to volunteer to yield their seats—to be bumped—in return for taking a later flight and a voucher for a future ticket. The backpack means that they have only carry-on luggage and are thus prepared. It may also mean they have been living at the airport for a couple of days while enacting this role. Week after week, the same flights are overbooked, and these people reserve them for that reason.

The airlines provide vouchers and other enticements to get passengers to surrender seats voluntarily, because if they are removed from a flight involuntarily the Department of Transportation regulation says that they must receive a certain amount of cash in compensation, which is more costly to the line than vouchers. (See **denied boarding compensation**.)

Two demon traveler friends, Danny and Annie Perasa, were aboard a full flight home from Las Vegas when the flight attendant asked for volunteers for bumping. "No way," Mrs. Perasa said. "Just let me get home to bed." Her husband asked a question of the attendant and returned. "You just gave up a round-trip ticket to anyplace in the United States," he said. "No way," Mrs. Perasa said. "I never give that up." And they got off the flight, Mrs. Perasa's fatigue having evaporated.

The price does rise once the passengers are seated although often enough a higher offer to the seated passengers will be matched for those who volunteered out in the gate area.

If you volunteer, ask about the voucher: restrictions on using it; its validity period (usually a year, but extensions may be available); can it be written in someone else's name? I had a voucher I wanted desperately to give to a friend because she had an urgent meeting and neither of us had the money for it. Because we were such inept cheaters, I almost ended up flying to Dallas myself. But as it turned out, when I volunteered to wait for the next flight with her in mind I could have had the voucher made out to her to begin with.

Certain flights are good candidates for overbooking and bumping: the Sunday noon flight from California to New York or Washington; Sunday flights from vacation areas to major cities in the summer; 5 or 6 P.M. flights from cities during the week. The rates vary by airline; see **bumping rates.**

A personal caution. Be sure that you are prepared to wait for whenever the next flight may be, which may not involve merely the one-hour wait that the gate agents predict. A friend and I agreed to be bumped from an American Airlines 8 A.M. flight to Barbados in return for a $300 voucher each and a two-and-a-half-hour wait for another airline's flight. When we got to the other airline's gate, it had never heard of us. American, embarrassed, increased our vouchers to $400 each, said it would arrange to cancel the lost night on our Barbados hotel reservation and promised to fly us first class the next morning. When the American flight attendant the next day heard what happened, we were offered champagne all the way, but we concluded that nothing was worth the loss of one day of sun from a one-week winter vacation. We wrote another letter of complaint, and we ended up with a total of $500 each in vouchers—the cost of our Barbados tickets. But if I could live it over, I would have stayed in that seat, mainly because we felt like such foolish victims and spent so much vacation time grousing about our maltreatment.

So far as bumping is concerned, whatever you want, either to get where you are going on schedule or to get there eventually but with a voucher for another trip, your song should be, "Get me to the airport on time." Hang on to your luggage, check in right away and if you anticipate a mob scene tell the counter agent right then that you will volunteer to be bumped.

Bumping Rates

Because **"denied boarding compensation"** is one of the few areas where the government still regulates domestic airlines, the Department of Transportation keeps track of how many passengers are bumped from their ticketed flights, whether by volunteering or otherwise. The airlines are then ranked by the percentage of passengers who are involuntarily bumped— that is, who must be paid a certain amount of money, not merely given a voucher for tickets.

American Airlines, with the largest number of passengers, has for several years had the lowest rate: For the first nine months of 1992, 0.37 passengers of every 10,000 of this line's passengers, less than a hundredth of 1 percent, could not get aboard their flights because of oversales. But in the same period, American gave a hefty total of 124,444 passengers, or 18 of every 10,000, vouchers to yield their seats and take the next flight—that is, to take them out of the "involuntarily denied boarding" column.

Trans World Airlines, operating in bankruptcy during this period, had an involuntary rate of 2.59 for every 10,000 passengers, six times American's rate, and gave vouchers to 17 out of every 10,000. Southwest had the highest involuntary rate in the period, 3.6 for every 10,000, and gave vouchers to only 10 in 10,000.

The Department of Transportation issues these figures monthly, along with other demerits such as lost luggage complaints and flight delays, by airline, flight and airport. A single copy of "Air Travel Consumer Report" may be obtained by writing Office of Consumer Affairs, Department of Transportation, 400 Seventh Street, S.W., Room 10405, Washington, D.C. 20590.

I love reading these tables, and there is a lot of information in them. But unless you organize travel for, say, a whole organization and you book enough flights to bring the averages into play, there is no real point in planning your travel around such statistics.

Cabs in a Strange Language

Everyone knows the nightclub routine about telling the Paris cabby where you are going. You can pronounce "Gare du Nord" with an accent that would satisfy the Academie Française and the cabby will say, "Eh?" which is probably spelled "Hein," and on it goes. Eventually, you get some passerby who translates, saying "Gare du Nord" just as you did, and then the cabby says, "Ah, GARE DU NORD!"

My friend Ursula Mahoney solved this one long ago. Because she is a sometime painter and calligrapher, she carries a nice unlined pad about the size of a stenographer's notebook. Before we leave the hotel in France, Italy or wherever, she writes out boldly, sometimes in fancy letters, the address we want. She shows this to the cabby with a "s'il vous plaît" and off we go.

Mercifully for us who barely hobble about in other languages, the electronic age has brought forth taximeters that all read in roughly comprehensible digits. Failing this, you can whip out a pocket calculator and ask the cabby to punch in the fare for you to read.

Getting back? Easy. Have your host, or the restaurant owner, call a cab and give your destination to the driver in an accent that causes no difficulty. For some other ideas on scaling the language barrier, see **symbols.**

Cancellation Insurance

This is insurance that will pay you back your deposit if you are unable to make a trip for reasons that the policy covers, such as a death in the family or a serious and new illness.

It should come with trip interruption or trip delay coverage so you can get home if you must, or catch up again if you have to miss a departure en route. Good policies provide reimbursement for lost deposits and entire tour payments in the event the tour operator defaults or goes bankrupt. (See **tour operator default**.) Minimal lost baggage coverage is usually thrown in.

Few topics generate so much angry mail to the Practical Traveler column as trip cancellation insurance. In the worst case I recall, a couple had paid $30,000 for a cruise in the Far East, including air fare to the embarkation port. They paid $179 extra each for trip-cancellation insurance. They flew to Asia, where the husband fell ill, and the doctor there told him to go home and be treated. So without ever setting foot aboard the cruise vessel, they returned home, where the husband was hospitalized and recovered. When they filed a claim for the cost of the cruise, the insurance administrator pointed out that the brochure stated that coverage ended when the couple left home to begin their trip. Although they collected for the emergency air trip home, they lost most of the $30,000.

Their travel agent blamed herself because she did not know of the policy deficiency in time to get the clients added—and essential—coverage for trip interruption or trip delay to fill the period after cancellation coverage ends. This sort of thing, unfortunately, happens all the time.

If you are booking an expensive trip, particularly one where you buy everything from one source—a cruise, for instance, or a big package tour—do your best to insure whatever part of the cost you cannot afford to lose. This means you want insurance that covers straight through: to protect your deposit or full payment if you must cancel any time up to the moment you leave, if you must interrupt the trip from that moment on or if you suffer a delay that keeps you from connecting with your tour at some point. Look carefully at the section that defines when coverage begins and when it ends. Some policies stop as much as 72 hours before the trip begins, so stumbling on your way to the airport would not be covered.

If your trip is a big investment, the small type will be important to you. When you go to buy, read limitations carefully, and not optimistically. Assume the company is going to interpret everything literally. If the policy does not list stepchildren, assume they are not covered.

These policies may bear any number of names—house brand names for the cruise company that offers them, or a tour operator's name—but the underwriter is an insurance company. They may be sold as freestanding coverage by a travel agent, by an insurance broker or directly by a company that administers insurance and deals with claims, known as an insurance administrator. When you examine the policy, you need to learn the name of the actual insurance company, the underwriter. Sometimes your own insurance broker can give an insight into how the company behaves on settling claims. I know the broker at my insurance agent's office has very decided opinions on which companies drag their feet on paying and which jump to it. The jump-to-it guys have higher premiums, of course, but her judgment was borne out when I had an auto accident.

Some of the underwriters involved in trip cancellation, interruption and delay insurance belong to the American International Group (or A.I.G.) of New York, to the Chubb Group, TransAmerica of Los Angeles, Mutual of Omaha, the BCS Company of Chicago, and Travelers of Hartford. Over the years, I have watched policies with the same wrappers shift from one carrier to another, which is genuinely the reason I cannot give you a list of the companies that behave well and are helpful and the companies that should get out of the field. Things move too fast, and this is a very profitable field.

If you are putting the trip together yourself, or with a travel agent, inspect the refund provisions for everything: the hotel deposits, the air ticket, the canal cruise, the rail pass. If you can claim a refund when you cancel out, minus some modest fee, the insurance will probably cost more than the fee. But if you stand to lose a lot on some section of it, insure that part. Friends of mine who had an alert travel agent reclaimed everything on six parts of a custom-planned trip when the husband unexpectedly had to have heart surgery.

I have become increasingly unhappy with most of the big brand-name policies. The letters I get indicate that people believed that because they bought a brand name—Access America, for example, or Travel Guard, or similar items seen in every travel agency rack—they were in a safe zone. Then when they could not get a claim paid they felt betrayed.

No policy is any better than what is written in it, and most of them are a lot worse. I have seen an insurance company deny a claim that was made by a policyholder when her daughter had a life-threatening illness because the insurance company ruled that an upper respiratory infection the previous summer constituted a preexisting condition. I have also seen denial of a claim based on destruction of the destination hotel by fire because such events were "not listed," and denial of a claim based on loss of the building housing the family business because it was not the principal residence. I was incredulous at all of these responses, but the insurers invariably pointed to the small type and the travelers had no real recourse, although many of them wrote to state attorneys general or state consumer affairs departments. Most policies will not pay when the traveler cancels because war has broken out.

All of these policies have clauses excluding major benefit payments when the policyholder, business partner, traveling companion or a family member has a preexisting illness. All specify what they mean by absence of a preexisting condition, that is, how long the person must have gone without requiring treatment, usually 60 or 90 days. All of these policies define which family members' illness or death is an allowable basis for a claim.

Get hold of the actual policy early, particularly if you are shopping for an expensive trip. If the policy differs markedly from the brochure, take action, including calling your state insurance department or consumer affairs department. At this writing, I believe that this is one of the most profitable and unpoliced areas in the travel industries, and only consumer action is going to change things. New York State, early in 1992, began to look more closely at what was being sold and at the prices and in 1993 began to tighten up so that the only companies that could sell trip insurance were those that filed their policies in advance so the state could approve or adjust the ratio of premium cost to benefits paid.

Do not imagine you are getting something valuable in coverage for accidental death and dismemberment, which are remote possibilities. The $500 baggage coverage probably would not buy the empty suitcases, but your home property insurance should have adequate provisions for your luggage. The real bottom line is what you will get if you cancel out after the operator's deadline, and how you will get home if you become ill. Under **emergency evacuation,** you will find information about buying coverage for a trip home on a stretcher, or by helicopter from Everest.

See **waiver** for information on the hazards of this type of protection.

Caribbean Medical Help

"Medical care is limited," say the State Department consular information sheets for country after country in the Caribbean. In the case of Cuba, the statement is couched in harsher, more political terms: "Medical care does not meet U.S. standards," which is certainly what the other entries also mean.

Every winter, the uncertainty about Caribbean hospitals—physicians may be well trained and plentiful, but equipment and supplies are scarce—is brought home again, both in requests for information about certified hospitals and in letters that say "Did my son-in-law have to die?" "I want to warn about . . ." or "Drs. Brady, Andujar and Arzola saved her life," but in truth were able to do it only because there was an ambulance parked at the beach.

There is a hidden issue here. When winter stiffens its grip, people who don't feel tiptop crave warm weather, relaxation and escape from the everyday grind. The tropical islands of the Bahamas or the Caribbean enable the fatigued to leave

behind sirens that scream at 2 A.M., but the fatigued will likewise leave behind the hospital where the ambulance is
headed.

Two basics. First, read **survival overseas** one more time,
with emphasis. Avoid the need for major emergency medical
care in a place that may have none by avoiding risks. Waterskiing, jet-skiing, high-speed motorboating, hang gliding, bun-
gee jumping, parachute waterskiing, skydiving and similar
daredevil undertakings, as well as using mopeds and motorcycles, should be limited to people who already know the
techniques, who are sober and have not lost a sense of caution. Yes, indeed, snow skiing, sailing, snorkeling and hiking
have their hazards, but they do not involve either overpow-
ered engines or taking risks for the thrill of it.

Dr. Stephen W. Hargarten of the Medical College of Wisconsin in Milwaukee, who has focused his travel medicine research on injury prevention, studied the emergency transport
cases in which members of the Association of Air Medical
Services were involved. Of 796 patients using air evacuation
from 1988 to 1990, injuries were the cause for evacuation of
44 percent of the patients; noncardiac medical illnesses, 22
percent; and acute cardiac problems—myocardial infarction,
angina, postcardiac arrest—for 18 percent. Infectious diseases
other than pneumonia constituted only 1.4 percent of the total cases and gunshot or stab wounds 1.6 percent. Sixty-one
percent of the cases were men. Mexico, the Virgin Islands
and the Bahamas were the source of 59 percent of the cases.

A letter describes the jet-skiing death of a 40-year-old man
on Aruba, who was struck broadside by the rental company's
speedboat, saying, "Jet-ski customers, who are tourists . . .
cannot be expected to be experts on jet-ski operation or the
rules of the sea." Precisely. Blaming the victim is a rotten

practice, but in these cases the responsibility of the victim cannot be ignored.

Scuba divers who have not received complete training at home, in a swimming pool perhaps, should probably not decide to take it up in the Caribbean; most Caribbean islands do not have decompression chambers, and with the possibility of inexperienced instruction a mistake could do great harm. (See also **diving and flying**.)

The second basic is to be fully aware of where you are going and how readily you can get out of there in an emergency. Little islands that are off other islands, where you can leave only by boat, seaplane or helicopter, are bad choices for chronic cardiac patients. Jerry Edwards, who has for years run telephone assistance services for credit card companies, said: "Some places, the best piece of medical equipment . . . is the next airplane out."

If you have a chronic problem that may act up, and you are likely to need a well-equipped hospital, look at the map and figure out whether Miami or Puerto Rico is the best shot, and then look at plane schedules to see how long it is between scheduled flights. There are airlift services available, but the price can be rugged.

Margaret Zellers, who keeps a close eye on the Caribbean for her Fielding's Guides, says no one with a chronic problem should leave for the islands without the name of at least one ɪ airlift service to Miami, or in the southern Caribbean to Puerto Rico. I would suggest membership in an **emergency evacuation** group, but in any case, some preparation should be made. In her 1993 edition, her rating-the-islands chart awarded stars for medical facilities to Barbados, the Cayman Islands, Cuba, Jamaica and Puerto Rico. But as she worked on the 1994 edition, she said that Puerto Rico and, for French speakers, Martinique and Guadeloupe were the only places where she considered the medical facilities could meet tourist needs. Supplies and equipment are short everywhere, she said, and hospitals are overcrowded with local patients. Jamaica, she said, is overwhelmed by medical problems. And throughout the Caribbean, Ms. Zellers said, the AIDS question is not being faced.

None of this should be interpreted as warning that a trip to the Caribbean is unwise; by this theory, you would never hike into backcountry, visit the third world or hike inn to inn. It just means that people with chronic problems should plan how to deal with them.

The question of which hospitals are accredited implies a failure to understand that the United States is not in charge of everything. Most of the Caribbean and the Bahamas consists of independent countries, which may inspect their hospitals or not. In the U.S., hospitals are reaccredited every three years, upon request and payment of a stiff inspection charge, by the Joint Commission of Accreditation of Healthcare Organizations, a creature of the American College of Physicians, the American College of Surgeons, the American Dental Association, the American Hospital Association and the American Medical Association.

In 1993, 34 hospitals in Puerto Rico held accreditation from this body. The Joint Commission, after an inspection, issues one of these ratings: accreditation with commendation (a level instituted in 1991); accreditation without a recommendation (established in 1993); accreditation with a "type 1" recommendation, which refers to a specific area needing work; conditional accreditation (established in 1989), where there are conditions that must be remedied in six months; and nonaccreditation.

On its customer service line, the Joint Commission will tell you if the hospital you have in mind is accredited, and at what level. It will also tell you, if you ask specifically, in case the hospital near you is not accredited, whether it did not seek accreditation, or it lapsed, or it could not pass. This is a check to make when you learn from a resort where the nearest hospital is. The commission will not recommend a hospital, however, only report on one you ask about. Joint Commission, 1 Renaissance Boulevard, Oakbrook Terrace, Ill. 60181; customer service: 708-916-5800.

As for finding a physician, get what information you can before you leave home. Your physician may have a classmate practicing in the area or may find a fellow member of some specialty group there. I heard once of a family who bought a vacation for their physician and family at a nearby resort, but that is beyond the reach of most of us.

Dr. Richard Dawood, a Briton who is editor of *Travelers' Health: How to Stay Healthy All Over the World*, says that there were a number of scandals at European resorts in 1993 where the tour companies' local representatives received kickbacks for recommending certain physicians. As a tourist, you may have no idea how the local back-scratching works, and if it is an emergency in a hotel in the middle of the night, and you have no number of your own, your choices may be limited.

Many gold credit cards offer a 24-hour assistance phone line for getting information in medical emergencies. I have watched the assistance aides work and they can be quite good, particularly when they have worked on an emergency in the same area recently and thus have a good line on physicians and facilities. Many of them are children of military families and have languages and knowledge of foreign countries. Take the number with you; the 800 numbers will work in the parts of the Caribbean that are on the 809 area code; otherwise you must call a U.S. number collect and say "medical emergency." (For more information, see **emergency evacuation**.)

The entry on **I.A.M.A.T.** offers added information.

A couple of other thoughts. Pack good, legible medical records. If heart is the question, and you have had a recent cardiogram, take it with you to enable a physician to evaluate any changes. Likewise, X rays. Carry your own physician's numbers, including pager number, because the phone service in the Caribbean has been upgraded since Hurricane Hugo and your doctor may be able to help the local doctor assess what is happening to you.

Medicare and Medicare B do not cover outside the United States, Puerto Rico, the Virgin Islands, Guam or American Samoa. "Foreign physician and ambulance services are covered in connection with a covered stay in a Canadian or Mexican hospital," the rules say. If you have a Medicare supplement, check what it will do elsewhere, or buy some added coverage. Check if the added coverage has emergency evacuation provisions. If an emergency strikes, be sure the insurance administration office first approves what you are going to do; it may consider that the local physicians can set your arm perfectly well, and faster.

And back to the State Department consular information sheets. The "medical facilities" entry for almost every country says: "Doctors and hospitals often expect immediate cash payment for health services."

Car Keys

On assignment in the tiny town of Whiteville, North Carolina, I locked my keys in the rental car at the motel. The
locksmith was a miracle of promptness, and I do not know
how he could possibly make a living on the tiny amount he
charged for driving over, sliding that metal strip into the
door and retrieving the keys. After that, I tried to imagine
how I would have coped if I had stopped in the mountains to
buy a bottle of birch beer and had pulled the same
boneheaded move. I have my own memory devices to keep
from locking myself out now—one hand for the key, one hand
for the latch—but the peril is still great with an unfamiliar
rental car on the open road.

One reader wrote to say that the first thing she did when
she rented an auto was to get a spare key made to keep on
her person. If several people rent a car together, this is a
sensible precaution because the guardian of the keys may go
in some other direction, still carrying the keys.

In our family, we have a joke derived from an old Charles
Addams cartoon showing the shadow of a huge flying bird
with a man in its talons, with the woman running down the
beach below shouting, "George! George! Drop the keys!"
Whenever it looks as if one of us in danger of falling overboard, or is drifting away from the shore accidentally, or sliding down a ski slope out of control, we shout: "George! Drop
the keys!" But it isn't always a laughing matter; keys on the
bottom of the deep end of a motel pool can be a problem.

Carry-on Baggage

Jim Burnett, former chair of the National Transportation
Safety Board who traveled by air a lot and never minced
words in my presence, said that he had been hit in the head
three times by huge bags that popped out of overhead com-

partments in turbulence. He said he failed to understand why anything heavy was allowed overhead, and I have the same view: Suitcases should be under foot and coats and hats overhead. But no one asked us and even though the government has given the airlines the power to limit strictly the size and number of bags that are carried into the airplane cabin, the airlines crumple under this task.

The real problem, in my view, is that although flight attendants' jobs are primarily safety jobs and only secondarily comfort jobs, the two components are so conflicting that the flight attendants can almost never bring themselves to be tough with the customers. The sales side of their jobs, "Thank you for flying Shagbird Airlines," quashes the "You have three valet packs and an elephant with a handle, and you must give us the elephant to check."

When the carry-on limitation went into force in the late 80s, I talked to all the airlines about what their limits would be, and they specified the types of planes and the suitcase dimensions down to quarters of an inch, whether briefcases and purses counted, and gave a lot of other information that sounded like a post office clerk describing how to wrap an umbrella for mailing. But we reverted almost instantly: big, bad and ugly customers coming aboard with huge bags and spreading them along the overheads—which are not so territorial as the foot space—over my head, your head, their heads.

A scene I saw aboard an American Airlines plane tore the veil from the personalities of people with gigantic carry-ons but also showed that flight attendants cannot be pushed forever. A film crew from Germany was leaving Albuquerque, and using a luggage puller they brought aboard many of those metal cases used for photographic equipment. A flight attendant, Sharon Harless, said later she told them that they had too many carry-ons, and one of the three men replied that they were needed for bombs. "I was pretty sure it was a joke," Ms. Harless said, "but I told the captain."

Within minutes, airport security, Albuquerque police, the F.B.I. and who knows what else arrived and brusquely marched the film crew and their cases off. A blasting mat was thrown over the cases, which I could see for a while beyond the tip of the wing. We took off, late, minus the film guys. I later got the rest of the story. Captain Don Mayhew of the Albuquerque police said he told the filmmakers that police could either X-ray the cases or blow them open with water cannon. Either would have destroyed the film. The leader of the Germans volunteered to open up the cases himself and did. The film crew was released on the understanding that they were leaving the country, and the government did not prosecute because of a lack of criminal intent.

At any rate, the bag limit is not supposed to be more than two, but if you are to fly a wide-body and it is underpopulated you can probably bring aboard more. If you travel as I try to, all carry-on, keep those bags from bloating like sausages lest you become unable to stuff them under the seat. If you are flying a tight-fit commuter plane, there are no options, but the benefit is that they take the bag away from you right on the tarmac and you know that it goes into the plane you are on.

I want to believe that the two-bag limit is enforced evenly, but my perception is that linebacker types, particularly if they have had a few beers in the airport bar, are likely to get away with a lot more than I can because the flight attendants dislike confrontations on boarding. "We are going to be spending several hours locked into a tube with those people,"

one flight attendant at a safety seminar explained, "and starting off on a bad note is going to make it tough." I try to
respect the two-bag rule, but the issue of whether my briefcase is a briefcase or a purse does not attract a lot of attention and sometimes I have a knitting bag underneath the coat
on my arm. But no elephants with a handle.

Centers for Disease Control and Prevention

This federal complex of organizations in Atlanta has been a
mainstay in the preparation of the health sections of this
book because they are authoritative and unbureaucratic.
They know everything a traveler needs to know, from when
malaria mosquitoes bite (at night) to how to protect against
cholera (not with a vaccine but by avoiding local water and
seafood and other foods.).

If you don't use a travel clinic, you can get information to
assist your doctor, or your doctor can get information, directly from the centers. The phone numbers are 404-332-4559
or 404-332-4555, and the number for ordering fax sheets with
information is 404-332-4565. To learn about using this resource, see **immunization help by fax or phone.**

Child Flying Alone

In 1986, the Department of Transportation assigned some experts to prepare a leaflet about children taking airplane
flights alone. With the rise in divorce and fractionated families, travel by children alone is probably still rising, although
no one keeps precise track. But increasingly bitter custody
fights combined with the vulnerability of children alone to
molestation probably mean no government agency would now
write about children traveling alone. And I would rather
there were no such question; I have heard a lot of bad news.

There are circumstances where a child's going alone appears unavoidable. When custody is shared by two hostile and far-removed parents, or when grandparents have visitation rights or care for a child while the parents work, a child must often move great distances at the end and beginning of the school year. My belief, five years after I first wrote about this issue, is that strong measures should be taken to avoid entrusting a child to an organization as large and impersonal as an airline, even for a short nonstop flight. It's not my field, but I think divorce lawyers should consider provision for payment to an accompanying adult, possibly a college student, to go with any child moving from one parent to another. If one parent travels a lot, frequent flier miles could provide for the child's ticket and the fare money could be used for an escort's trip.

If there is no way out of this situation, here are some basics. The child must be at least five years old to travel alone on a domestic flight. (Arrangements for the transportation of an infant overseas can be sometimes made with an airline, which uses an off-duty flight attendant to carry the child.) Most airlines will accept children five, six or seven years old on a flight that involves no change of plane. The child will pay a regular adult fare. From eight to eleven, the child will be accepted on a flight involving a change of plane or a connection, if a fee is paid for the child to be escorted to the connection. At twelve, the child will be allowed to make a connection alone, although the parent who wishes may still pay the fee and request an escort through the change. This decision should be based on how mature the child is, and a parent should be aware that if the twelve-year-old is unescorted the airline will have no power to keep the child from settling in a video game room and missing the next flight.

Every step of how this is going to work should be confirmed with the travel agent or airline, and the name of the airline agent preparing the reservation should be written down.

A child should never be scheduled so that he or she is to connect with a flight that is the last one out of the airport that night. I have heard of flight attendants, both on and off duty, who have taken children home overnight when a flight was canceled, but I do not want to think about that or, worse yet, the alternatives.

A child alone should be wearing or carrying a tag with full information written on it, including phone numbers for the people who put the child on the flight and those who will meet the flight.

The person taking the child to the airport bears a great responsibility, and if it is not the parent the helpful friend should be warned not to be in a hurry: The escort must see the plane take off, even if it is delayed, the gate is changed, or the flight is canceled and another substituted. Then the escort should be able to call the party at the other end and give the details on any changes. The departure escort should then be at an arranged phone number in case the child calls to report being grounded at some intermediate point, or to hear from the receiving family that the child is safe on base.

I would also want to know the phone number at the arrival gate of the airline at the other end. This is not easy to worm out of airlines, but if you have a child about to board you have a maximum opportunity to learn this. (The airlines know this number because it is the one you must call to tell your waiting party if your flight has been canceled.)

Probably the meanest problem is whether the airline will be willing or able to require identification from the person

who is meeting the child. Even when the sending parent
specifies that this must be obtained, or that the child may be
picked up only by a specific grandparent, it is clear that an
airline is nearly helpless if the child rushes into the arms of a
waiting person. Once again, in this sort of situation you
should find an escort for the child.

The child should be rehearsed in certain responsibilities.
The ticket and information tag should be shown to the flight
attendant at each step so any errors can be caught. The child
should know how to make a collect phone call or should have
a **debit phone card** and know how to use it.

You are not out of the woods, alas, when the child becomes
a teenager. Some motels do not permit independent registration of guests under 21, and the teenager needs to understand that being stranded at an airport in midtrip may mean
—oh, grisly humiliation—asking the airline to help get a bed
instead of an airport bench to sleep on. If the child looks
particularly mature, this may be a hard one. Also, if your
adolescent child carries a credit card with your name embossed on the front and the child's signature on the back, be
aware that certain charges like a refund to change an airline
ticket may not be permitted.

Child Safety Seat

For some, this entry may seem didactic. But if you are the
parent of a child under 40 pounds or 40 inches, it is important.

Every one of the 50 states, however benighted its speed
limits or adult seat-belt requirements, has enacted some law
requiring that a child ride "restrained" in an auto, meaning
the child must be in a safety seat or a seat belt. These laws
may be enforced laxly, but they exist as a reminder that

children are a more important natural resource than petroleum.

The airline business is something else. A child under 2 is the only person at this writing who is permitted by law to ride in an airplane without wearing a seat belt. And economics encourages parents to carry infants and toddlers on their laps, because such a lap ride is free.

You may already have heard that riding to the airport is more dangerous than the flight itself. So why am I chewing the curtains about safety seats on airplanes? One reason. The likelihood of being *killed* in an airplane may be remote; the likelihood of being *injured* in an airplane if you are a unbelted child under two is rather greater. It takes minimal turbulence to cause an adult to lose a grip on a "lap child." In January 1993, two lap children were tossed around a plane over Florida; one was injured and the other landed in someone's arms two rows back. The National Transportation Safety Board has once again urged the Department of Transportation to require the use of safety seats or seat belts for *all* passengers.

In the past, the department has conducted studies and concluded that parents, faced with the expense of buying extra plane seats to hold the safety seats, would decide to drive instead.

This response strikes me as not only misguided but specious. If safety seats were required, airlines would certainly manage to offer some competitive fare for kids under two that would net more than they are now getting—$0—but less than the full child fare that is required over the age of two.

I feel entitled to speak sternly because I have watched tests of child safety seats holding special wired-up dummies. In the Oklahoma City Civil Aeromedical Institute laborato-

ries of the Federal Aviation Administration, sleds of airline
seats holding safety seats were slammed to a stop at a mere
30 miles an hour. The safety seats kept the airline seats up-
right. I did not have to look more than once to understand
what could happen to a child riding in an adult's lap in such a
stop.

The tests were being conducted at the request, and expense, of the Canadian Government. In the United States,
there may be a tacit national policy that says children are not
entitled to protection if it might hurt the airline business, but
you as a parent do not have to subscribe to it. Do whatever
is required. Use your frequent flier awards, or even money,
to get a child a companion ticket, but have your child ride
safely buckled in.

Children and Museums

My sister has an ingenious way of avoiding being dragged
out of a museum before she has time to buy postcards and
pencils for the children. She shops before she goes inside. If
you have kids with you and the place has a good display of
postcards, I have found it works well to take them in there
immediately and tell them they may select one or two cards
that interest them most. Then they are really tickled when
they see the original. A postcard in the hand also gives them
the power to ask an attendant where they may find Hopper's
"Nighthawks" even if they cannot pronounce the title.

The order of entry to a museum, as any grandparent will
tell you, is: Get ticket, check coat and bookpack, buy postcards, use toilet, see museum. Refreshments at the end.

Child-friendly museums always have a stash of inexpensive
souvenirs to protect those of us who must buy for more than
one grandchild. But I have found the rule we set for children

still works for grandchildren: Yes, we'll always get you a postcard or a small book, but there will be no impulse buying.

China

Most countries do not get a separate entry in this book, but China deserves a couple of caveats. First, if you have chronic upper respiratory problems or do not feel that your immune system is in fighting trim, China is going to be a hard trip for you. The incidence of pneumonia, flu, chest infections, bad colds and similar problems in tour groups is legion. When China first reopened to foreign travelers, information was sparse, but it is not any more and this is the word.

Second, the travel business in China is in flux. It is neither capitalist nor communist but a disorderly condition between. If you read the provisions in the back of any tour operator's brochure, you will see that no one can guarantee even an approximate itinerary let alone specific cities on particular days. Larry Kwan, vice-president of Pacific Delight, a major U.S. operator in China, agreed with one disgruntled customer that the loss of six items on a 26-day tour was terrible but there was no refund because the brochure warned of this possibility. The president of Pacific Delight said he had told Chinese officials that such lax performance by the China International Travel Service was inevitably going to diminish travelers from overseas as a source of hard currency.

There are two potential remedies. One is to be sure you get on a tour with an escort from the United States. More often than not, this depends on the size of the group, but keep tabs on it and pull out if the tour is undersubscribed. A U.S. escort comes equipped with the bargaining power of his or her tour operator, and with dollars. The combination of dollars and future business may repair a crumbling itinerary.

The other remedy is to have a travel agent put together an independent tour for you. In China, the independent tourist may be subject to huge anxieties about catching flights and trains if no one is running interference for you but you may be able to get what you want as you go along. I think again of Phileas Fogg, buying the vessel with his carpetbag full of money.

Church Suppers and Clambakes

Signs along the road for church suppers, firefighters' chicken barbecues, clambakes and the like gladden the heart. The price is always modest and the evening meal is usually early, to get the kids home in time or to leave time for a country auction where everyone holds a 25-cent head of cabbage and swats mosquitoes with the other hand. There is still time to find a motel or B & B down the road.

It is also an ideal time to meet local people, who are happy you are there—you're bringing in out-of-town money—and want to tell you about the good places to visit or the beach access that no one knows about. We went to a church social on the lawn in Low Country South Carolina where we ended up sitting with someone who was apparently one of my half-million half-cousins. What a time! We were introduced to everyone by a combination of my name, my mother's name and my great-grandmother's name.

If you go to a local supper, keep a tactful but wary eye on your food choices. Super-hot baked beans can't hurt you, nor a piece of chicken or fish or a hot dog plucked blazing from the grill. Chowder steaming in a cauldron is probably okay, but skip lukewarm soup and lukewarm chili. Cornbread, biscuits, certainly, since it would be hard to find a bread that will hurt you. I would avoid chicken salad, potato salad, egg salad—the traditional hazards—unless it is clear that they have been on ice until now. You want to save space for the pie anyway.

Closing Up the House

When we got home from Europe once to find a little collar of ice in the toilet bowl, I realized that a few more hours and we would have come home to a house full of burst pipes—a grisly possibility.

Here's a quick checklist to help you create a departure list. The best recourse of all, of course, is to have someone live in your house while you are gone and cope with everything including your calls.

Deal with the mail as well as newspaper and any other deliveries.

Get a device to attach to the phone line that creates a busy signal if the temperature drops. Ours is called Telefreeze, but they come by other trade names. Ask your plumbing contractor if you cannot find one. Give your plumber a key and a payment to keep checking the number in cold weather.

In season, arrange for snow clearance.

Set the thermostat low.

Fill the boiler and water heater.

Close and latch the windows.

Post over the phone a list of emergency numbers for the plumber, the electrician, anyone else who might be needed, along with your itinerary and phone numbers.

Pour out the leftover milk and dispose of anything else likely to go bad in the refrigerator. Since no one will open the door, ease up on the cold setting.

Decide what you want to do about an answering machine. If you get a lot of messages, it may overload.

Leave a list of your credit card numbers and passport numbers, an itinerary with phone numbers and a house key with a friend who will be easily available. I ask an office friend to perform this role because I know when she will be available.

Ask a neighbor to drop by periodically to take free samples off the doorknob and fliers off the mat.

Plants to water? Put them in one place with the pitcher nearby.

Have a neighbor change the configuration of the burning lights periodically. (We do not trust devices that turn lights on and off on a time clock because a power failure unhinged one friend's gadget and the lights flashed on and off every few seconds for weeks. The signal read: "House empty! House empty! House empty!")

Lawn mowing? Other regular maintenance? Make the necessary arrangements.

Check the stove burners, the iron, the faucets. Be sure any washing machine has finished its cycle and shut off.

When you get on the doorstep, check again to see that you have your front door key.

Do not hide things. Don't put the key under the mat, in the mailbox or the milk box. Do not put your jewelry in the laundry hamper. Do not put a car key under the hood. Burglars know all of these and some you think you made up.

Collision Damage Waiver

By whatever name, this is the provision that the auto rental company wants you to agree to and pay a daily fee for. If you accept and the car is stolen or damaged in a collision, the rental company will pay for the repairs because it has waived its right to collect from you the repair costs. Hence, collision damage waiver, loss damage waiver, C.D.W.

In 1987, when I began writing the Practical Traveler column, New York was trying to regulate sales of the C.D.W. on the grounds that it was insurance, charging that the rental companies were making unconscionable profits on these daily fees. On the basis of a daily payment of $10, the annual charge would be $3,650, which beggars even my auto insurance.

Unfortunately, although a great hullabaloo has been created and now we know what the initials stand for, the situation has not improved a great deal. New York State and Illinois have legislated the C.D.W. away, forbidding auto rental companies to charge extra daily amounts for relieving the renter of financial responsibility if the car is stolen or damaged, and have put a cap on what the renter may be required to pay in a theft or accident. But the rates in those states have risen a commensurate amount and some small auto dealerships that rented cars as a sideline say they cannot afford to be in the rental business anymore.

Other states have taken other steps. California and Hawaii put caps on the daily C.D.W. charge. Others require that the renting company make a full disclosure of the terms, not just in what lawyers call "mice type," or specify that the renter be told the coverage is purely voluntary.

The really intimidating part of the C.D.W. is the small type that cannot possibly be read while you stand at the counter. It probably specifies that no one but you may drive the car unless you declare this at the outset, that you may not take the auto into certain states and other bans, including driving under the influence of drink or drugs. If any provision is violated, the C.D.W. is voided and you are going to pay for the repairs anyway.

There is another unchewable potato in the stew and that is

criminals who decide to rent a car, with a C.D.W., for use in a theft or a drug run: Witnesses do not link the car to the driver, the rental saves damage to the criminals' own cars and, in an accident, the C.D.W. protects the renter's insurance rates. Because the rented cars are often never returned or are totaled, rental agencies have been experiencing heavy drains in certain areas. This has caused what amounts to redlining: In high crime areas, car rental companies will not rent to local residents. In states where the C.D.W. is still legal, the companies may rent to local people but will not sell them a C.D.W. Ironically, for downtown people who own no auto but rent for weekends and vacations the inability to buy a C.D.W. may be a problem more serious than the outlandish price.

This distressing situation aside, what preparations should an auto renter make to deal with the C.D.W.?

Get to the counter prepared. Once you have done this research, you can initial the "rejected" box and not listen for one minute to the threatening words a counter agent may speak. Many agencies pay the counter people extra if they have a strong record in selling waivers and employees of these companies do not hesitate to engage in strong-arm arguments.

If you own an auto, find out if your collision policy covers a rental auto. Be clear when you call your broker: You are not talking about whether the policy will pay for you to rent an auto if your own is in the shop; you want to know if the car you rent is covered for collision, rollover and theft. Don't forget that your deductible will apply to the rental car, too. Get a value for the total coverage for your car; you are going to rent a newer car in all likelihood and you want to know what you owe on the deductible at the bottom and the overage at the top. If it's more than you want to deal with, ask your broker what you can buy.

Examine what your credit card will do for you. In the C.D.W., the charge card companies found a place to offer an added benefit. If you have a gold Visa or MasterCard or a Diners Club card, or an American Express card, it may give you C.D.W. coverage. As the crime situation has gotten tougher and the economics of car rental more trying, some of these cards are cutting back. Increasingly, the cards are limiting what they will cover overseas.

Except for Diners Club, domestically this provision is "secondary"—that is, it covers what your own auto insurance does not cover. You may or may not have to pay for damage yourself until the credit card company learns what your insurance has paid for and reimburses you for the rest. Diners Club covers up to $25,000 and you need not use your own insurance at all.

You do not need to tell the counter agent why you are rejecting the C.D.W., but agents may ask and then say that their rental company does not deal with that card. Most of us do not have the patience of a renter in this situation who goes to a pay phone and calls the credit card company and then returns to say "You're wrong." Likewise, a rental company would not be able to force you to stay in the state until the claim is paid; a court can do that if there is an accident and you are implicated, but that won't have anything to do with an insurance claim.

There is one other evil possibility. A rental company, particularly overseas, may put a "hold" on your credit card if you refuse the C.D.W. If the hold is for anything like the value of the car—as opposed to the cost of the rental—it can eat up your credit line in one gulp. If you are going to deal with a company you have never heard of before, in a town with few options, or on a busy holiday, call in advance and ask if this is a possibility. Get an authoritative answer from someone with a name. Write down the name. Prepare for the worst.

In Italy and New Zealand, your credit card may not be any help in meeting C.D.W. requirements. If you can manage, reserve in the United States before you leave and get all the details specified on the agreement.

Computer on Board

In 1990, when the Practical Traveler column first got an inquiry about taking a portable computer through airport security, it took a lot of research to find answers for the executive who found herself crawling around on the airport floor to plug in her machine to show the guards it was really a computer. Today, everyone has an answer and some hackers have more than one.

But if you have never had the experience, take certain precautions. Have new batteries in your laptop or notebook computer. Carry a spare set. Keep your computer and all its disks in its own case, or at the top of the case it's in. Hand the computer and its disks outside the metal detector and outside the X-ray machine to the security guard. When you are asked to turn it on, turn it on with battery power. Many experts say they fling their computers through the X-ray machine, but cooler heads warn against it.

On the plane, put the computer on the floor under your feet where you can watch it. Don't make the error of dropping the disks into your pocket when you're done but put them back into the computer case so their precious data will bypass magnetic fields if you go through security again.

The matter of using the computer while in flight was suddenly thrown into turmoil in mid-1993. Some business flights began to look like offices, with computers clicking away all down the aisle. Then pilots began to complain that they were seeing interference on their instruments, so flight attendants asked that all computers be shut off and stowed. Several airlines banned their use in flight, along with use of cellular phones and some other electronic devices.

As with all airline safety regulations, the government establishes the minimum requirement but the airlines may make more stringent rules of their own. The use of laptop computers seems a likely area where airlines will all move in a conservative direction because no one wants pilots receiving distorted information. It may revive the pad and pencil, if anyone remembers how to use them.

Connecting Times

The Official Airline Guide, one of the principal tools of a travel agent, specifies in all its versions the minimum connecting time for each airport listed. Usually, it's 45 minutes. Some airports like Dallas–Fort Worth or Denver's Stapleton are huge and complex and even have rail lines to connect separate terminals. If the arriving flight is the least bit late, even the specified connecting time will not save you in one of these mazes.

A recommendation: Either allow yourself overadequate connecting time and take a good book, or be sure you are not trying to catch the last flight out of your connecting airport, that is, that you have some further options. If you need a golf cart to get from one gate to the next, have the agent at your first airport order it up for you.

There is no way of knowing when a airline will hold a con-

necting flight, although Delta has a reputation for doing it
more often than the other airlines and this shows up in their
on-time ratings collated by the government. There are im-
ponderables; for example, many airports have curfews dic-
tated by noise regulations. In such a case, a flight that could
easily have been held 10 minutes longer for the incoming connection may not be held.

When you're coming in late for a connection, get out the
diagram in the back of the airline magazine that shows the
arrangement of the gates at the airport. Then listen for
the flight attendant's announcement of the gate for your next
flight. The diagram may show your connection is a piece of
cake or on the contrary, that it is hopeless and you can concentrate on making the next possible flight rather than gear-
ing up for a mad dash.

Consolidators

Since getting there on an airplane is a dreary undertaking at
best, I see no reason to pay more for this experience than
one must. Consolidators, which go under the more descriptive
name "bucket shops" in Britain, sell cheap tickets and there
is no blanket reason not to buy from them. There is not even
a legal one, since the federal Department of Transportation
has elected to ignore their flouting of a 1958 law that says
international tickets should not be sold below the published
price. There is no such regulation on domestic tickets; consolidators simply do not deal in them much.

First, the explanation of how consolidators work, and then
a long list of caveats:

Airlines cannot sell all of their tickets at advertised prices.
Rather than realize no money at all for vacant seats, they
assign these seats at a bulk rate to a wholesaler, or consoli-

dator, who then marks up the price and resells them to the public. Sometimes, the airline itself is a partner in the consolidator, much as a regular bakery will operate a day-old outlet down the road.

Big consolidators have contracts with airlines to buy a certain number of seats a year at an agreed price. George Chen, head of C. L. Thomson Express in San Francisco and Hong Kong, was the first consolidator I ever interviewed, and it was a break because he was candid and forthcoming. (Before you dive for the phone book, C. L. Thomson Express sells only to travel agents, not to the general public, which makes it something of a rarity.) Thomson has dozens of choices for ways to cross the Pacific; in common with most consolidators, however, it hasn't many for getting across the United States. Like most consolidators, Chen got his start as a travel agent in what the trade calls "the ethnic market," that is, by selling tickets to expatriates—Asians in Chen's case, but who might just as easily be Indians, Pakistanis, Africans or Jamaicans. One factor in the success of such agents is the eagerness of new residents to discuss travel arrangements in their native tongue and to deal with someone who looks and sounds familiar.

Chen, who now heads the biggest operation in his field in the United States, gave me a computer printout of the flights he had available; it was half an inch thick. When I went to Washington to interview officials at the Department of Transportation about consolidators, I took this printout and the way hands reached for it you would have thought I was showing a Gutenberg Bible to book collectors. But none of this information is covert and government officials could have easily asked Chen for the same printout. They were apparently reluctant to make direct contact with someone openly undercutting international tariff rules.

What's the catch? First, be aware that you are dealing with an ephemeral business. Although I am often asked for a list of "reliable consolidators," I cannot create one that will stand up for more than a few weeks. A change in airline fares can obliterate an operator in 24 hours. *The New York Times*, to cite only one publication that carries consolidator ads, may run an ad for weeks and then block it when the bill is not paid, a sure sign of trouble. But people using, say, a previous Sunday's paper have no way of knowing the company cannot pay its bills. When one consolidator collapsed overnight, I learned of its fate when I got a call from a travel agent in Boston who had paid for a number of tickets, had clients waiting and now could get no answer on the phone. She wanted me, as an outsider, to go look at the office. I did. The security gate was padlocked and there was no sign of life, and that was all I could tell her. Perhaps her agency's money bought the operators' getaway ticket out of the country.

And if the consolidator slices the markup too thin, the company collapses, as one of New York's biggest did in the fare war of the summer of 1992. An almost infinite number of layers can be placed between the airline and the customer. Someone who advertises a ticket may be buying it from yet another consolidator and marking it up a little more. As the middle people bargain with each other and slice the margin thinner each time, one company may become so marginal that it buys no tickets and decamps with any payments and the others tumble after.

You should also note that the fabulous ticket price in the little ad is probably a come-on and that you will almost certainly pay more—perhaps only $20, but more. No one, least of all the newspapers that carry the ads, has yet tried to make consolidators live up to their published promises. Moreover, when airlines are waging fare wars, the consolidator's wares may not be much of a bargain. A saving of $10 or $20 is probably not worth the anxiety inevitably entailed in dealing with a consolidator. I would want to see a savings of $100 per ticket before I did.

Consolidators have generated letters of complaint for not delivering the ticket until after receiving the whole payment, sometimes on the day of the flight. Then when this last-minute ticket is delivered, the return coupon for the round trip, instead of having an "O.K." under the "status" column, meaning your seat is confirmed, may instead have a "wait listed," which may well mean the return flight is full. Some consolidators do not deliver until you are at the airport, a trial not for those with unsteady nerves.

Nuts and bolts: When you see an appealing consolidator ticket price in one of those tiny ads, employ these safeguards:

Take the ad to a travel agent and say that you want that ticket at that price. The travel agent can get it for you and should also be able to find out within 24 hours if you have a confirmed seat. The agent may ask you to sign a release saying you are aware that this is a consolidator seat, a reasonable protection for the agent because you have declared that price is your first consideration.

Almost all travel agents subscribe to a monthly publication called *Jax Fax*, which has virtually all listings of consolidator wares including air flight–tour combination offers. Clif Cooke, the editor, is pretty fussy about whose ads appear because if one of his subscriber travel agents gets burned he has to mediate. *Jax Fax* probably won't sell you a subscription, but you can see what's available in a trip to a particular place by reading it in the agent's office. (Also, if getting there cheaply is all that matters, look at **courier travel**, or if you are under 26 or a student up to about 35 years old, look at **student fares**.)

In some cases, travel agencies are also consolidators and also operate charters. One such is Council Travel on East 42d Street in New York, which also has 41 offices elsewhere in the United States and is the commercial agency arm of the Council on International Educational Exchange. A big operation like this is a good bet to deliver what it offers. S.T.A., also an operator that began life for student travel, is another. It has 10 offices in the United States.

If you feel certain you are getting a better deal by buying directly from a consolidator, make your reservation and then call the airline 24 hours later and see if you indeed have a reservation. Do not pay until you hear you have a reservation or the airline tells you that your consolidator is known to the line and has an arrangement to deliver the names later. Some companies, however, once they get your credit card number, consider it a done deal and exact a penalty if you pull out.

Another safeguard in dealing with a consolidator is the Better Business Bureau, which is a private nonprofit organization largely supported by businesses. In metropolitan New York, the bureau uses a pay-per-call number, 900-463-6222, to provide data on complaints or investigations of companies in the city, Long Island and the mid-Hudson region. You will pay 95 cents a minute for listening to reports that you activate by punching in the consolidator's phone number. I picked a couple of ads at random and ran an eye-opening test, learning that one company charged $100 for canceling a reservation and another company had refused to respond to information requests from the B.B.B., which I consider damning. I have not yet heard that B.B.B.s in other major cities have a 900 number, but they do keep track of complaints as do many state consumer affairs departments (see the listing for the state under **consumer assistance**).

One last lecture in the consolidator course. The New York B.B.B. ran a test on 20 companies selected at random, seeking a round-trip ticket for dates 18 to 20 days later, and not one could provide a ticket at its own advertised price, which is why I point to a come-on element. The savings in comparison with the airlines' own prices for a New York–Paris round trip ranged from $619 down to $1. One consolidator was charging $90 more than the airline.

Consumer Assistance

If you have really been done, undone, rooked, robbed or ripped off by a telephone salesperson who took your money and left you on hold, you need some state legal help. It may end up being a federal case, in the literal sense, but you need to start where you live. There are lots of arguments about where a phone transaction takes place, but increasingly the law sides with the view it took place where you live or made or received the phone call. So start with where you are.

Every state has some channel for consumers to bring forward what has happened to them, and to see if the state can remedy it or, if not, take some action in behalf of the bilked citizens. Understand, states are not able to do anything about a trip where it rained all the time, or a room less glorious than the catalogue. For the moment, states have also been prevented from dealing with slippery advertising, that is, ads that show air fares in big type that are half of round-trip fares but are available only with a full round trip. States are concerned about companies that take money and do not deliver anything, whose representations are totally false. When a company that sold trips to school kids shut its doors on the 1993 summer day just before the airlines expected deposits, leaving 4,462 students and teachers in 49 states out $7.8 million, it was the attorney general of Massachusetts that took court action first because the company was in business there.

The listing below, alphabetized by state or territory, gives the identity of the organization or office that deals with such complaints at the entry level, plus a phone number and address. The original research for this was carried out by *Travel Weekly*, a publication for travel agents and operators, and it was a formidable piece of work. Most 800 numbers operate only in the state involved. Be aware when you call that you will spend a long time on hold with 800 numbers, or hearing busy signals, because there is a lot of grief out there. But state offices open early in the morning and usually close early, so start calling at 7:30 or 8 A.M. until you find that the hours are different.

Alabama. Consumer Protection Division, Attorney General's Office, 11 South Union Street, Montgomery, Ala. 36130; 800-392-5658 or 205-242-7334.

Alaska. Alaska has only one person in its attorney general's office to deal with consumer complaints, so the state has a contract with the Better Business Bureau to hear complaints and refer along only those cases where the state must act. Better Business Bureau, 2805 Bering Street, Suite 2, Anchorage, Alaska 99503; 907-562-0704.

Arizona. Consumer Protection, Attorney General's Office, 1275 West Washington Street, Phoenix, Ariz. 85007; 800-352-8431 (in Arizona); 602-542-3702 or 602-542-5763. Or, Consumer

Protection, Assistant Attorney General, 402 West Congress Street, Suite 315, Tucson, Ariz. 85701; 602-628-6504.

Arkansas. Consumer Protection Division, Attorney General's Office, 2000 Tower Building, 323 Center Street, Little Rock, Ark. 72201; 800-482-8982 (in Arkansas); 501-682-2341.

California. Consumer Affairs, 400 R Street, Suite 1040, Sacramento, Calif. 95814; 800-344-9940 (in California); complaints: 916-445-0660; information: 916-445-1254.

Colorado. Consumer Protection Unit, Attorney General's Office, 1525 Sherman Street, Fifth floor, Denver, Colo. 80202; 303-866-3611.

Connecticut. Department of Consumer Protection, State Office Building, 165 Capitol Avenue, Hartford, Conn. 06106; 800-842-2649 (in Connecticut); 203-566-4999. Or Assistant Attorney General, Antitrust/Consumer Protection, Attorney General's Office, 110 Sherman Street, Hartford, Conn. 06105; 203-566-5374.

Delaware. Division of Consumer Affairs, Department of Community Affairs, or Assistant Attorney General for Economic Crime and Consumer Protection, both at 820 North French Street, Wilmington, Del. 19801; 302-577-3250.

District of Columbia. Department of Consumer and Regulatory Affairs, 614 H Street, N.W., Washington, D.C. 20001; 202-727-7000. (This is the right number, but I have never gotten anyone to answer it.)

Florida. Consumer Services, Department of Agriculture, 218 Mayo Building, Tallahassee, Fla. 32399; 800-435-7352 (in Florida); 904-488-2221. Or, Consumer Division, Attorney General's

Office, 4000 Hollywood Boulevard, Hollywood, Fla. 33021; 305-985-4780.

Georgia. Governor's Office of Consumer Affairs, 2 Martin Luther King Jr. Drive, Atlanta, Ga. 30334; 800-869-1123 (in Georgia); 404-651-8600 or 404-656-3790.

Hawaii. Office of Consumer Protection, Department of Commerce, 828 Fort Street Mall, Suite 600B, Box 3767, Honolulu, Hawaii 96812; 800-468-4644 (in Hawaii); 808-586-2630 or 808-587-3222.

Idaho. Consumer Protection Unit, Attorney General's Office, State House, Room 119, Boise, Idaho 83720; 800-432-3545 (in Idaho); 208-334-2424.

Illinois. Governor's Office of Citizen Assistance, 222 South College, Room 106, Springfield, Ill. 62706; 800-642-3112 (in Illinois); 217-782-0244. Or, Consumer Protection Division, Attorney General's Office, 100 West Randolph, 12th floor, Chicago, Ill. 60601; 312-814-3580.

Indiana. Consumer Protection Division, Attorney General's Office, 200 West Washington, Room 219, State House, Indianapolis, Ind. 46204; 800-382-5516 (in Indiana); 317-232-6330.

Iowa. Consumer Protection Division, Attorney General's Office, 1300 East Walnut Street, Des Moines, Iowa 50319; 515-281-5926.

Kansas. Consumer Protection Division, Attorney General's Office, Kansas Judicial Center, 301 West 10th Street, Topeka, Kan. 66612; 800-432-2310 (in Kansas); 913-296-3751.

Kentucky. Consumer Protection Division, Attorney General's Office, 209 St. Clair Street, Frankfort, Ky. 40601; 800-432-9257 (in Kentucky); 502-564-2200. Or, Consumer Protection Division, Attorney General's Office, 107 South Fourth Street, Louisville, Ky. 40202; 502-588-3262.

Louisiana. Consumer Protection Section, Attorney General's Office, Box 94095, Baton Rouge, La. 70804; 504-342-9638.

Maine. Bureau of Consumer Credit Protection, State House Station, 35, Augusta, Maine 04333; 800-332-8529 (in Maine); 207-582-8718.

Maryland. Consumer Protection Division, Attorney General's Office, 200 St. Paul Place, 16th floor, Baltimore, Md. 21202; 800-969-5766 (in Maryland); 410-528-8662.

Massachusetts. Consumer Protection Division, Attorney General's Office, 1 Ashburton Place, Boston, Mass. 02108; 617-727-8400.

Michigan. Consumer Protection Division, Attorney General's Office, Box 30213, Lansing, Mich. 48909; 517-373-1140.

Minnesota. Office of Consumer Services, Attorney General's Office, 1400 NCL Tower, 445 Minnesota Street, St. Paul, Minn. 55101; 612-296-2331.

Mississippi. Consumer Protection Division, Attorney General's Office, Box 22947, Jackson, Miss. 39225; 601-354-6018.

Missouri. Consumer Complaints, Attorney General's Office, Box 899, Jefferson City, Mo. 65102; 800-392-8222, 314-751-3321.

Montana. Consumer Affairs Unit, Department of Commerce, 1424 Ninth Avenue, Helena, Mont. 59620; 406-444-4312.

Nebraska. Consumer Protection Division, Department of Justice, 2115 State Capitol, Box 98920, Lincoln, Nebr. 68509; 402-471-2682.

Nevada. Consumer Affairs Commissioner, Department of Commerce, 1850 East Sahara Avenue, Suite 120, Las Vegas, Nev. 89104; 702-486-7355.

New Hampshire. Consumer Protection Bureau, Attorney General's Office, 25 Capitol Street, Concord, N.H. 03301; 603-271-3641.

New Jersey. Division of Consumer Affairs, 134 Halsey Street, Newark, N.J. 07102; 201-504-6200. Or, Department of the Public Advocate, 25 Market Street, Trenton, N.J. 08625; 800-792-8600 (in New Jersey); 609-292-7087.

New Mexico. Consumer Protection Division, Attorney General's Office, Box 1508, Santa Fe, N.Mex. 87504; 800-678-1508 (in New Mexico); 505-827-6060.

New York. State Consumer Protection Board, 99 Washington Avenue, Albany, N.Y. 12210; 518-474-8583. Or, 250 Broadway, 17th floor, New York, N.Y. 10007; 212-417-4482. Or, 120 Broadway, New York, N.Y. 10271; 212-416-8345.

North Carolina. Consumer Protection Sector, Attorney General's Office, Box 629, Raleigh, N.C. 27602; 919-733-7741.

North Dakota. Consumer Fraud Section, Attorney General's Office, 600 East Boulevard, Bismarck, N.Dak. 58505; 800-472-2600 (in North Dakota); 701-224-3404.

Ohio. Consumer Frauds and Crimes, Attorney General's Office, 30 East Broad Street, State Office Tower, 24th floor, Columbus, Ohio 43266; 800-282-0515 (in Ohio); 614-466-8831.

Oklahoma. Attorney General's Office, 4545 North Lincoln Boulevard, Suite 260, Oklahoma City, Okla. 73105; 405-521-4274.

Oregon. Financial Fraud Section, Department of Justice, 1162 Court Street N.E., Salem, Oreg. 97310; 503-378-4320.

Pennsylvania. Bureau of Consumer Protection, Attorney General's Office, Strawberry Square, 14th floor, Harrisburg, Pa. 17120; 800-441-2555 (in Pennsylvania); 717-787-9707.

Puerto Rico. Department of Consumer Affairs, Box 41059, Minillas Station, Santurce, P.R. 00940; 809-721-0940.

Rhode Island. Consumer Protection Division, Attorney General's Office, 72 Pine Street, Providence, R.I. 02903; 800-852-7776 (in Rhode Island); 401-277-2104.

South Carolina. Consumer Fraud and Antitrust Section, Attorney General's Office, Box 11549, Columbia, S.C. 29211; 803-734-3970. Or, Department of Consumer Affairs, Box 5757, Columbia, S.C. 29211; 803-734-9452.

South Dakota. Division of Consumer Affairs, Attorney General's Office, 500 East Capitol, State Capitol, Pierre, S.D. 57501; 800-300-1986 (in South Dakota); 605-773-4400.

Tennessee. Consumer Protection Division, Attorney General's Office, 450 James Robertson Parkway, Nashville, Tenn. 37243; 615-741-3491. Or, Division of Consumer Affairs, Department of Commerce and Insurance, 500 James Robertson

Parkway, Nashville, Tenn. 37243; 800-342-8385 (in Tennessee); 615-741-4737.

Texas. Consumer Protection Division, Attorney General's Office, Box 12548, Austin, Tex. 78711; 800-621-0508 (in Texas); 512-463-2070.

Utah. Division of Consumer Protection, Department of Commerce, Box 45804, Salt Lake City, Utah 84145; 801-530-6601.

Vermont. Public Protection Division, Attorney General's Office, 109 State Street, Montpelier, Vt. 05609; 800-649-2424 (in Vermont); 802-828-3171.

Virginia. Consumer Litigation Section, Attorney General's Office, Supreme Court Building, 101 North Eighth Street, Richmond, Va. 23219; 800-451-1525; 804-786-2116.

Virgin Islands. Department of Licensing and Consumer Affairs, Property and Procurement Building, 8201 Subbase 1, Room 205, St. Thomas, V.I. 00802; 809-774-3130.

Washington. Consumer and Business Fair Practices Division, Attorney General's Office, 111 Olympia Avenue Northeast, Olympia, Wash. 98501; 800-551-4636 (in Washington); 206-753-6210.

West Virginia. Consumer Protection Division, Attorney General's Office, 812 Quarrier Street, 6th floor, Charleston, W.Va. 25301; 800-368-8808 (in West Virginia); 304-558-8986.

Wisconsin. Division of Trade and Consumer Protection, Department of Agriculture, Trade and Consumer Protection, Box 8911, Madison, Wis. 53708; 800-422-7128 (in Wisconsin); 608-266-9836. Or, Consumer Protection Bureau, Department of Agriculture, Trade and Consumer Protection, 927 Loring Street, Altoona, Wis. 54720; 715-839-3848.

Wyoming. Attorney General's Office, 123 State Capitol Building, Cheyenne, Wyo. 82002; 307-777-7874.

Converter

See **electric current.**

Country Inns

Alas, I have never had much time to visit country inns; it seems I am always on the way to someplace down the road. But Mariana Field Hoppin, a far-traveled friend, stops at a lot of them, sometimes as part of projects for the prestigious Relais & Chateaux hotel group. Mariana says that when you check in, you should tell the hosts you plan to eat in their restaurant, which is a major source of revenue for them. A better room will materialize for you, she predicts. This is probably ineffective if there is no place else to eat anyway.

Coupon Broker

Also known as a discount travel agent. Either way, the agent sells coupons that have been awarded to other travelers on the basis of frequent flier miles, usually first class or business class tickets, which are ordinarily expensive.

This subject lurks in a messy thicket created by lack of legal agreement on what a frequent flier coupon is. One side believes it a product the customer has earned or bought and may dispose of in whatever way she or he chooses, including selling it to someone else. The other side, namely the airlines, believes that while the coupon can be given away to an aunt it cannot be sold to that same aunt.

The litigation in state courts is endlessly tangled. At this writing, the airlines are ahead and the coupon brokers, or discount travel agents, are behind.

That ad for a first class or business class ticket overseas at a price comparable to charter prices was probably placed by a coupon broker, because even a **consolidator** cannot offer such a price. In the same newsletters that carry the brokers' ads, the airlines place white-on-black ads warning of dire legal action against anyone who buys or sells a coupon. The sellers are not often pursued, because they are indeed the airlines' prime customers, business travelers who rack up more mileage points than they can use. Nor are the buyers prosecuted, but when they are identified—and computer data make this easier to do all the time—the tickets may be seized right at the counter. If this happens when you are overseas, you may pay an outlandish price for a replacement ticket home. It is the brokers who are almost constantly in court.

If you have a high-roller disposition, you may want to buy a coupon; it is not a crime regardless of what the airlines say because the owner wanted to sell it and got a price. But listen closely to what the broker says to do in the event the airline questions you about where you got the ticket. I have interviewed people who have made uneventful round-trips to Italy and France on coupon-based tickets. I have interviewed enraged people who got caught in the Pacific because they refused to tell the crucial lie that the broker told them was essential to the game. Only you know if this is something you would be at ease doing.

Officials at Ralph Nader's Aviation Consumer Action Project say they really cannot see why something that can be given away cannot as properly be sold, but it is not the sort of burning legal issue that inspires reformers to bring suit. Conceivably if the revenuers again begin to look at taxes on frequent flier tickets, the issue will again arise of whether someone who is weary of travel can dispose of coupons for something more tangible than Aunt Millie's goodwill.

Courier Travel

A curious business, traveling as a courier. Marion Donnelly, pivot woman of the *Times* travel section, reports that she gets a steady flow of calls asking the dates of columns on traveling overseas as a courier. Going as a courier is about as inexpensive as you can get but involves limitations that rule out the trip for most people. Marion and I believe that people call in because the word "courier" sounds romantic, like a State Department employee gliding aboard with a briefcase chained to one wrist.

If you want to travel with someone, if you need a lot of luggage, if your trip needs to be scheduled a long time in advance and if you tolerate anxiety poorly, courier travel is not for you. It is closer to a trip grab bag: If your passport is up to date and you would like to go someplace, but no place in particular, and don't mind giving up your luggage allowance because it will be used for the material you are escorting, and if you are able to go in the next few days, it may be, well, the ticket.

I had an enjoyable four-day $199 trip to Mexico City, and an exercise instructor of mine got a free trip to Jamaica for a week in the dead of winter, but another friend wrote me pages of woe about his trip to Geneva. All of us were sent by the same agency. The crucial difference may be that the Geneva-bound friend wanted to see a particular person there, who had a schedule, too, and every one of the many false starts and returns created a problem for him.

Here's how courier travel works. Many companies have material they need to ship overseas promptly, such as bank records. These can be sent as cargo, but they are then held up in the customs shed for someone to claim them and this usually means a delay of one business day. If these records are sent as personal luggage, which is perfectly legal, they can be picked up as soon as they are unloaded and the accompanying courier has turned over the luggage check and an envelope of documents. There is also material traveling in the other direction—back from Geneva or Mexico City—and the timing of the trip back may affect how long you may stay at the destination. Usually, it's a week, and you will travel on a weekday at both ends, but it may be longer if the need for you to accompany documents on your return is not tightly scheduled.

The closer to departure date, the less you will pay, and if it's for tonight it may be free. Our exercise teacher got his trip free because he had twice showed up at the airport for trips that were canceled.

Courier travel is neither so cheap nor so diverse as it once was; tight times affect this business as any other. Even so, many companies that ship records still find it a bargain. At one time, the companies, or their brokers, paid salaried employees to take the trip, but then it became obvious that nonemployees would do it for nothing or even pay part of the fare to get the trip. Thus arose the courier travel business, which is carried on by courier companies, which have contracts to deliver the documents, and employees at both ends, and by agents, who may charge a fee to register the courier, give a briefing and check out the passports.

The leading agent, Now Voyager of New York, was started in 1984. It charges $50 for a year's registration, and has a phone message that now tells of charter flights as well as the courier trips for which it is famous. (74 Varick Street, New York, N.Y. 10013; 212-431-1616.)

The most used newsletter, Steve Lantos's *Travel Unlimited*, a mimeographed monthly publication, now reports on travel bargains other than going as a courier because of the thinness of courier choice. (Travel Unlimited, $25 for 12 monthly issues a year; $5 for a single issue; Box 1058, Allston, Mass. 02134)

A paperback book, *The Insider's Guide to Air Courier Bargains*, by Kelly Monaghan, is in its third edition. It has lots of names and addresses but obviously cannot keep up with the ebb and flow of demand as a newsletter can. It is $14.95 plus $2.50 shipping from Upper Access Publishing, Box 457, Hinesburg, Vt. 05461; 800-356-9315. Both the newsletter and the book, frankly, pad out a reasonable amount of courier data with personal views and other travel material.

If you are like me, hearing a list of places I can go for a couple hundred dollars brings on a zany kick-over-the-traces wanderlust. When I was depressed once, a dear friend said, "Go to Amsterdam and ride a bike," and the prospect sounded like almost the only thing I would like to do. While I was booking my '92 trip to Mexico City, I heard a recorded announcement of a two-day $50 round-trip to Stockholm, Madrid or Brussels. The trip was in a couple of hours, and I was holding my passport, but I truly had only the clothes on my back and things at the office were in a mess. But sometimes I just dial up Now Voyager to see what I could do on the spur of the moment. The magic carpet simplicity of it is liberating: Go just for the joy of going.

Courses and Classes

Travelers often write to ask how to find a cooking school in Hong Kong or a photography workshop in Maine, thinking to combine pleasant travel with improvement of a skill and contact with people interested in the same hobby.

With the help of a lot of stamps and some dogged computer work, Dorlene V. Kaplan of Florida has compiled guides to these topics: cooking schools, photography workshops and schools, arts and crafts workshops, writers' conferences, academic travel and golf schools and camps. The cooking schools guide is the largest, at 326 pages, and the golf schools the smallest at 164. The cooking guide is $19.95, plus $3 for shipping: Shaw Guides, 625 Biltmore Way, Coral Gables, Fla. 33134; 800-247-6553 or 305-446-8888.

Interested people hope there will be lists compiled for adult tennis camps, or baseball camps for the Over the Hill Gang.

Credit Cards, Lost

See **lost documents.**

Cruises

Cruise taking is booming, and the *Times* travel section devotes acres of space to it. But, oddly, I have never seen a letter asking for guidance on selecting a cruise. Lots of unhappy letters about reroutings, yes, or lost days, or failed trip cancellation insurance or accidents. (Judging by the outpouring of anger about poor communication with the passengers, the *QE2* grounding in New England the summer of 1992 must have been very educational for Cunard Lines.)

But there's nothing in the mailbag about picking a ship in the first place. I think this is because most people get the idea from a friend, and perhaps travel with friends on the basis of someone else's recommendation, or have a travel agent who can discern the swing-all-night ships from the more staid ones.

One reason that travel agents have become so expert on cruises is obvious: Selling a cruise is good business. One sale wraps it all up: room, food, daily entertainment, airfare to the port of embarkation, and it all comes with commissions. Whenever I drive my travel agent nutty with three plane tickets for $318 each on the basis of a coupon from the airline, with no hotel because we are staying with relatives, and I know his agency will earn barely $85 from the sale, I wish I could compensate him by buying a big fat cruise.

Right now cruises are comparatively inexpensive because the market is very competitive, and almost no one pays "full price," whatever that is, for a cruise. The cruise companies themselves discount to try to fill their cabins, and there are many discount "cruise only" agencies that will offer all sorts of deals. Travel agents that specialize in the cruises of certain lines get "preferred supplier" privileges, that is, super-commissions. Some agents pass these discounts, or part of them, along to the customer.

The cruise companies are now trying to reverse the public tendency, heightened since the Gulf War, to wait until the last minute to buy a trip, particularly a cruise. The closer the date got, the more the price was discounted, and the cruise business approached chaos. Everyone knows the chilling sensation of sitting next to someone who paid half what you paid —be it theater ticket, plane trip or cruise—and is not shy about telling you about it.

Aware of this, the cruise companies early in 1993 began to offer discounts for early booking. Carnival named its plan "fun ship supersavers"; Costa, "fettucini fares"; Holland America, "keeping it simple" and so forth. Auctionlike, the prices ratchet up as the ship fills up or sailing date approaches.

This practice has one great advantage for a traveler: You don't mind hearing that someone got a better price if they paid far in advance. You, after all, had the use of the money in the meantime, or perhaps made up your mind only at the last minute.

If you buy one of these early-discount cruises, ask the travel agent or cruise company if the price will be revised downward if there is a last-minute discount.

A few warnings derived from travelers whose cruises did not work out well. If you are going to take a cruise around spring break time, try to learn if cabins are being sold as individual berths, which may mean that groups of students are booking them four or more to a cabin. Some cruises, both from the West Coast and into the Caribbean, have virtually been taken over by student groups and have evolved into messy situations, with drunken young people in the corridors and public sexual and other sports activities. The cruise lines say they know which agencies are violating their rules about sale of individual berths, and I haven't heard much about it lately so it may be under control. But it is highly profitable for travel agents in college areas.

Sometimes, bargain cruises that include airfare to the embarkation port involve air trips with many connections—New York to Miami via Cincinnati, for example. If your cruise is in winter, be aware that every airport connection provides another possibility for delay, and if the connection is too tight you may miss the sailing.

Buying a cruise is a good time to get **cruise cancellation insurance** because your investment is in one big lump. Check carefully to see whether the policy covers you up to the moment of embarkation, or expires several days ahead. You are not restricted to a policy sold under the cruise line's name. Your travel agent will sell you a freestanding policy if you ask for it.

Cruise Cancellation Insurance

Few people are so much in need of trip insurance as those who buy a cruise. They have paid for the whole thing in a lump: transportation, room and meals and often air travel to the port. If you cancel at the last minute, and are not covered by the right insurance, you may lose the whole amount.

Many basic questions are covered under **cancellation insurance** , but the cruise industry dotes on **waivers**, a big pitfall. Cruise brochures may describe them in reassuring phrases such as "cancellation protection," "travel coverage and cancellation penalty waivers" or "cancellation fees waiver." Modest coverage for lost or damaged luggage may be included. However, the brochure often does not contain the price or crucial terms of the waiver, especially the hour at which coverage ceases.

Among the many lines that have offered waivers are American Hawaii Cruises, Paquet French Cruises, Holland America Line, Princess Cruises, Regency and Renaissance Cruises. As an example, one line's At Ease waiver was described this way in its brochure, with italics added for emphasis:

"The At Ease Program, a cancellation-fee waiver and baggage protection, is offered for $65 per person for cruises offered up to and including seven days, $75 per person for Mexico and Caribbean cruises longer than seven days; and $85 for all other cruises longer than seven days. Available as a single package, this covers (1) cancellation charges normally assessed if you cancel your cruise *between 60 days and 72 hours prior to sailing* and (2) loss and/or damage of your baggage to a maximum of $500."

The line levies these penalties for cancellations in advance of departure: from 59 to 31 days, the amount of the deposit, which may be $250 or $450 a person; 30 to 15 days, 50 percent of the fare; 14 days to 72 hours, 75 percent of the fare; and less than 72 hours, 100 percent of the fare.

Buy the waiver or not, if you cancel less than 72 hours— three days—before sailing, you lose the whole fare.

Another line offers a Cancellation Fee Waiver, or C.F.W. Purchase of the C.F.W. waives penalties if the trip is canceled more than 24 hours before "commencement of travel." A spokesman for the company said that its legal department interpreted this phrase to mean the start of any travel for which the line provided "air, hotel or cruise." Its regular penalties for cancellation are as follows: 90 to 60 days before travel, $200; 59 to 30 days before, $300; 29 to 15 days before, 50 percent of the fare, and "up to 14 days" before, 100 percent. The waiver is priced according to the cruise; for a Mediterranean cruise, the cost is $159 a person.

This brochure, however, is specific: "C.F.W. is not insurance; it provides no rights other than those explained above . . . nor does it cover expenses or unused services due to trip interruption." The brochure also suggests discussing cancellation *insurance* with a travel agent.

Still another line offers "travel coverage and cancellation penalty waivers" that have some of the earmarks of insurance—a $1,000 payment for an emergency return flight, for example—but the waiver does not offer any repayment of costs for an interrupted cruise or one that is canceled later than the outbound departure date. The cost is $149 per person for a one-week cruise.

The use of waivers is declining, and increasingly cruise lines are offering more realistic insurance policies under their own name that provide coverage for trip cancellation, delay and interruption, accident and medical protection, lost baggage and accidental death or dismemberment. These policies are profitable and, as one official said, they mean the line can offer protection that passengers, who are frequently older, like to have. But no passenger is restricted to buying the house brand; freestanding policies are available, as they are for any sort of trip.

American Hawaii Cruises formerly offered only a waiver, but on January 1, 1993, it began offering cancellation and interruption insurance along with baggage and medical coverage. The waiver, which cost $70 a person, could be bought alone; the policy, Cruise Guard, available only in conjunction with the waiver, costs $65 a person. The waiver ceases effect 72 hours before cruise departure, and the cancellation coverage picks up at that point. American Hawaii's policy was underwritten by the Monumental Life Insurance Company of Baltimore except in New York, where it was handled by International Life Investors Insurance Company. The administrator was Trip Mate Insurance Agency of Kansas City, Missouri.

In 1993, 16 cruise lines offered insurance policies under their own names that were administered by Berkelycare in Mineola, Long Island, and underwritten by one of three companies: a member of the American International Group of New York, a member of Chubb, or the Hartford Insurance Company. These lines were the Bergen Line, Carnival, Clipper, Crystal, Cunard, Dolphin Hellas, Epirotiki, Norwegian Cruise Line, Premier, Diamond, Royal Cruise Line, Royal Vi-

king, Seaquest, Seven Seas, Special Expeditions and Sun
Line.

The prices reflect the duration or cost of the cruise. Insuring a three-day Premier cruise would cost $35 a person; an 11-day cruise on Royal Cruise Line, $139. As a percentage of the cruise cost, the premiums hovered around 5.5 percent, typical for most trip insurance. Royal Viking charged 6 percent, and 8 percent on its world cruise; Special Expeditions, 6.75 percent.

Elizabeth Koch, president of Travel Headquarters in Short Hills, New Jersey, sells many cruises and has a subspecialty in cruise insurance. A big stumbling block for customers, Ms. Koch says, is trying to get information on what a policy covers. Often, she says, the cruise line puts through a single charge for a deposit, port taxes, a cancellation waiver and cancellation insurance "and you haven't got a scrap of paper to show the client.

"A travel agent has to press hard to get an insurance policy ahead of time," she said. "They don't even give you a brochure footnote on what it covers."

Krysti Rom Hamlin of Carolina World Travel in Tryon, North Carolina, reports similar experiences. "Unless you get the policy, you don't know which relatives are covered under illness, or the definition of preexisting conditions," she said. She cited difficulty in learning even the cutoff date on a Princess waiver.

However, if the cruise industry continues in the direction of offering better buys to early purchasers, the frantic last-minute search for coverage may stop, eliminating nightmares for clients who fall ill and for their travel agents. Shopping for good coverage will become possible and older people who shop for a cruise need not fear losing the whole price.

Cruise Ship Sanitation

All passenger cruise ships that call at U.S. ports are given sanitation inspections by agents of the Federal Centers for Disease Control and Prevention. All but two of these 140 vessels are registered in foreign countries, mainly the Bahamas, Liberia, Panama, Norway and Italy, but 80 percent of cruise passengers are U.S. citizens so the government is concerned about preventing outbreaks of gastrointestinal disease, which can be quite serious aboard ship, particularly if the problem is the water supply.

After unannounced inspections, the ships are rated for water quality, food preparation, potential contamination of food and general cleanliness, storage and repair. A score of 86 is considered satisfactory. Ships that do not meet this level are reinspected as soon as possible, or after the ship reports that corrective action has been taken. The government can recommend that a ship not sail if conditions appear threatening, particularly the condition of the water supply.

The lag between inspections can be quite long—six months, for instance—so the figures are not always a good guide to an individual ship's conditions. The real goal is to keep the shipowners and operators enforcing appropriate rules: For example, if a salad maker cuts a finger, cleanliness requirements for covering the cut should be met as a matter of course before the worker again touches food.

Any potential passenger may request the most recent sanitation inspection report on a particular vessel by writing: Chief, Vessel Sanitation Program, National Center for Environmental Health, 1015 North American Way, Room 107, Miami, Fla. 33132.

Customs

The only time I ever got stopped coming back into the
United States was when I was carrying a nice big orange I
bought from a fruit stand in London, but didn't eat on the
plane. The orange was seized by Customs in New York, acting on behalf of the Agriculture Department. I could have
eaten it while standing in line, but as I found out later when
I was doing research, it was ground up and sent into a waste
container so it would not enter the U.S. soil and water cycle.

All the other times, we fill out our forms and are waved
past. I have a travel companion with a profile the same as
mine: white, female, a New Yorker, a Columbia graduate and
a journalist. She gets stopped every time and none of us un-
derstands it. One time when I was bringing home virtually
nothing, I listed her gift perfume on my declaration and they
still stopped her, not me. Although she has never been fined,
she must by now give off some sort of aura of panic.

Except for the Generalized System of Preferences (see
third world duty-free goods), Customs rules are pretty simple. As a "returning resident" after a trip to a foreign country, you are entitled to bring in $400 in things acquired
overseas, and if you are a family the exemptions, including
one for each U.S.-born infant, can be combined.

If you are returning from a U.S. island possession—that is,
American Samoa, Guam or the U.S. Virgin Islands—the exemption is $1,200.

Although many Caribbean travelers are not aware of this,
if they are returning from one of the 24 following places in
the Caribbean or Central America the exemption is $600: An-
tigua and Barbuda, Aruba, Bahamas, Barbados, Belize, Costa
Rica, Dominica, Dominican Republic, El Salvador, Grenada,
Guatemala, Guyana, Haiti, Honduras, Jamaica, Montserrat,
Netherlands Antilles, Nicaragua, Panama, St. Kitts and

Nevis, St. Lucia, St. Vincent and the Grenadines, Trinidad and Tobago, the British Virgin Islands.

Of this $600, up to $400 worth may have been obtained elsewhere. That is, the regular $400 exemption for return from an industrialized country continues to exist inside the $600 allowed for countries where the United States wants to encourage trade.

There are different rates of duty for material that exceeds the limit. The first $1,000 beyond the limit will require duty of 10 percent, except for people returning from the U.S. islands, where it is 5 percent. After that, different rates of duty are applied, depending on what the object is: 3 percent of the value on a camera, for example, and 32 percent on cotton clothing. The items with the highest rates of duty will be placed under the exemption, and the duty will be applied to the surplus. Inspectors are required to say they'll accept a revised declaration at each step in the process, and the likely payments rise as this is refused. The inspector may add a fine and double the duty or raise it to six times its basic amount if the traveler has concealed the objects, produces fraudulent receipts or shows up as a multiple offender.

Foreign-made articles that you take abroad, including such likely items as cameras, camcorders and field glasses, will be charged duty on return to the U.S. unless you can show they were bought here before departure. Good proof, like a bill of sale, insurance policy, appraisal, should be taken along if the issue is likely to come up. Expensive new objects with serial numbers may be registered with Customs in advance on form 4457 and this registration will serve for any number of reentries. This form may be requested ahead of time by mail or phone from the nearest Customs office, but the object must be shown to a Customs officer before you leave and your signature on the form must be witnessed.

As my orange demonstrates, the Agriculture Department rules are harder to explain and understand. The stakes for U.S. agriculture are very high, as the Mediterranean fruit fly infestation in California in the eighties proved. A homemade salami will always be seized, but I have seen all sorts of fruits and vegetables from the Caribbean come through with people returning from a visit to their family homes who knew exactly what is allowable and what not. I once declared two yams from Grenada, and the Agriculture inspector said that would be okay, but he had to satisfy himself that they were yams, not sweet potatoes. I dug them out, saying they were sold to me as certified yams, but he sliced off one tip before ruling: Yes, yams.

Probably the most frustrated people are those who have bought, say, a refrigerated can of goose liver pâté in France, the same brand that is available at a higher price in their local fancy food store, and cannot get it past the Agriculture rules. "The importer gets it through," the traveler contends. "Why not me?" An Agriculture inspector explained the difference. The commercial importer demonstrates to the Agriculture Department that certain required processing rules have been followed, to eliminate whatever danger exists in the meats of the country of origin. A permit to import this product implies that the processing has assured that something like foot-and-mouth disease cannot sneak into the United States in the meat. The same product, packed for domestic consumption, may not undergo the same processing. If the canned meat product can be kept without refrigeration, it is probably a safe bet to bring home.

"Travelers' Tips," covering Agriculture Department regulations, is available free from the U.S. Department of Agriculture, Animal and Plant Health Inspection Service, Room 613, Federal Building, 6505 Belcrest Road, Hyattsville, Md. 20782; 301-436-7799. To ask a question about a specific item, call the quarantine department, 301-436-7885.

"Know Before You Go, Customs Hints for Returning Residents," is a crisp little booklet issued by the Customs Service that covers other details, including how to send things home, what the alcoholic beverage allowances are and where to get more information. This is available free from the Customs Service, as is the leaflet on the Generalized System of Preferences for third world countries. There are a couple of more exotic leaflets that may be appropriate: "Pets, Wildlife" and "International Mail Imports."

To find the nearest Customs office, look under Treasury Department, Customs Service, in the blue U.S. Government listings in the phone book. There are 44 Customs districts in seven regions. Here are addresses for the seven regional headquarters that may be able to send you the leaflets or direct you to a district office for help:

Northeast, 10 Causeway Street, Boston, Mass. 02222

New York, 6 World Trade Center, New York, N.Y. 10048

Southeast, 909 Southeast First Avenue, Miami, Fla. 33131

South Central, 423 Canal Street, New Orleans, La. 70130

Southwest, 5850 San Felipe Street, Houston, Tex. 77057

Pacific, 1 World Trade Center, Suite 705, Long Beach, Calif. 90831

North Central, 55 East Monroe Street, Chicago, Ill. 60603

Customs Surprises

 If you bought a tidy amount of stuff overseas, say $5,000 worth, and on return either pay United States Customs duty for the total above your regular exemption or apply further exemptions for particular imports from developing countries (see **third world duty-free goods**) you may still find yourself facing a new tax bite. If you live in New York, California, Illinois, Connecticut, Pennsylvania, Florida or Texas, this is particularly likely. These states want to collect the equivalent of the sales tax you would have paid if you had made your purchases at home. The tax is called the compensating use tax, and all states with sales tax have legislation providing for this tax at the same rate. If you ever bought an automobile in an adjoining state, you are probably familiar with this one.

Since early 1990, New York State, which is a big port of entry, has been pursuing returning travelers with tax bills and interest at 1 percent a month, although apparently not with penalties, because this tax is more secretive than the Sphinx. I wrote about it in April 1991, a year after experts from something quaintly called the New York Revenue Opportunity Commission began poring through several years of Customs declarations for state residents bringing in a lot of stuff. By then, the state had harvested just under a million from its exertions, $575,000 from one payer who when asked to go over earlier records coughed this amount up in a single check.

California warns its residents with posters in the Customs shed. New York said it was a nice idea, but I have not seen any warnings. It appears that you have your choice: ask how to get a state form and pay up promptly or wait for your state to come get you and pay interest, too.

You can ignore this whole thing if you are returning with

purchases below the Customs exemption, and it is not likely that your state will send a Customs bloodhound letter to collect taxes of less than $500. However, don't expect me or any state to tell you what the working lower limit is, because that constitutes encouragement to break the law.

Daylight Saving Time

This begins a week earlier in Europe than it does in the United States, and no one seems concerned enough to warn you about it. If you are bumping around Europe at the end of March, keep your eye on the situation, or ask the concierge, or you might miss your train, plane or bateau mouche because the departure time on the ticket will be European daylight time. At least it will start on a Sunday, same as in the United States.

Debit Phone Card

These cards, which provide almost the only way you can use a phone booth in France or Japan, involve buying call units in advance. To use the French or Japanese card, you stick it into the pay phone, much as you do an A.T.M. card, and use up the value of the card as you make calls.

In Japan, the cards constitute a rare bargain since you can make a local phone call for the equivalent of 10 cents. They are so common they are given away as souvenirs, including at funerals. The cards, available in vending machines, stores and post offices, sell 50 local calls of three minutes for 500 yen ($4.50 in 1993), or 100 calls for 1,000 yen.

In France, a card providing 50 local calls costs 40 francs ($8 in 1993), but you get 120 calls at a slightly better rate on the 90-franc card. They are sold in tobacco shops, post offices, subway booths, stationery stores and the airport. Do not buy a Télécarte before you go; they cost a lot more in the States: Marketing Challenges, Inc., in New York, for example, sells the 50-call card for $12, plus a handling charge of $7. You can call the United States and charge it to the Télécarte, and you will get about four minutes on a 50-unit card. But you can use a Télécarte simply to connect to United States long-distance carriers through their regional access numbers and the call will not be deducted from the card.

Incidentally, the designs on the French cards change all the time and the cards are collected avidly, so hang on to them after you use them up; the cards make distinctive take-home gifts for teenagers and other collectors.

With the upsurge of "shoulder surfers," thieves who learn your telephone credit card number by watching you punch it in and then make potentially thousands of dollars of calls, some American companies have started selling debit cards for use in the United States. But since the phone system is not electronically set up for them, the cards work by giving you an 800 number to call for access, and a personal identification number to identify your account. The switching station then deducts the call from the remaining value of the card.

This involves a lot of dialing, but if I had children traveling I would urge them to carry debit cards to assure they could call me even when I was not able to accept a collect call. They do not offer much of an opportunity for thieves because the number expires with the card. A big sales target is foreign tourists because the cards eliminate the need to juggle unfamiliar coins and most permit calls home. One executive said many of his sales were to people who could not afford home phones.

The cost for a one-minute call to anywhere in the United States is 50 to 60 cents, depending on the card. The time is rounded up, so a call of only a few seconds will be recorded as a minute. For a call in the same city, this is a poor bargain; for a call to the opposite coast, a better one. For comparison, an A.T.&T. pay phone call from New York to Los Angeles in business hours Monday to Friday might cost $2.19 in coins for the first minute, 25 cents for subsequent minutes, putting a three-minute call at $2.69. The same pay phone call charged to an A.T.&T. credit card could be $1.06 for the first minute, 26 cents for subsequent minutes, or three minutes for $1.58. At a flat 60 cents a minute, the debit card call costs $1.80 for three minutes, a price right between the two alternatives.

Here is the lineup of available cards at this writing:

A.T.&T.'s Teleticket. Sold in denominations of $6, $15 and $30, with calls in the United States, Puerto Rico and the Virgin Islands costing 60 cents a minute. Overseas calls are possible at a higher rate, $1.80 a minute to Canada or England, for example. This card feeds through 10 separate 800 numbers for calls to be made in different languages—Dutch, English, French, German, Italian, Japanese, Korean, Mandarin Chinese, Portuguese and Spanish—and cards bear instructions in these languages. Teleticket is sold at A.T.&T. Phone Center Stores and tourist centers, including tourist bureaus in Orlando and San Francisco. It does not work on rotary dial phones. For information on phone stores carrying the card: 800-462-1818.

World Telecom Group's Amerivox. It has a different price structure from the others, and also provides free calling time for renewals, referrals and the like. The initial card costs $20, $10 of which is used as an activation fee, payable only once.

The card buys 36 calling minutes to anywhere in the United States, Puerto Rico and the Virgin Islands; adding in the cost of the $10 fee, the cost per minute on the first card is 55 cents. When the minutes are used up, another $20 in value may be added to the original card and this provides 72 minutes of calling time at 27 cents a minute. After $500 in calls, the per-minute fee drops to 23 cents. Does not work on rotary phones. The company sells its cards through regional agents. Information: 415-694-4977.

Global Telecommunications Solutions' Global Card. Sold in denominations of $10, $20, $40 and $50, with calls in the United States and Puerto Rico costing 50 cents a minute. Calls may be made overseas at a higher rate. Does not work on rotary dial phones. The card was sold initially in New York, Florida and Los Angeles. Information: 800-929-4301.

Western Union cards. Sold in Western Union offices for $5, $10, $20 or $50; calls in the United States and Puerto Rico and the Virgin Islands cost 60 cents a minute. Calls may be made overseas at a higher rate, Canada or Britain at $1.80 a minute, for example. This card, even if not used up, expires six months after purchase. A Western Union recording at 800-325-6000 will give the address, but not the phone number, of the nearest office.

Sprint's Instant Fōncard. Sells in $5, $10 and $20 versions; calls in the United States, Puerto Rico and the Virgin Islands cost 60 cents a minute. Calls overseas are also possible. Sprint also makes a debit card that is distributed by tour operators and airlines overseas for use in 32 countries. Information: 800-877-1992.

Other companies are coming into the market, and my sense
is that if your travel involves a lot of pay phone use, particularly on open highways, having a debit card in reserve is a
smart idea.

Denied Boarding Compensation

This weird phrase is what the Department of Transportation
calls the payment you are to receive if you had a ticket (1)
with a firm reservation for a flight (2) on a plane holding
more than 60 passengers (3) leaving from the United States
and (4) even though you got to the airport on time you (5)
still were not at your destination within an hour of the scheduled time (6) because too many tickets were sold for that
flight.

Cutting to the bottom line, if you get where you are going
more than one hour late and less than two hours late you are
entitled to the amount you paid for your one-way ticket, or
half of the cost of your round-trip ticket, to a maximum of
$200. If you get there more than two hours late, you are
entitled to double that amount, to a maximum of $400. And,
of course, the airline still has to get you to your destination
however tardy the flight may be.

Overbooking is a game all airlines play, because the percentage of no-shows becomes more predictable each year that
the lines store computer data on flights. An airline's yield-
control functionaries want to fill the flight beyond its capacity
only to the level of the no-shows, and they are playing poker
with the odds in mind. News, weather, traffic jams and other
events can upend the odds, however.

Even so, the airlines do not pay denied boarding compensation every time the passengers cannot be fitted aboard because the lines prefer to persuade excess travelers to be

"bumped"—to take a later flight in return for vouchers, much cheaper for the airline than giving cash. If you want to see how this works out, look at **bumping rates.**

Each year, fewer passengers are paid denied boarding compensation. Department of Transportation figures for 1992 showed the lowest total in 20 years: 45,732 passengers were paid, a rate of 1.03 for every 10,000 passengers (a hundredth of 1 percent). The department pointed out that the decline was linked to the airlines' efforts to persuade volunteers to wait for the next flight, which causes them to drop off the compensation chart. These figures, incidentally, include domestic airlines' flights going overseas but not their flights coming into the United States. What happens to you if you are bumped overseas will be governed by any regulations there, and there are regulations in the European Community. Reconfirming your return flight is always a good idea anyway, since an airline's unannounced switch to a smaller plane may create a problem.

The European Community in 1991 adopted minimum rules for denied boarding compensation that roughly parallel the U.S. regulations, including the quest for volunteers. These rules are to be made available to passengers at airline offices and at check-in counters. Roughly, if the flight is up to 3,500 kilometers (2,100 miles) and you are denied boarding and the airline cannot get you to your destination within two hours of your original arrival time, you are to receive the local equivalent of 150 European Currency Units. (These sound like the Space Credits we once received in cereal boxes, but it is a synthetic figure derived from a selection of European Community currencies and its value is quoted in the paper.) If your trip is more than 3,500 kilometers and you do not get there within four hours, you are to get the equivalent of 300

European Currency Units. If you are denied boarding but get to your destination within the allotted time, you receive half the appropriate compensation.

In addition to these compensations, the European Community rules say any involuntarily bumped passenger must receive the price of a telephone call, fax or telex message to the destination; meals and refreshment in "reasonable relation" to the waiting time; and hotel space if an additional overnight stay is required.

Diarrhea

L. R. Shannon, a nearby coworker, has hanging over his desk a map showing the areas of the world where traveler's diarrhea is prevalent. The map is published by a diarrhea remedy company, and for Larry it is a *Far Side* desk decoration deliberately offsetting our pretty posters of the moon over Charleston and Nantucket whaleboats.

But, truly, a world map is appropriate for traveler's diarrhea. It is hard to avoid. So we might as well get done with basic information and turn to something more pleasant.

Men and women are equally vulnerable, but young people are more vulnerable than the elderly possibly because of their immature immunity and certainly because of more daring eating habits. Dr. Herbert L. DuPont, the first president of the International Society of Travel Medicine, is probably the world's leading expert in this undramatic area and his research subjects are thousands of students who go from Texas to Mexico for a semester or less and who all apparently suffer from traveler's diarrhea at some time.

Dr. DuPont inelegantly introduces himself at meetings and forums as "the shit doctor" because, he says, that is what the young people call him as soon as they learn what his field is.

Dr. DuPont says that anyone who has six or more "unformed bowel movements" a day is suffering from the disorder. The problem will continue three or four days; the Centers for Disease Control and Prevention say that only 10 percent of the cases persist longer than a week and only 2 percent longer than a month. "Rarely is T.D. life threatening," the C.D.C. says. In other words, it's common and it's not likely to kill you, but that does not make it any less painful and embarrassing. If you are sick longer than the averages indicate, or have symptoms other than the runs and cramps, or possibly nausea, or, rarely, fever, you should go to a clinic.

Dr. DuPont, who gives free pretravel inoculations for other ailments to the students in return for their keeping a diary of their attacks and what they ate just before, describes a pretty standard curve that he says has not changed in the two decades he has been doing this research. The initial attacks are brought under control once the students settle into Mexican life and begin buying their groceries and preparing their own meals, including boiling their water. There is almost always an attack, he said, after the student visits Mexican friends during some holiday and eats a home-cooked meal. The local people obviously do not suffer the same consequences, he said, so the issue is acquiring immunity to contaminants in the food and water. The usual suspect in Mexico is the street vendor, but this is not the same in all of the developing world; Jamaica and Tobago, for example, have many street vendors but only minimal occurrence of diarrhea from cooked foods.

The major risks are raw or rare meat, raw seafood, raw fruits and raw vegetables and several kinds of fluids such as tap water, unpasteurized milk or other dairy products.

Probably the biggest peril is water, because you need it so

often during the day wherever you are, and ice, because you may forget (once) that freezing does not kill fecal contamination. Water in sparkling streams in national parks is not advisable to drink because of the possibility of giardia parasites. Dr. DuPont presented a paper at a 1993 convention assessing the bacteria-killing impact of various liquors upon bacteria in ice cubes. The results indicated tequila was more effective than Scotch, but the margin was narrow, and nothing did much good.

Take boiled or chlorine/iodine-treated water with you if you are uncertain of the supply in the day ahead, or order soda or beer. Unless the bottle of mineral water arrives sealed, assume it has been filled from the local supply. Soda with an internationally known brand name—Coca-Cola, Pepsi, 7Up and similar brands—is probably manufactured from water that meets international safety standards (see **water**).

Confirmed hypochondriacs will hate this: In 20 to 50 percent of the researched cases, no specific cause for traveler's diarrhea can be found. My mother used to say that bowel misbehavior, either diarrhea or constipation, was brought on by the change of water, and researchers can't do much better than that. The stresses of travel probably play a role.

The Centers for Disease Control and Prevention concludes that the strongest weapon for avoiding traveler's diarrhea is careful attention to one's own food and beverage preparation. Go easy on medications. It warns that prophylactic use—advance use—of difenoxine, which is the ingredient that is supposed to make Lomotil stop the flow after you get diarrhea, can actually increase the probability of incidence of traveler's diarrhea in a well person. Nor is either Lomotil or Immodium effective in prevention, according to the agency. Rather large preventive doses of bismuth subsalicylate, which everyone

knows as Pepto-Bismol—two-ounce doses four times daily—
do work. They have decreased the incidence of diarrhea by 60
percent in tests, according to the agency, but Pepto-Bismol is
hazardous for many people—those allergic to aspirin, those
on anticoagulant therapy, people taking salicylates for arthri-
tis, among others—and in any case should not be taken for
more than three weeks at a time.

There are more formidable medications but C.D.C.'s *Health
Information for International Travel* recommends against
them. And if you are thinking about preventive doses of anti-
microbial agents and the like, you should read the entry on
Traveler's Diarrhea in this government book. The nub of it is
that the side effects of the medication may be worse than the
ailment.

What can you do if afflicted? Since most cases are self-
limiting, the most important thing is to keep from becoming
dehydrated. The World Health Organization has worked out a
formula for rehydration salts, and the product may be found
under various trade names in packets in the baby supply area
of the supermarket and in most stores or pharmacies in the
developing world. If you are in a pinch, particularly if the
diarrhea sufferer is a child, Dr. Richard Dawood, editor of
Travelers' Health: How to Stay Healthy All Over the World,
recommends mixing a similar drink: eight level teaspoons of
sugar or honey, ½ teaspoon of salt and a quart or liter of
clean (bottled) water.

If your diarrhea persists, particularly after you return
home, it may be caused by giardia, a parasite found in water
in many parts of the world, notably the American West, ski
resorts, Glacier National Park and the like. See a doctor.

Diphtheria

This appalling old disease has had a resurgence. See **Russia**.

Direct Flight

This phrase is a wretched deception. It sounds fast, efficient and, well, sort of nonstop. Only one thing is certain: It will not be nonstop, it will have a stop, perhaps more than one. You may have to change planes and even airlines, as you will read under **airline code sharing**. The one thing that a "direct flight" is not supposed to be is a "connecting" flight to or from a hub where you change planes or airlines according to a design of your own, not the airline's design.

On a direct flight, if you must change planes the gates should be adjoining, and the airline has a responsibility to see that you get from one plane to the other. If the first plane does not make it in time for boarding the second plane, the airline has the responsibility.

Most of the time, a direct flight is a flight with a stop, perhaps a good long one.

Disney World

"The attraction that ate Florida" is what one writer calls it. And it is the biggest tourist magnet in the country, the one thing everyone goes to see eventually, America's drawing card in the international tourist stakes. If you've done it, you don't need me to tell you it's an expensive and tiring undertaking. If you have not done it, here is a modicum of advice: Make a plan.

The biggest times of the year are Christmas Day to New Year's Day, Thanksgiving weekend, the Presidents' Day week, the whole cycle of spring breaks and Easter. Then comes summer vacation. In other words, it's busy when the kids are out of school. There are also curves in the week, which you can understand if you imagine a huge amusement park ride in which the families board their cars on Saturday morning in New York and Philadelphia and drive like fiends to Florida, crowding into Disney World on Sunday night or Monday morning.

Disney will send you a lot of material, and since the Disney hotels and resorts started paying commissions to travel agents there is no shortage of information there. I think the most useful book is *The Unofficial Guide to Walt Disney World* by Bob Sehlinger. He breaks the rides down into two basic types, continuous loaders and stop-and-go loaders, and assesses the waiting time for every 100 people in line ahead of you. If Space Mountain is the way your kids want to scare themselves out of their wits, the author tells you what steps to take to get them on it; he includes some letters indicating that some people think Space Mountain and even Big Thunder are a lot scarier than he does.

He has a number of plans for seeing the highlights in a particular number of days; and each time I write about Disney World, including this time, I am indebted to his on-site research team.

We went with a mob of kids and their cousins, and we may be oddballs, but the children enjoyed playing in the motel pool at their doorstep overall more than they did Disney World. Likewise, the playground in Mickey's Starland (then Mickey's Birthday Party, I think) was a relief from standing endlessly in line. We adults really enjoyed the Circlevision 360-degree theater, where you stand in the cool dark for 20 minutes to watch a movie all around and above you, in our case "American Journeys."

I cannot imagine how you might find a motel without a pool in Orlando, but don't do it. Plan to get back to the motel at least by 4 P.M. and allow for long-muscle exercise time, even if you return to Disney World in the evening.

If you plan to drive to Orlando and belong to A.A.A., get a map custom-made. The interstates' underpinnings are showing signs of age and there are many sites of heavy repairs. Take sunscreen, straw hats and water bottles for everyone.

Diving and Flying

Not a good idea on the same day. According to the Civil Aeromedical Institute, the research arm of the Federal Aviation Administration, taking that last scuba dive on the day you are leaving and then flying to an altitude of 8,000 feet involves the same hazards of decompression sickness, or the bends, as flying to 40,000 feet in an unpressurized cabin. Most commercial airliners fly well above 8,000 feet.

The institute's *Physiological Training* manual gives this advice:

After a dive to a depth that does not require stops for decompression on the way up—the need for such stops depends on the time spent at a particular depth; for example, divers who have been at 60 feet for at least 60 minutes must stop while ascending—there should be a wait of at least 12 hours before any flight rising to 8,000 feet. After a dive to a depth that requires a stop on the ascent, there should be a wait of 24 hours before a flight to 8,000 feet. Before a flight that will go above 8,000 feet, there should be a wait of 24 hours after a dive, whether or not it involves a decompression stop.

A 24-hour phone number, 919-684-8111, is maintained by the Divers Alert Network at the Duke University Medical Center for help in a decompression emergency; ask for the D.A.N. emergency line. General diving safety questions may

be directed to D.A.N., Box 3823, Duke University Medical
Center, Durham, N.C. 27710; 919-684-2948 on weekdays from
9 A.M. to 5 P.M.

Driving Classes

Who's the safer driver, the young driver or the old one? It
depends on who's arguing the case, but the statistics show
where the argument comes from.

If you look at the death rate of drivers on the road, the
older driver is twice as safe. In 1988, for example, there were
26,912,000 licensed drivers aged 16 to 24, and 20,808,000 aged
65 and older. The National Highway Traffic Safety Administration, a government agency, said that 8,521 drivers in the
younger age group, which has the worst safety record of any
group, were killed on the road as opposed to 3,237 in the
older group. But if you apply the rate to miles driven, the
gap is not so great: There were 3.38 driver deaths for each
100 million miles driven in the younger group and 2.75 in the
older group. Nothing to be proud of in either case.

Leave aside the various reasons why driving safety im-
proves after 24 and then begins to decline at 50; people over
50 know what the reasons are, however little they want to
acknowledge them.

Being over 50, I can testify that you learn things from a
refresher course that can protect you on the road and the
time is well spent, particularly if it's been years since you
first got a license. I learned about the two-second and three-
second safety rule in one class, and I learned that I was
making left turns the wrong way in another. These classes
are reality based. One problem presented to a class involved
a grandparent with three rambunctious children in the car
who realizes at the end of a Sunday trip from the beach that

he or she has forgotten to pick up a gallon of milk and reaching the mall will mean a sequence of left turns across heavy traffic. (Instead, do a square of right-hand turns to reach the mall entrance, or, better, drop the kids off at home, confess failure and go back to get the milk.)

Further, insurance companies have had it shown to them that refresher courses improve performance, and more than half the states mandate a reduction in liability premiums for older drivers, and sometimes younger ones, who have recently taken a no-exam course of eight hours or so in one or two days.

Your state motor vehicle department ought to be able to tell you if there is an insurance impact for taking a course, and who teaches it. Some states send out information cards with license or registration renewals. Here are some organizations that offer courses in several states; I would prefer them to storefront driving schools, which may be effective with beginners but not necessarily with those being retrained.

55 Alive/American Association of Retired Persons offers volunteer-taught classes in all states and the District of Columbia at a nominal cost. Membership is not required. Send a stamped, self-addressed envelope to 55 Alive, 601 E Street, N.W., Washington, D.C. 20049.

The National Safety Council offers classes in all 50 states and the District of Columbia. These classes are taught by professional drivers or driver's ed teachers and cost more. Information: 1121 Spring Lake Drive, Itaska, Ill. 60143; 800-621-7615 or 708-285-1121.

American Automobile Association clubs offer classes in half the states, sometimes restricted to members. Call the local auto club.

Duty-Free

This phrase is a headache maker. Whatever duty the purchase is free of, usually the host country's "sin tax" on liquor, cigarettes, jewelry and other luxury items, it will not be free of duty in the next country down the road unless it fits within your exemption for entry there. Airport departure lounges all over the world are chockablock with duty-free shops, which will not hand over your purchases until you are irrevocably boarding the plane and are therefore taking your camera, perfume, silk scarf or souvenir porcelain plate out of the country and will not be offering it for resale, having evaded the luxury tax.

That's the end of duty-free. But when you get to United States Customs, if you are over your limit for purchases while you were away—$400 or whatever it may be—you are going to be charged duty on the camera, perfume, silk scarf or souvenir plate.

I have seen multitudes of baffled people try to get their minds around this one, but it is simple if you remember that one country cannot control taxes or duty in another.

When you are leaving the United States, you may likewise buy liquor for less than at your corner store because the government is not levying its taxes, but that liquor is leaving with you. Incidentally, when I used to put in a week or two in the *Times*'s London bureau in the spring, I bought United States bourbon at the airport in the United States and took it with me because it was terribly expensive in London. One homesick member of the bureau loved to receive maple syrup. I had to hire muscle to heft my gurgling luggage.

If you are making a trip and want to buy a particular item, most probably a camera or a watch, on your way home from the Caribbean or the Far East, do yourself a favor and clip and take along ads from a U.S. newspaper showing good prices on the particular item. I find that a model number is easy to forget and that I tend to get confused thinking in two currencies. At one point, a popular duty-free shop in Bermuda was selling cameras well above the U.S. price because legislators had neglected to include cameras in the rules covering duty-free exports. One purchaser rejected the camera, knowing it cost too much, but the shop later said the sales clerk would have explained that because of the fluke in the law the camera price included Bermuda duty.

Ear Problems in Flight

If your ears hurt on the ascent or descent of an airplane flight, you can yawn or try the Valsalva maneuver, which I learned about in an F.A.A. flight chamber in Oklahoma City. Hold your nose and squeeze your diaphragm to exert air pressure to open the passageway between your mouth and ears. The F.A.A. experts had also warned me that if I had a bad root canal, I could get a dreadful toothache when I went into the sealed chamber to experience rapid depressurization of the type that would occur if a hole was poked in a plane: The air in the tooth cavity expands painfully. So if you get a toothache on board, check it with your dentist later.

East Coast Intensive

For those who like to take a week to explore an area, *The Discerning Traveler* newsletter is a good bet. It confines itself to the Northeast, a somewhat elastic concept that now includes North Carolina.

The 16-page newsletter usually focuses on one area or town in each issue—there are eight a year—talking about things to do there, where to stay and what to eat. Penobscot Bay, Newport, R.I., the Eastern Shore of Maryland and the Blue

Ridge Parkway represent typical issues. The places to stay are generally bed-and-breakfast houses, inns or small hotels. By keeping its focus narrow in each issue, the editors and publishers, David and Linda Glickstein of Philadelphia, find nooks that may be missed by all but a few.

In the issue on Newport, a place I know fairly well, the editors reviewed 13 restaurants and spotted a couple of up-and-coming places—a storefront seafood restaurant called Scales and Shells and a Northern Italian spot called Puerini's —that you could still have gotten into at the time they wrote. We thought they were private stock, but quality will out.

The Glicksteins go to all the places they write about. In restaurants, they remain anonymous, they say, and pay cash. When they get to an inn that they like, they find that their questions immediately cause the innkeeper to say, "Whom do you write for?", so they do not try to hide their purpose. They pay the full room rate, Mr. Glickstein says, or sometimes barter a subscription but take no other discounts.

A sample issue may be obtained by sending $8 to *The Discerning Traveler*, 504 West Mermaid Lane, Philadelphia, Pa. 19118; 800-673-7834. A year's subscription is $50.

Economy Class Syndrome

This is a snobbish, pseudomedical name for a serious problem, namely the development of phlebitis in the leg. This can lead to the loosing of a blood clot in a vein, which can be life threatening. The *Merck Manual* depicts one risk factor for phlebitis in a Merckish way: "prolonged immobilization with the legs dependent while traveling"—that is to say, stuck in coach seats again.

If you have a tendency toward phlebitis or varicose veins,

see your doctor before you take a plane flight where you are
going to be cramped into economy class or, more seriously,
into the minute spaces some charter operators fancy as accommodating the human form. Pregnant women, women taking birth control pills and people with blood disorders are
also vulnerable.

For others, there are simple steps that can be taken to
lower the risk.

First, do not wear tight socks or stockings or round garters
unless you must. Try to avoid wearing panty girdles or the
like. Better off bulging than ill, as one physician said. Dr.
Selig Epstein of Philadelphia, who treated a friend of mine
who developed phlebitis on a transcontinental flight, also de-
nounced one-size-fits-all stockings. "One size does not fit all,"
he said. "They are mass-produced by the carload and they do
not take account of the needs of the public. Some are too
tight and they occlude venous circulation." I like to wear cot-
ton or wool ankle socks without elastic when I fly.

Do not cross your legs while you are sitting, even if you
have room to do so. It's not great for circulation even on the
ground, but it's perilous in a high altitude; most aircraft cabins are pressurized not to sea level, but only to the altitude
of Mexico City. Try not to jam your knees into the back of
the seat in front of you. The dry airplane air adds to the
problem, so you should keep your liquid intake up. Drink a
lot of water or juice, perhaps a cup an hour; this will have
the added benefit of getting you out of your seat frequently
for a therapeutic walk to the toilet. Get an aisle seat if you
feel self-conscious about this.

If you find your waistline swelling unaccountably, ask the
attendants if the pressurization is okay. Without blinking
they will tell you it is, but reiterate that you have gas pains.

Often enough, an adjustment is made and you will be more comfortable and safer.

Between aisle walks, contract and relax your abdominal and thigh muscles and do some deep breathing to increase blood flow. One exercise is to imagine you are operating an old-time parlor organ with your feet.

Ruth Bocour, who has experienced phlebitis, now does some of her dancers' exercises while flying: pelvic tilts, pressing down the heel, then the ball of the foot, then the toes, and rotating her ankles. She has not had a recurrence.

In any event, if you experience a pain in your calf during a trip and it goes away, don't assume everything is fine. Dr. John M. Cruickshank, one of three Britons who created the term "economy class syndrome," got a calf pain on a flight to the Far East but went ahead and played tennis when he felt better. He had to be treated for a blood clot that had found its way to his lung.

Educated Travelers

A newsletter called *The Educated Traveler*, in the words of its editor, Ann H. Waigand, focuses on places and events about which information "isn't easy to get."

She has covered auction tours offered by various sources, a self-guided tour of an Italian Renaissance village in Poland and a report on a little-known nature preserve in Venezuela. Most of the companies whose tours Ms. Waigand writes up, she says, "are small entrepreneurial tour operators who have no budget for ads or publicity."

The eight-page newsletter, begun in November 1990, has a circulation of 1,000. It does not cover restaurants or lodgings, except something like a temple inn in Japan. Ms. Waigand's writers are mostly in the travel business—in her previous

life she was a group travel manager—but they do not
write about their own offerings. The bylined writers are not
identified, however, so one has to take her word for their
objectivity.

Her writers often travel on discounts or free because they
are taking the trip for another purpose, possibly a speech.
"You can't ride the *Queen of Scots* on what I am going to
pay," she says of a five-day, $4,000 rail trip in Scotland, add-
ing that writers are often not paid at all. She says that she
knows her writers and what they are writing about and does
not feel that their objectivity is affected by the way their
trips are paid for. "We took the position that we would not
write about something unless it was good," she said.

Two valuable features: Each issue has a full-page chart
rounding up tours—for fans of performing arts, for example,
or barge or rail tours—with notations on the size of the tour
group; and a column called "A Guide's Guide," with data on
finding knowledgeable people to guide you individually or a
small group in a new place.

The Educated Traveler, Box 220822, Chantilly, Va. 22022,
703-471-1063. Six issues a year, $45; a single copy or back
issue, $7.50. Subscription includes an annual guide to mu-
seum-sponsored tours.

800 Numbers, Hotel

Many of us who book a lot of hotels have concluded that
these numbers are the poorest way to reserve a hotel room.
The telephone marketer for the hotel chain or group reads
the price off the television screen and has little idea what
rates a particular hotel may be offering, or how eager it may
be for the business, or whether the room faces on the pool or
the parking lot. "Don't ask me," a clerk said one time when I

asked about a room in Newport, Rhode Island, "I'm in St. Louis." Her candor was refreshing, if not exactly great sales work. I think it is valuable to call direct, and the dollar or two at the most it may cost is quickly recouped with a better value.

However, 800 numbers are useful to learn the real number of the hotel you want. My phone company charges 45 cents for in-state directory assistance calls and 65 cents for those out of state, so it saves at least that much to get the number from the 800 sales person. Start by calling 800-555-1212 and ask for the number of the chain you want. Then call that number and ask the marketing agent for the number of the chain's motel in, say, Washington. This process is circumvented if you have a directory for the chain you are interested in. See **motel chains** for a start.

One other piece of cheese paring: Take advantage of the clock if you can. Some big hotels shut their reservations offices in the evening, but you can save money by calling while it is reduced-toll time in your area—early morning or early evening—and the reservations office is likely to be open.

Electric Current

When you're in another country and the plug on your hair drier doesn't match the holes in the wall, that cute plug adapter kit you got as a going-away gift may not be the best solution. You can still burn the whole drier right out because it's the type and frequency of the current, the voltage and the stability of the output, that matter, not just the plug contour. To understand the basis of the problem, be aware that standard household current in the United States is 110 volts, 60 cycles. Most of the world uses 220 volts, 50 cycles. Plug your U.S. gizmo into the wall and it will overheat and burn out, and clocks and timers will run behind. To put it briefly: An adapter (plug arranger) is not a converter (current changer).

Electric Current Abroad, published by the U.S. Department of Commerce, is designed for companies that want to set up overseas, but when I looked at the entry for Grenada I understood what had happened to my beloved one-cup automatic coffeepot. The booklet covers all the details, including variations within a country showing the contour of the plugs you are likely to find there.

If you travel with a lot of electrical stuff, or want to recharge your Water Pik on the road, this is your book. It is Department of Commerce publication PB-91-193383, National Technical Information Service, 5285 Port Royal Road, Springfield, Va. 22161; 703-487-4650. It costs $9.95 plus $3 for one-week delivery. If you buy it from the Superintendent of Documents, Washington, D.C. 20402, it is document 003-008-00203-2 and costs $3. (I heard an explanation why the price varies, but like a lot of things I learned in 1991, it didn't make a lot of sense.)

If you are going to be abroad for a long time, and you want appliances, including refrigerators and heavy stuff, that will operate in your future home, my favorite place is Appliances Overseas, 276 Fifth Avenue, Suite 407, New York, N.Y. 10001; 212- 545-8001. Among their thousand items, they have stereo systems and other luxuries that may be the right gift for someone going into the Peace Corps. They say they ship parts, too.

Emergency Evacuation

If you suffer a sudden illness or an injury overseas, your anxiety is intensified by difficulty with a foreign language, problems with the telephone and a lack of friends and family to help out.

Assistance companies are set up to give help by phone, consult with medical people on the spot and to arrange and authorize an emergency evacuation if that is the wisest course. Assistance organizations may be in business for themselves, selling memberships or coverage; they are also retained by credit card issuers to deal with cardholders' emergencies, from damage to a rental car to finding a lawyer in a foreign city to arranging for a patient to be flown home.

Assistance companies operate 24 hours a day and the employees know several languages; medical consultants are available. The "benefits" lists sent by credit card companies when you first get the card, and then occasionally later, detail what assistance comes with that type of card. The card company usually also sends a wallet-sized card that gives numbers for various types of help—lost card, getting cash, how to reach assistance help—usually through "800" numbers in the United States and numbers to call collect from overseas.

Different credit card issuers may use the same assistance company, which works with the same database of doctors, hospitals and air ambulance companies to assist all callers.

The decision on whether evacuation is the safest course is made by the doctor on the scene in telephone consultation with the assistance company's medical officials. The assistance company may arrange for credit card advances to pay for medical care or the trip home, but the amount must be paid by the traveler or his or her insurance company.

Once the decision is made to move sick or injured travelers, says Jerry Edwards, president of the Worldnet Services assistance company near Dallas, "whether an insurance company pays or not, we go in and get them back." The cost can be high. For example, a patient who must lie down, accompanied by a medical aide, may take the space of five first class seats. An air ambulance with medical personnel is expensive, with distance a factor; from Nepal to the United States, for instance, could cost $50,000.

When you are choosing whether to join an assistance plan that provides evacuation insurance or to rely on the assistance that comes with a credit card, preexisting medical conditions should be weighed in. Recurrence of a condition that was treated in the previous 60 or 90 days may void coverage sold by an insurance company for medical evacuation, although, as Edwards makes clear, it does not void the assistance company's commitment to get the patient out.

Here is information on four major assistance companies that sell their coverage direct to the public.

International SOS Assistance has been in business for 18 years, mainly providing service to companies with personnel overseas. It sells individual memberships based on trip length, which provide assistance services and emergency evacuation when approved. There is no exclusion for preexisting conditions. Membership costs $35 for one person for the first 14 days of a trip, $60 for a couple; $70 for one person for a month, $120 for a couple. Additional days are $3.50 each for one person and $6 for a couple. The underwriter for the evacuation and repatriation is Cigna of Philadelphia. International SOS Assistance, 8 Neshaminy Interplex, Suite 207 Trevose, Pa. 19053; 800-523-8930.

TravMed and its assistance service, Medex, were founded in 1977. Assistance services and up to $100,000 in medical and hospital expenses are provided at a cost of $3 a day for people under 70, $5 a day over 70. The deductible is $25; preexisting conditions that required treatment in the previous 90 days are not covered. Students are covered up to $25,000 for $2 a day with the same 90-day exclusion for preexisting conditions. The underwriter is the Monumental General Insurance Company, except in Minnesota where it is Lloyd's of London. TravMed is not available from travel agents. TravMed, Box 10623, Baltimore, Md. 21285; 800-732-5309.

USAssist, founded in 1988, sells mainly to companies but offers an individual policy for assistance and medical evacuation with a benefit limit of $100,000. The cost of other actual medical expenses may be advanced but are not covered. The annual enrollment fee for someone making a trip or trips of 90 days or less is $95; for longer trips the annual fee is $150. Preexisting conditions treated 60 days before a trip are not covered. The underwriter is Federal Insurance of the Chubb Companies in New Jersey. This is not available from travel agents. USAssist, 3400 International Drive, N.W., Suite 3L, Washington, D.C. 20008; 800-756-5900.

Travel Assistance International is linked to Europe Assistance Worldwide Services, which was founded in 1963. It provides assistance and evacuation with no limit when approved by the assistance company; local ambulance and emergency care up to $15,000 a person are included, with a $75 deductible. An individual membership for a trip of 9 to 15 days costs $50, $75 for a family. A trip of 60 days costs $120 for one person, $220 for a family. Conditions treated in the previous 180 days are not covered. For an extra fee, trip cancellation and other coverage is available. The underwriter is Clarendon of Baltimore. This policy is available from travel agents. Travel Assistance International, 1133 15th Street, N.W., Suite 400, Washington, D.C. 20005; 800-821-2828.

Trip cancellation and baggage policies may also include evacuation coverage. In all likelihood, the assistance and approval for evacuation come from one of the companies listed above.

Emergency Oxygen

If you are like me and are instructed to put the oxygen mask over your nose and mouth *before* you put it over your child's, you probably said to yourself, No way, I'll save my child first. I wish the emergency cards in the seat pockets of airplanes would explain this bit of direction because it wasn't until I once went through F.A.A. physiological training that I learned the reason for it. Let me preach to you about that most unlikely event: a decompression.

I went to a big medical center to get a special pilot training medical examination. Then when I went to the decompression chamber in Oklahoma City, I was rehearsed several times in how to seize and don an oxygen face mask similar to a pilot's. We were to make rudimentary notes on a clipboard. Then the chamber was rapidly deprived of oxygen in an imitation of what would happen if the plane lost a door at cruising altitude. I thought I was doing okay with my pencil, but after a very few seconds of no oxygen I grabbed my mask and saw that my pad was covered with scrawls, not notes.

Apoxia, or lack of oxygen, deprives you of good sense, but without your knowing it, and it affects your eyesight as well. It will take you only a couple of seconds to get your mask on, and your child, with no tasks to perform, will be in no danger in the meantime. Then you can get the mask on the child. If you try to do the child's mask first, you may never be able to manage your own. The consequences are obvious, particularly if you consider the possibility that you must seize your child and make an exit.

Every time you read that a door flew off in flight or that a plane had to make an emergency landing, you know that the oxygen drill was performed, and in lots of other less severe situations, too.

As to the question you should now ask: Yes, there is a spare mask in the overhead for each row, but usually only one, which is why only one "lap child" is permitted in each row. For more immediate child safety, protecting your nearest during a rough flight, see **child safety seat**.

Facecloths

Or washcloths. The absolute first hotel I ever stayed in, in Boston during World War II, had forgotten to make up the beds or put towels in the bathrooms for the wrinkled little campers coming from the railroad station to stay overnight before taking the Maine train in the morning. We were perplexed but finally concluded, incorrectly, that the camp had neglected to tell us to get a couple of sheets and a towel out of the footlockers before we left them at the railroad checkroom.

The hotel apologized in great embarrassment the next day, but this early imprinting has never been erased: When I get to a hotel room and find no facecloth, I assume that I have somehow neglected to read the small type. But in fact many European hotels do not provide facecloths, and there is little way of predicting which ones will. In Rome and Paris, I had great fun shopping for them at neighborhood stores, but if you arrive dusty from travel and want to wash your ears you don't want to go shopping first. Take a facecloth with you, in a plastic bag in case you have to pack it damp. My smart sister keeps it in her carry-on luggage for use on the plane, too.

Family Reunion Trip

The magic number is 10: 10 tickets, 10 rooms, 10 rides and you are a group. Just like the professional convention or the business meeting, this number for a family reunion gets a discount. It may be a lower fare for everyone, or it may be one free room, or a free hospitality suite. At the hotel, you should be talking to the banquet department or the marketing department. With the airline, group sales. For the boat trip, call in advance and book and get a free ticket or two. At every step, be sure that the people know you are buying for the whole group. Ask for a private room at the restaurant and a waiter who is patient with children if that is a factor. Check on wheelchair entrances if that is a factor, too.

Many people hate to bargain and find it embarrassing, but try to overcome this by thinking in terms of lowering the price for everyone and, often, getting special billing or favors. Start in plenty of time and do not neglect anything, including a call to the local paper some months in advance to see if you can get in a notice of what is coming up. My husband's family did this when they returned to the Midwestern town of their origins, and on the appointed day the bank president brought over a huge decorated cake for the picnic.

The travel section of the *Boston Globe* carried a little notice, "Wades Wanted," one spring when the Wades of Canada were holding a reunion and were trying to find other descendants of Nicholas Wade of Scituate, Massachusetts. So don't neglect the possibility of finding lost acorns that fell close to the tree.

The Econo Lodge in Orlando, which messed up the reservations for us one year, compensated by posting a welcome to the family on the big sign out front and it made a perfect backdrop for the group picture. And the hotel at Paradise, on the slope of Mount Rainier, trotted out the summer's first clear sky and a full moon for us.

There are lots of books and even a magazine, *Reunions* ($28 a year, Box 11727, Milwaukee, Wis. 53211; 414-263-4567), about running reunions, but they mostly pertain to school or military reunions, a special breed. Family reunions are increasingly important in a day when relatives are so widely scattered, so borrow the expertise. Recently, motels, including the Best Western chain and Holiday Inns, have been offering leaflets to family reunion planners, but the commercial content has a precious thin veneer of advice. You can do it yourself: Take out a calendar for the coming year, settle on a date and count backward to establish deadlines for invitations, responses, hotel deposits and the like.

T-shirts are the most common keepsake, but these involve a survey of sizes. One year we went one-size-fits-all and got a friend to design a beach towel with the right mountain in the background, the family name, the place and the year. It was more expensive than T-shirts, but it was a big hit. The company that supplied the towels and printed the design advertised in the Yellow Pages under "Screen Printing." The next year it was coffee mugs with a custom design and our name.

Best souvenir idea: one-use cameras for all the children.

Fare Wars

My crystal ball needs a good polishing, but I suspect that these screwy battles will continue unless the government decides to reregulate the airline fare structure. So the question is, What did you do in the fare wars, Mom?

The answer is, Try very hard to schedule our important trips well in advance. I use a travel agent and I tell him what we will need to do when and with how many people, and he watches the fares for me. If I see one in the paper that looks good, I call and ask him to check if we can get in on it. I send him discount coupons from my frequent flier programs with instructions to give them away if they don't fit my plans.

If the fare for your ticket drops after you have reserved but before you have paid, the new fare can be used. If you have paid, you may have to fork over $25 or whatever the fee has become, to change the ticket to the lower fare, an irritating aspect to the semirefundable ticket that evolved from the nonrefundable ticket, but if you are saving more than $25, just do it.

In my job, I get hundreds of letters about the irrationality of fare structures and furious accounts of trying to take advantage of an advertised special only to find tickets in that class were sold out apparently before the ad was printed. The states' attorneys general tried for a time to control the advertising but were ruled out, and usually the small type now required at the bottoms of the ads does not say what everyone wants to know: How many seats at that price? As it says, the fare has "limited" availability or is "capacity controlled." So don't count on a last-minute killing; take Mom's advice and plan ahead and then try to adapt to changing circumstances.

Fire Safety

Questions about selecting a hotel or motel with adequate fire protection are discussed under **hotel safety.** Here are some other considerations that should be on a card in your room, but just in case . . .

If you cannot select a motel with wired-in smoke detectors and sprinklers, get a room on a low floor.

If you do not smoke, get a room on a nonsmoking floor.

When you arrive in your room, check out the exit routes that do not involve elevators. If you find a stairway exit blocked or barred in some way, report it to the front desk immediately. State and city laws protect the usability of those exits and a hotel is not permitted to chain them to prevent employees from using the stairwell. Try to fix the location of the stairwell in your mind.

If the motel has a battery-driven smoke detector, check to see that it has a battery in it.

When you go to bed, put the room key within reach on the table beside your bed. If you leave in an emergency, take the key with you because if the corridor is impassable you will need to get back into your room.

If there is a fire, get out of the room, use the exit and get as far away from the building as you can.

Irrelevant but important: Change the battery in your home smoke detectors when you change your clocks for daylight saving time in the spring and fall. It's easy to remember, which is why fire departments recommend this.

Flight Insurance

Forget it. The likelihood that you will be in a plane crash is so remote that this is an insurer's bonanza. You are paying a $10 premium to be covered for $500,000 against a near impossibility in the next seven hours. Buy several magazines instead and enjoy the flight.

Frequent Flier Plan

If you belong to one, you already know that the rules change all the time and handbook information is out-of-date by the time you read it. If you plan to join one, here are the basics:

If you live in and regularly travel to cities served by several airlines, pick the best combination of plans of airlines that (1) serve cities you fly to often, (2) offer high mileage points for the trips you make ("minimum mileage") and (3) perhaps throw in points for a hotel or car rental agency you use anyway. (You should know that the hotel stay or car rental usually needs to be made within a day of your flight on the "partner" airline.)

There is no reason not to join the program of any airline you use, but the idea is to concentrate your points on one airline so you can collect. If you are buying a handful of tickets for the family, be sure they all join the plan just in case they fly enough to get a free trip or upgrade.

Be sure the ticket and the plan membership are in the same name, including initials and periods because computers are dumb that way. One airline kept sticking a "Ms." on my name that caused the system to find me a nonperson.

Have your travel agent enter your membership number when she books the ticket but check the desk at the airport to be sure. Save the bottom sheet or card of your ticket and all your boarding passes.

If you have to appeal to the plan to give you credit, send photocopies, not the originals.

American Express has a linkup with some airlines, Membership Miles, where the dollars you spend past a rather steep minimum—which has not always been the same amount —can be converted into frequent flier points. This can be helpful in "topping off" an award where you are falling shy. Many airlines let you top off in cash, but this is cheaper.

When collecting your earned trip, be sure you reserve early. I asked one airline's spokesman if it was possible that only one frequent-flier seat was set aside on a New York-Paris run in April; his reply was that such a thing would never happen. This is the man who in another context said, "But I never say never." I shifted to another airline and used the points I had there to get a companion ticket that was far easier to book. But I had to buy a refundable ticket to go with it, which was an extra $200-odd. When I read of a much cheaper fare on Tower Air, I concluded that I had been taken by the idea of the free ticket but should have shopped harder because it had really cost me $200.

Passengers have inevitably accumulated millions of points more than they have used. From a business standpoint, these unclaimed miles represent a big liability on the books of hard-pressed airlines, but no one discusses this situation much so it must be that the airlines do not expect the majority of the miles to be collected. Periodically, the airlines offer merchandise catalogues to their big point accumulators in hopes they will expend points for gadgets and lop off some of the burden.

At the same time, many consumers are interested in getting rid of their surplus. Most airlines let you give your coupons away to nonrelatives, but no airline agrees to your selling them. See **coupon broker.**

A few newsletters keep track of the now-you-see-'em-now-you-don't aspects of these plans. Here is the name of one if you wish to join in:

Inside Flyer, 4715-C Town Center Drive, Colorado Springs, Colo. 80916. $33 a year for 12 issues.

Gadgets

Lord save me from gadgets. That's what it may take, in fact, since I go insane when exposed to hardware stores, luggage shops, travel gadget shops, catalogues of little gimmicks or even thrift shops. My friends have had to drag me from the Museum of Modern Art Design Store in New York, where I want everything from the $1 plastic holder for subway tokens to the bike that folds into a canvas bag at several hundred dollars.

But wish and fulfillment diverge. Most gadget stores and catalogues look as if they were created for use in the days of the 40-year assignment to India: Who on earth is going to cart around a leather case with three decanters of brandy or an umbrella that will never fit in any luggage?

Every year, I survey the new crop of goodies, and while I crave liberally, I actually buy—whether the trifle is intended for me or somebody else—only if I consider the item valuable enough for me to carry it in my suitcase. Yes, I would love to emerge from the Underground and pedal off on that bike, but not enough to drag it to London.

What can I recommend? You will recognize a number of gadgets listed in the entry on **packing**. I will elaborate on some of them here:

The Zeiss 8×20 pocket binoculars my sister gave me years ago rank at the top of any list. They are so expensive that when I wrote about them I waffled on the brand and the price and after a raft of letters ended up having to give the specifics. The price in 1987 was $440. As of this writing, it is $475. I guess the readers understood better than I that bog-

gling at the price of such a treasure was like asking the cost
of the sunset. These seven-ounce wonders fold up very small
and go into a pocket or fanny pack, causing scarcely a lump.
You need never leave them behind in a hotel room when you
go out, and probably shouldn't. For birds, seals, whales,
shorelines, architectural detail, mountains, the children in the
park below the hotel window—these binocs provide crisp
magnification but are not so powerful that you need a tripod
to hold them steady. I hate to rhapsodize but they are the
essence of a good gadget: unique, convenient, portable. They
come with a little leather case with a wrist strap, plus a light
string for the neck so if you want a grandchild to have a look
you need not fret that they'll be dropped overboard. But
frankly, if you are climbing in the wilds or just need something for everyday use, less expensive binocs that fold up will
do the job. We have two pairs for that reason.

Item two is a small powerful flashlight. Ever since Hurricane Hugo caught me in a brand-new economy motel in
North Carolina without lights, TV, smoke detector or much
of anything else, I have not traveled without a flashlight,
which I put on the bedside table along with my room key
when I call it a day. (See **fire safety**.) I have long used the
Tekna-Lite 2, which is 1¼ inches in diameter and 5½ inches
long. Made of plastic, it weighs 3½ ounces with two AA batteries and goes into a purse easily. More expensive is the
metal Mini-Mag of aluminum, which is five inches long and
weighs 4¼ ounces with two AA batteries. L. L. Bean in
Freeport, Maine (800-221-4221) and Campmor in Paramus,
N.J. (800-526-4784) both carry these, as do lots of hardware
stores. Incidentally, both of these babies use peculiar bulbs,
and if replacements do not come with the light, order one or
two when you buy.

A high school friend in California who read about my experience with Hugo quickly sent me a waterproof plastic MityLite from the Pelican Company in Torrance, Calif. (213-328-9910) that weighs a piddling two ounces with two AAA batteries. It has performed well. For some reason, it reminds me of pictures I have seen of "ladies' pistols." This one is also in a lot of catalogues, most recently that of the Nature Company.

In our family, we are strong fans of the Swiss Army knife. For years, I carried a model with only two blades and a tiny pair of scissors, but the writer Thomas Hoving, once the head of the Metropolitan Museum of Art, picks the seven-ounce model with the miniature eyeglass screwdriver inside the corkscrew and pliers and scissors. Despite its capacities, such a folding, short-bladed knife apparently does not arouse the interest of the security monitors at the airports: Hoving says he has had only one taken away from him, by security for a domestic Italian flight. Male friends who serve as Manhattan jurors say, however, that a Swiss Army knife will set off the protective devices in the courthouses. I concur with Hoving that having a corkscrew at all times is a plus: It means a spontaneous roadside picnic need not confine itself to soft drinks or screw-top wine. Swiss Army knives are pretty easy to find, and this is the top of the line at $70 to $100.

Scissors are needed amazingly often on the road. I buy the children's snub-nosed models, but with sharp edges. They will clip clippings, open parcels, trim a hangnail or cut a flower. They are inexpensive and have always passed through airport security.

For the essential calculator, I select one with big buttons and numbers that is solar and battery powered. Every once in a while, I can't get it to work in a cellar restaurant that uses only candles, but usually it tells us what we owe or divides the check cleanly. I try to stick to an inexpensive model because I lose them readily and sometimes even give them away. I know Radio Shack has been selling these at $10 or so. I do not need to do square roots on the road, so I take a basic model.

At the top of my old packing list was my travel alarm clock, and it was like the gong for the fire dog; putting it into a suitcase told me I was, like Willie Nelson, on the road again. With the advent of hotel television sets and alarm radios and telephones with digital time displays and automated wake-up calls, the travel alarm is less essential, but there are still places that lack such gadgetry. So pack one. These have gotten lighter lately and are sometimes given away as promotions.

Since I mangled our one-cup automatic coffeemaker using it in Grenada, I have tried to avoid dealing with **electric current** overseas, so my rechargeable battery-operated Water Pik is a heavy (1¼ pounds) but essential companion. It recharges on 220 or 110 volts and then works fine for five days or so. Before you set off with it, give it a charge. If you cannot find this model, call Appliances Overseas in New York (212-545-8001).

A flask is a peculiar business. John Cheever's "Diary of an Old Gent" in *The Wapshot Chronicle* lays down one of those deathless-wisdom rules: Never carry liquor in a hot-water bottle because it imparts a funny taste. In a moment of enthusiasm, I once bought an translucent plastic flask with an extra cap usable as a tiny shot cup and it had the same problem. I have never had confidence in the idea since. I bought a pint of vodka in a light plastic bottle at a duty-free shop once before boarding the Hovercraft in England, and the empty has served as a vodka carrier for years. It does not have an aroma. If I lose it, I won't be crushed. In any case, avoid glass as both heavy and breakable.

These days, I take a fanny pack so I can stride around with both hands free without abandoning my wallet, passport, pen and tissues. I notice that some very sharp tour operators are now distributing these instead of the flight bags of yore, and I can hardly imagine a better promotion than having your clients tromp everywhere with your name at their waists for all the world to see. When buying one, test to be sure it will hold your essentials.

Giardia

This disagreeable parasite causes a long-lasting diarrhea and is one more important reason to worry about the quality of the water. It was once something people worried about only when visiting the Soviet Union, but a physician got giardiasis from an ice cube in Thailand and it is common in ski resorts in Colorado. A candid brochure on day hikes in Glacier National Park in Montana says this: "Glacier's water is clear and cold, but not always pure. . . . Giardia is present in the park's water." So however you may wish to imitate the pioneers and drink from the crystal-clear stream tumbling down the mountainside, take your drink from your water bottle filled from a banal tap.

Gloves

If you are going overseas but not to the tropics, pack a pair of leather or knit gloves. They take no space, but weather can get miserably cold unexpectedly and gloves will save your sanity, because you cannot safeguard a bag while your

hands are in your pockets. Of spring in France, almost everyone says, "I didn't expect it to be so cold."

Grandchild on Board

The tough economy, the prevalence of the two-job young
family and the increasing vigor of the grandparent generation
have given rise to something called "intergenerational
travel." What it is is the old extended family, where everyone nurtured the kids, in a new life as a road show.

It is fun, but it is not like traveling with your own children
because it's a generation later and your relations with these
children are different. It does take planning and a renewed
awareness of children's needs: for physical activity, for rest
for the legs, for liquids and toilets, for contact with other
children. If you are about to try it for the first time, you may
want to hook up with a group of others doing the same: It
provides other children to play with, other adults for you to
sit with, and some expert guidance.

Here are some possibilities, but be prepared, these are not
budget offerings.

Grandtravel invented the idea of selling these tours in 1987,
and Hilda T. Koenig, the owner, has branched out from simple tours to Washington (almost the prototype for grandpar-
ent-grandchild travel) to barge trips in Belgium. Ms. Koenig
says that children 7 to 14 enjoy her trips most. The Grand
Canyon is a big draw, as is the Southwest, to learn about
Native American life. Grandtravel, 6900 Wisconsin Avenue,
706, Chevy Chase, Md. 20815; 800-247-7651.

Rascals in Paradise while not catering to just to grandparents, plans some trips for this pairing. In 1993, for example,
there was one to New Zealand. Most tours with this com-

pany, founded in the mid-80s, involve activities like snorkel-ing and scuba diving. The prices reflect this adventurous orientation. Rascals in Paradise, 650 Fifth Street, 505, San Francisco, Calif. 94107; 800-872-7225.

Elderhostel (minimum grandparent age, 60) provides a really structured trip, focused on an educational venture at a cam-pus or a natural site. In 1993, courses in 24 states and three Canadian provinces were designed for grandparents and grandchildren, and some thought went into the programs. In Vernal, Utah, for example, there was a program called Dig-gin' Up Bones: Unearthing Dinosaurs and Human History, which included field work at Dinosaur National Monument, rafting the Green River and some study of Native Ameri-cans. Elderhostel's problem is that it has been tremendously popular and courses fill up early. Elderhostel sends cata-logues: 75 Federal Street, Boston, Mass. 02110; 617-426-7788.

Interhostel administered at the University of New Hamp-shire, where the now much larger Elderhostel was born, has begun offering some overseas courses for grandparents and grandchildren. The Grandparents-Familyhostel effort began in 1992 and was expanded to five programs in 1993. Interhos-tel: University of New Hampshire, 6 Garrison Avenue, Dur-ham, N.H. 03824; 800-733-9753.

Other tour companies offer one or two grandparent-grand-child trips, so ask.

The authoritative newsletter in the field is Dorothy Jor-don's *Travel with Your Children*. She keeps an eagle eye on hotels that promise activity programs. See **kids along.**

Guidebooks vs. Travel Literature

There are too many new guidebooks published every year.
Few of them contribute anything really new and a lot of
them, especially the ones that bear a new date on the cover
each year, have been insufficiently revised and probably not
even by the nominal author but by people using phones instead of travelers using feet, eyes and mouths. Yes, I do a lot
of reporting by phone, but I don't pretend to tell you what
the place is like, how the air feels, what you will see if you
cross the bridge over the Serpentine. That takes being there.
Publishers, I guess, command that a book on a fast-changing
area like the Caribbean or Mexico be bought up to date regularly, and I find that patchwork updating causes the book to
lose any cohesiveness.

Publishers will hate to hear me say this, but really good
guidebooks never go entirely out of date, as you can see under **W.P.A. Guides**. No one will ever replace Kate Simon's
New York, Places & Pleasures, even if the bulldozer has
rolled over some of her places. Same goes for her London
and Paris books, and if you have come to feel blasé about any
of these cities, get these books from the library and sip a
little vintage Simon before you go. We used Henry James' *A
Little Tour in France*, more than a century old, in Provence,
and since Roman ruins don't move around a lot it was wonderful. Our family has also given hard use to the
Londonwalks, Romewalks series published by New Republic
Books. We used *Viennawalks* for a tour of the former Ghetto
on the Passover-Easter weekend the year it fell close to the
50th anniversary of the Nazi takeover of Austria, and while
the country was in an uproar over Kurt Waldheim's past as a
Nazi. The authors in this series are teachers of history as
well as travelers. Although not all the walks in all the books

are equally stimulating, there is something respectful and vigorous about their tone that engages me.

I think the selection of such discursive books must be personal; you must like the author and be interested in what he or she wants to talk about. A good public library is the first place to look for such books because, depending on the time of year, the bookstore selection is usually spotty and based on what publishers are trying to sell at the moment. But I suggest you not try to make such a book also do duty as a hotel finder and meal suggester. That is something else—the kind of book where you need up-to-dateness. If you are going to allow a more intellectual book in your suitcase, try to pick something relatively light for the purpose of finding current addresses and prices.

I have made do with stapled publications put out by city tourist agencies. For example, the Chamber of Commerce and Industry of Paris put out a 28-page booklet, "Insider's Good Value Guide to Paris," with inexpensive restaurants, wine bars and hotels by arrondissement, which we found invaluable in the spring of '93. The French Government Tourist Office distributed it, but the publisher was listed as Corporate Word, 420 East 51st Street, New York, N.Y. 10022. The leaflet device works less well in the countryside because it can be a long way between oases. The Michelin red guides are dense and reliable.

People who travel with backpacks and hiking shoes—including me on occasion—get a wider choice of omnibus guides than others do. You should shop through the Lonely Planet Series, the Harvard Student Agencies' Let's Go Guides and their new West Coast competition, the Berkeley Guides, and see if the volume on the place you are going appears up to

date and meets your needs. These have identifiable points of
view and generally youthful authors.

Thalia Zepatos, in *A Journey of One's Own* (Eighth Mountain Press, Portland, Oreg., 1992) as an "independent woman
traveler," describes her method for selecting guidebooks. One
is to think of three questions you want answered about the
place you are going: How can I get to Machu Picchu? What
is the cultural background of Machu Picchu? What will a hotel cost me in Cuzco? See how the various books respond to
the same questions. The other is to pick a guidebook to a
place you already know and see if its judgments match yours,
and use this as a touchstone to the series. I think this
method is less reliable.

For Latin America, the venerable British *South American
Handbook* (Trade & Travel Publications in Bath, England,
distributed in the United States in 1993 by Passport Books in
Chicago) has been broken into pieces: Mexico and Central
America, the Caribbean and the original. When I am doing
research, these seldom lead me wrong and people who travel
a lot in the third world swear by their reliability.

Reliability takes me into a complex area I might as well
deal with here. The question is whether the writer is be-
holden to someone other than the reader who buys the book,
and how much this may affect the book's credibility.

My sister swears by the Karen Brown series on country
inns and chalets and the like, which are published by Ms.
Brown's own enterprise and distributed by Warner Books.
Ms. Brown, herself the keeper of a country inn in California,
writes some of these guides, her mother, a travel agent,
writes some and there are a couple more authors. As innkeepers and travel agents, they are involved in the business
rather than being the famous but incognito inspectors whose

work creates the Mobil Travel Guides. In an area where each inn is one of a kind and has a small capacity, it is probably impossible to disguise oneself without acting like Inspector Clouseau.

Four in our family used an outdated Karen Brown on our Henry James tour of Provence and got wonderful treatment when, on the basis of the writeup, we reserved at the Old Mill Inn in Villeneuve-lès-Avignon. But when we left, we learned that the owner was crushed that Ms. Brown was leaving him out of the new edition. We said we would let her know how much we had enjoyed the midnight arrival supper, the bathtub with a view of the river and the whole place generally. And we did let her know. In small country places, the proprietor wants you to tell people if you enjoyed it, including disaffected guidebook authors. Having given my view, I never checked later whether the Karen Brown team considered that the Old Mill Inn deserved another look.

Karen Brown says her researchers visit anonymously the first time they go and pay their bills at the regular rate. The next time around, she said, if the writer is recognized and is offered a better rate or a free stay she or he may accept it. Ms. Brown said in 1992 that a proper first visit, with meals and tips, usually cost $500, which can add up in a book that reviews, say, 120 places.

The late Norman Simpson was known, recognized and lionized at the country inns he wrote up, first as the Berkshire Traveler and later under his name, and in fact he organized the inns into an association that created a logotype for bars of soap and shampoos that the inns used. Our favorite lodge would practically disintegrate with excitement on the day before his arrival. It's terribly hard to know how to judge such a book, and the Simpson *Country Inns and Back Roads* matter is still further confused by a new author who continues to print old Simpson essays saying "I arrived," etc., mixed among new entries with the new author writing in the first person.

The number of bona fide freelance writers who sustain themselves wholly on travel writing is very small, and the majority manage it by using discounts or taking trips for other purposes and writing about it as a sideline, which may be the genesis of much of the material in the Let's Go series and similar guidebooks. Freelance writers often also write guidebooks, and may get an advance to use for expenses.

Some guidebooks to hotels and restaurants will tell you what their policy is on accepting discounts or free stays, called "comps" for "complimentary." I think they owe it to readers to do so. But I also think that you can tell on the second or third try whether you are getting fair-minded reviews. If you are told that the host is gracious and attentive and the one you meet is rude and ignores your reservation, you know what has happened. It's like the joke about the people who get a glimpse of hell and decide it looks fine, but when they get there it's frightful: "The first time, you were on a familiarization trip," the authorities say.

Then there is the sponsored book, like the Birnbaum guide to Disney World. Some people like guides that are endorsed and subsidized by the place being reviewed, but I am amazed that I must pay for them. Once upon a time, maps were given to us free at the filling station, but those days are gone, too. Of course, the Mobil Travel Guides cost about $15 now and the link to the oil company has become vestigial, and no one thinks twice that the Michelin guides, likewise now sold in bookstores, are sponsored by a tire company.

I sense that the dividing lines are more blurred by the

year. For example, the A.A.A. Tour Books have careful inspection standards and are now phasing in requirements for fire safety. But A.A.A. members get special rates at some places, and this certainly must skew a reader's judgment. Similarly, the Mobil guides have pages of coupons in each issue that are good for that year. Newsletters do the same. Gene and Adele Malott, who publish *The Mature Traveler*, have offered subscribers discounts on cruises and like.

Health Overseas

Curiously, the statistics indicate that the things that you never encounter at home that can make you sick overseas—malaria, yellow fever, cholera and the like—are not the things that are likely to kill you. If you want to worry about dying on a trip, read **survival overseas** and **safety overseas**; you will learn there that if you are going to buy the farm overseas your undoing will likely come from the same things that do you in at home, plus the enhanced danger of motor accidents in the third world.

But because millions of Americans each year visit countries with malaria and practically none die of it—there were two fatalities out of 550 cases reported in 1991—does not mean that malaria prophylaxis should be ignored. Malaria is frightful. One physician who gave himself malaria as part of his research described a grisly sequence of being ill, feverish and out of his head. The government is curt: "Deaths from malaria are preventable," it says in its annual reference book, *Health Information for International Travel*, which also talks about ways of avoiding malaria. You need to be protected if you are going to an area where you will be exposed to tropical diseases.

Travel to the tropics, or probably any travel more daring

than a trip to Disney World, should begin with an updating of your basic inoculations: tetanus, diphtheria and polio vaccine. Other protections, including rabies, yellow fever and malaria, will depend on where you are going and in what order. If you are taking a cruise to a malarious area but will return to your vessel at night, you are not likely to encounter malaria mosquitoes, which are active after dark. You should receive detailed information about traveler's diarrhea and cholera and eating and drinking safely.

The family doctor is not the best person to sort this out unless he or she is a tropical medicine specialist. Dr. Frank James, director of a county health department in Washington State, says he has for a long time been pressing "the good old local docs to stop scribbling out prescriptions" for what they fancied prospective travelers might need, and send them straight to him. A couple of years ago, Dr. James' argument was bolstered when a traveler who had seen only the family physician returned with malaria; the doctor had not immunized him.

A still more worrisome case was recounted by Dr. Leonard Marcus of Newton, Massachusetts, who said that a group of five or six missionaries who were preparing to visit Liberia were told by their travel agent that a vaccination would be required only for yellow fever, which is true, and for cholera, which is not true. Malaria was not mentioned. One missionary fell ill and returned home with chills and fever, telling her family doctor she had been in West Africa and thought she had malaria. The doctor disagreed, treating her for flu. The patient ended up with pulmonary edema and eventually recovered; a second missionary got malaria but was diagnosed correctly and recovered. The travel agent made a bad mistake, but had the family doctor been asked for pretravel advice he would not have done much better.

A "shot station," a place authorized by a city or state to administer yellow fever shots, is not the best place for help either. The patient's history needs to be taken. For example, Larium, a malaria prophylactic, should not be given to people using beta-blockers.

The best recourse is something new under the sun: a travel medicine clinic. These first appeared in the early 1980s and there are probably 500 in the United States now, although it is impossible to evaluate which are real clinics and which are subpractices for tropical medicine specialists. If you are planning a complex trip where medical care is not going to be easily available, you want a clinic, which will have a long questionnaire and various sorts of literature for you to take away. Travel clinics often operate as part of a bigger medical center, and an efficient way to find one is to call the nearest information number at a medical center or teaching hospital. Sometimes, a good county medical department will know where you can go. (For more details and how to get a list of 100 clinics, see **travel health clinic**.)

One other thing. Your family doctor is probably not going to ask you if you plan to engage in casual sex while you are gone. And should your new professional at the health clinic fail on this score, bring the question up yourself. A professional ought to give you some clear idea of how high the hazard level for unprotected intercourse is, whether you are in Amsterdam or Nairobi, if you are in any doubt.

Dr. Jonathan Mann, now professor of health and human rights at the Harvard School of Public Health and formerly head of the AIDS program for the World Health Organization, sees a dilemma for physicians here. The doctor who brings the issue up may seem to be endorsing, or at least accepting, the possibility that the patient may visit a prostitute while traveling. The doctor who does not bring it up may fail in a duty to counsel a patient about a mortal danger.

Holidays

Many a traveler has had a dismaying experience overseas encountering an unexpected holiday shutdown, a day of historic importance, a religious observance. When newlywed, we took a long July weekend and drove into Canada, figuring we could buy a few plates to go with our Wedgwood wedding pattern and have a nice time looking at, yes, Niagara Falls. Well, it was July 1, Canada Day, then known as Dominion Day, and not even the souvenir stands were open. We were crushed, but the Canadians seemed disinclined to excuse our ignorance. It was then I learned that almost no place in the world, except perhaps New Orleans, is so dedicated to tourism that it stays awake and in business 365 days rather than send a visitor away empty-handed.

The British tradition of virtually shutting down the day after Christmas—Boxing Day—and Easter Monday has come to the attention of the traveling public. But every place from Iceland to Fiji has a day or more when operations cease, trains run on sparse schedules and museum gates clang shut. Even American states have holidays little known to outsiders —Rhode Island's Victory Day on the Monday in the week of V-J Day, August 14, for instance. Decent guidebooks will give you dates, and if you call or write a consulate it will, too. This is important to learn if you are planning a visit of only two or three days and risk getting into no museums, no restaurants, no historic sites. If a holiday falls in the middle of a longer trip, get enough cash in hand to function and, because restaurants may be shut, too, make it the night you eat in the hotel dining room.

Hostels and Dorms

For the solo traveler, hostels and dormitories are as cheap as they come; the hostel is not renting you a room but a bed or a bunk in a room with others of your sex, with a toilet and shower in all likelihood down the hall. In New York, it may be $20; on the road, as low as $6 or $7.

Hostels come in two types: those affiliated with the American Youth Hostels nonprofit group, and those operated privately under independent rules, with rates that may fluctuate.

Some are in fantastic locations or wonderful buildings in renewed big-city downtown areas. Others are in lighthouses, former stores, Coast Guard stations—you name it. Even if you are a family of four and the cost margin between a budget motel room and four hostel beds, possibly even a hostel room, is not that big, your hostel dollars may get you a night in the middle of everything, in a restored building, perhaps near a railroad station. Hostels serve the bus and bicycle crowd, or overseas student groups on their way to the Liberty Bell, the Capitol, the Grand Canyon and the Golden Gate.

Some hostels now have rooms available for families of four or more, with baths. The trend is in this direction. If you want to try for these, you must call early and reserve.

This discussion is not entered under "youth hostels" because that is a misnomer. Anyone of any age can join A.Y.H., the American Youth Hostel Organization, and the rates for older and younger people are lower than for those of the middle years.

A.Y.H. hooks into the International Youth Hostel Federation in 74 other countries, so a U.S. membership card provides member privileges elsewhere.

The hostel chains that do not link into A.Y.H. likewise do not restrict their clientele to young people. Many of them lease floors in regular hotels that are chronically unfilled, build bunks and run a dormitory within a hotel. Others buy languishing hotels.

I have visited such places as the Penthouse Hostel near Times Square, where $17 to $24 a night bought a bunk, bedding and a shower, and I have no profound argument with what they offer. I would prefer that my own child stay at the A.Y.H. New York Hostel at 103d Street and Amsterdam Avenue, which has money-saving cook-it-yourself facilities, but I know that the visitors, mostly European, like being in the nonaffiliated Times Square hostels close to movies, theaters and restaurants. They also enjoy drinking wine in the common room in the evening, and wine is not an option at the A.Y.H. hostels.

Because they do not want a long-term population of local people, these unaffiliated hostels require guests to show a foreign passport and their stays are limited unless there is no demand from new guests. By the same token, A.Y.H. members from New York cannot stay at the New York Hostel. Some unaffiliated hostels are eager to have bona fide American students but haven't found out how to reach them.

Jim Williams, who operates the Sugar Hill International Guest House in Harlem, which attracts almost entirely Europeans, has put together a list of all sorts of hostels, affiliated and not. He says it is "strictly nonjudgmental." This list, in its second edition in 1993, is available for $1 plus an addressed, stamped business envelope. Jim Williams, Sugar Hill

Guest House, 722 St. Nicholas Avenue, New York, N.Y. 10031; 212-926-7030.

For A.Y.H. information: American Youth Hostels, Inc., 733 15th Street, N.W., #840, Washington, D.C. 20005; 202-783-6161, or any state A.Y.H. council. Membership comes with an identification card and a directory of North American hostels, which may also be bought by nonmembers for $8.

A list of private hostels linked to the American Association of International Hostels may be obtained by sending $1 to the Santa Fe International Hostel, 1412 Cerrillos Road, Santa Fe, N.Mex. 87501. This group recently opened a hostel in San Miguel de Allende, Mexico, at 34 Organos.

College and university dormitories provide roughly the same possibilities, although most college rooms are quads at their biggest and groups of 10, say, will not be able to get a room together as they might in a hostel. Schools without summer sessions or conferences like to rent the space, and if you try a place like Stevens Institute in Hoboken, N.J. ($25 to $34 a night in 1993), with its view of the Manhattan skyline, you may give up motels.

Campus Travel Service, which also publishes a directory of **retreats** that take guests, publishes *U.S. and Worldwide Travel Accommodations Guide*, listing what it says are 765 colleges and universities in the United States and overseas that rent available student rooms, 49 of them said to take guests year-round. Like all computer directories, this is apparently updated in fits and starts; prices may be out-of-date. The book costs $14, including shipping. Campus Travel Service, Box 5486, Fullerton, Calif. 92635; 800-525-6633.

For Canada, the Canadian University and College Conference Officers Association offers a leaflet, "University Summer Accommodation in Atlantic Canada," and a listing of Canada-

wide campus conference facilities that may also accommodate
families. Write the association at Room 311, Hatcher House,
St. John's, Newfoundland, A1C 5S7; 709-737-7590.

The British Universities Consortium provides a chart of 50
member schools with price details, including some campus
"self-catering holiday flats," which in American English
means temporary rentals of apartments with kitchens. Write
to the consortium, Box 91, University Park, Nottingham, England NG7 2RD.

Hotel Safety

The *Federal Travel Directory*, published for employees and
others on government business, since January 1993 has included only hotels and motels where each room has a wired-
in smoke detector that is also linked to the backup power
source, and in buildings taller than three stories, where the
rooms have sprinklers, too. This book, which is issued
monthly, costs $13 for a single copy; an annual subscription is
$77. Ask for G.P.O. 722-006-00000-3, Superintendent of Docu-
ments, U.S. Government Printing Office, Washington, D.C.
20402; 202-783-3238.

In December 1992, before the Hotel and Motel Fire Safety
Act of 1990 went into effect, this directory included 9,900
properties; just after, the total dropped down to 4,100. This
doesn't necessarily mean that less than half of the places had
these protections; some of the impact may have been failures
in the state reporting systems. In any case, the total is
slowly climbing again.

This directory has never been comprehensive because some
places that meet the criteria do not provide a government
discount and thus are not included. A bigger list, 13,000
places conforming to the Fire Safety Act, is available as the

National Master List, first published in its new form in the *Federal Register*, vol. 57, no. 227, publication 069-001-00049-1. It costs $4.50 from the Government Printing Office, as above. It is updated regularly.

The American Automobile Association Tour Guides, which are free to members, are instituting new rules. As of the 1995 guides, a motel that wants to be listed must provide a dead bolt in the door in addition to the basic lock and a peephole or window in the door. The Tour Guides and the Mobil Travel Guides (about $14 a volume) both indicate if there are smoke detectors and/or sprinklers in the rooms, although there is no notation if the smoke detector uses a battery, which is less reliable than one that is wired in. Some hotel and motel chains, among them Sheraton and Travelodge, have dropped motels out of the chain for not meeting fire-safety standards.

Check the listing in any of these guides for an insight into what you may expect.

In a high-rise hotel where the construction does not strike you as modern, avoid a ground floor room to lessen the possibility of break-ins, but try not to get higher than the seventh floor because of the difficulty of getting out in a fire. Decipher the chart on the back of the room door so you know where the stairway is. (See also **fire safety**.)

Hotels, having long avoided even saying the words "fire" and "crime," joined forces through the American Hotel and Motel Association, and have combined with the A.A.A. and other organizations to prepare a card with 10 safety tips to be placed in hotel rooms. These are pretty basic, such as not opening the door to strangers including those identifying themselves as repair people, but the value is the increased awareness by all guests.

Sometimes, chain motels that were once on tourist routes are orphaned when new highways or bypasses are built. These places end up in areas that are deserted at night or, perhaps worse, are filled with activity that most tourists would like to avoid: prostitution, drug dealing, and other crime. Do what you can to assure yourself you are not booking at such a place. Motel 6, after two expensive rape lawsuits, put up for sale a few places it owned that were no longer on tourist routes. An officer of the company said these motels were removed from the handbook and the 800 number reservation service, too, but when I checked they still had listings in regular phone books.

If you have reserved at such an establishment, and do not like its looks or the look of its neighborhood, drive on and phone from elsewhere to cancel the reservation. If you have guaranteed your reservation with a credit card number and the deadline is past, call anyway; I have had places accept a too-late cancellation. If I got billed for a cancellation at such a place, my impulse would be to write to the chain's headquarters and describe the situation; my bet is you would get at least a voucher. But whatever happens, it's cheaper to pay for a room you do not use than to be injured or robbed, or just scared.

If you are traveling, as we often do, with a van full of stuff and a canoe or bicycles on top, unloading the whole works into the motel room at night is not feasible, although we have done it. My choice in such a situation is a motel where we can park the van right outside our window and can keep the outdoor light on. I am told that motels heavily used by truckers often have all-night security guards on patrol, and for this reason in the days of Jim Crow friends of mine going south often parked in these places to sleep in the back of their station wagon.

If you are worried for any reason, ask for a room near the check-in desk. It may not be as quiet as you like, but help will be nearer at hand. Test the phone. Shut and bolt the door and put on the chain, or flop over the hasp. Sleep well.

Hotel Tipping

I think the minimum for the person who cleans and changes your room is $2 a guest a night. The price of the hotel does not matter. The French tourist board recommends about the same level in francs. If you use extra towels or ask for spare water glasses, or prevent the cleaner from getting into your room on the normal tour time, leave more. At conventions of identifiable groups, such as unions, the level is higher because no group wants to be known as ungenerous when the members are probably on expense accounts. Many hotels list charges for getting suitcases, and 50 cents to $1 a bag is usual. If it is a full-service hotel, when I arrive I want to be escorted to my room and have it opened by a bellhop-desk employee to be sure everything works and no leftover guest is in residence. This is worth $1 or $2.

About concierges. I have interviewed the leaders of this elite group and they waffle feverishly about not expecting a thing, but they accept tips. If you plan to call from out of town for special theater tickets next time, do the tipping this time, with a note. In an envelope, too. People who like to get the best from a concierge send Christmas presents. One of the great tourist sights in New York is Tom Wolfe—no, not *that* Tom Wolfe—at his post at the Plaza, his back to the park, coping with everything. Don't miss him.

I.A.M.A.T.

The International Association for Medical Assistance to Travelers, a voluntary group, publishes a roster of physicians who meet certain standards, who speak English or another second language and who agree to charge certain fees. Like the question of whom a gold card medical assistance service will connect you with, the value here depends on how recently I.A.M.A.T., now in the person of Assunta Uffer-Marcolongo, has toured the area to enlist physicians.

If you want to join, I.A.M.A.T. will on request send the directory, a membership card and other useful information, including a "traveler clinical record" to fill out in advance. There is no charge but contributions are accepted to sustain the program, begun in 1962 by Dr. Vincenzo Marcolongo of Toronto, who died in 1988. Write to 417 Center Street, Lewiston, N.Y. 14092. Miss Uffer-Marcolongo will never specify the size of the contribution she hopes for from her 80,000 members. My guess is $25 would be right, but gifts of any size are welcome. She believes that information for good health and world peace should be free. May she be strong forever.

Ice

If you are uncertain about drinking the water, do not use the ice cubes. A physician friend believes this is the only way he could have gotten **giardia** in the Far East, which would prove that parasites can survive freezing. One other peculiarity. No U.S. regulation requires the labeling of bags of ice to show their source, and this presented difficulties to researchers working on an intestinal problem that laid low spectators at a football game who had held tailgate parties. The ice proved to have been made in an area that had recently suffered the overflowing of a river into the local wells.

Immunization Help by Fax or Phone

If you want reliable information about what vaccinations are *required* for travel to particular countries or, just as important, which are *recommended*, you may call an information line at the Federal Centers for Disease Control and Prevention in Atlanta on a Touch-Tone phone, to get information either by voice or by fax, if you have access to one.

These are not 800 numbers, so make routine calls when the tolls are low and be prepared with pencil and paper. The voice numbers, which operate 24 hours a day, are 404-332-4559 or 404-332-4555 and the number for ordering a list of documents available by fax is 404-332-4565. The voice-line numbers may also be used to order the fax list.

It is important to understand before you call that *required* shots are for the protection of the local population, to keep them from catching something you might bring in. The *recommended* safeguards, on the other hand, are of no interest to the immigration authorities but serve to protect you from catching diseases endemic or epidemic in the country you are visiting.

Call six weeks before your planned trip, particularly if protection against malaria, yellow fever or Japanese encephalitis is likely to be a question. Be sure your itinerary is firm, because various countries' requirements for yellow fever shots depend on where you were before you got to their country. Yellow fever shots are just about the only required inoculations that will affect the average traveler. (The World Health Organization reported in 1993 that no country required cholera shots any longer.) Tetanus, polio, diphtheria and malaria are among the dangers you want to avoid, so interpret that word "recommended" as "urgent," depending on where you will visit.

The C.D.C. automated voice line went into operation in

1990, and the logical follow-up, the fax line, in the spring of 1993. The fax line has a particular advantage in that it allows a traveler to order authoritative printed material to guide a physician unfamiliar with tropical medicine or in need of vaccine requirements or recommendations for a particular area of the world. A secondary advantage is that while either type of call to the C.D.C. is a toll call to Atlanta, the fax sheets you get in return are transmitted on the government's nickel. Before you try this trick with a commercial fax that charges for each sheet you receive, check how many sheets there will be in each document—there may be as many as 10. Like the voice line, the fax line operates 24 hours day and it will be faster and cheaper to call in the evening or before or after business hours.

On the fax line, call 404-332-4565 and follow the instructions to order a directory sheet, punching in your fax number with the order. This brings a single sheet that will show a six-digit number for each document. You then call back and order by number, a maximum of five documents at once.

The main headings are "reference documents, including immunization schedules," "disease risk and prevention information by region of the world," "bulletins on disease outbreaks" and "additional information on diseases," which now has a new recommendation on the Japanese encephalitis vaccine.

When you punch in your order, the automated voice tells you how many document orders are in front of yours so you can estimate when to return to the fax to pick up.

These information lines were designed by the C.D.C., but a commercial organization was hired to record the information and organize the trunk and branches sequence. This means that when their budget is tight the recordings may not be up-to-date, which is deplorable. If you think your question may be a tricky one, call between 8:30 A.M. and 4:30 P.M. Eastern time, so you can to talk to a person.

The C.D.C. publishes a yellow-backed book, *Health Information for International Travel*, annually. The 1993 edition was publication CDC-93-82-80, and costs $6.50 from Superintendent of Documents, U.S. Government Printing Office, Washington, D.C. 20402; 202-783-3238. This has charts to help you understand the difference between *required*, that is, by law of the country you are visiting, and *recommended* for your own protection. (Yes, it's a repetition, but this is an important distinction.) Also, for avid hypochondriacs, this book is a winner and cheaper than the *Merck Manual*. Did you know that the mongoose of the Caribbean can carry rabies?

Information provided by the individual consulates and embassies on vaccinations is most unreliable and the embassy people who give it to you over the phone are not medical experts, but simply read from a list.

See also **travel health clinic** and **health overseas**.

International Driving Permit

These official looking folders cost $10 from your local A.A.A. club; you do not need to be a member. They have no validity at all without a current U.S. operator's license, but they specify what type of license you hold, probably for "motor vehicles used in the transport of passengers and comprising, in addition to the driver's seat, at most eight seats," or vehicles that carry a maximum of 7,780 pounds of materials. This information is given in nine languages, including Arabic and Russian, and the description of the appropriate license type is rubber-stamped on each page. Your picture and address are in the back.

Europe, Austria, Greece, Spain and Germany have been reported to require a permit, but I have never seen one asked for. If you are going to Africa or the Far East, you are more likely to run into a country where a U.S. license is not recognized unless it is accompanied by an international driving permit. If you plan to rent a car or drive in one of these countries, ask the tourism office or the consulate ahead of time if you will need one. Their principal use is to demonstrate to someone not conversant in English what your driver's license permits you to do.

Bill Meier, in his book *Autorental Europe*, says that he has heard of travelers using the driving permit as a form of identification when the passport is being held by the hotel. It doesn't hurt to try. A photocopy of the opening pages of your passport would probably also work.

Mariana Field Hoppin, Avis's international driving expert, has a succinct view. "You never need it until you are in trouble," she says. "But when that happens, it really soothes the police officer to see something in a familiar language with your picture on it saying you are licensed."

International driving permits are valid for a year. When you go to get one, take along two passport pictures and your current driver's license. Pay the 10 bucks, it can't hurt.

Jet Lag

I have met one actual human being who went through the whole rigmarole of the anti-jet-lag diet, and she did it for research. Read the book *Overcoming Jet Lag* by Dr. Charles F. Ehret and Lynne Waller Scanlon (Berkley Books) and try the diet if you like, but some basic rules will avoid most of the weirdness that follows a shift of many time zones.

First, remember E-E—if you are going east, travel as early

as you can; westbound, it matters less because the day is lengthening and adjustment is easier, although a westbound transpacific flight will really put you out of whack and you should either pause a day on the way or consider your first day there pretty much a loss.

Second, do not drink any alcohol in flight.

Third, the inside of the airplane is as dry as the Sahara and you should drink water—noncarbonated bottled water—steadily. Juice is also a help, but coffee and tea tend to dry you out. If I drink anything carbonated, I balloon up because of poor pressurization in most planes. To give myself a head start on water before the carts are wheeled out, I take aboard a couple of bottles of water I have chilled or frozen at home and wrapped in a hand towel. Lots of water also means you get up and down to visit the toilet, which keeps your blood circulating and avoids other problems (see **economy class syndrome**).

Fourth, when you arrive, go for a walk, especially if it's daylight, and try not to flake out immediately.

There are a couple of other solutions I'd love to try if budget was no object. First, the Concorde to Europe, a short day flight that does not discombobulate you either way. For the other, British Airways set up a system in 1992 where first class passengers on regular night flights could have their airline dinner in the lounge at John F. Kennedy Airport before leaving and then get the maximum sleep available en route. Or try the old-fashioned way, by steamship, and let the day be shortened or lengthened one hour each day and you should be well adapted on arrival.

Journal

I think that keeping a record of where you travel is an integral part of the enjoyment of the trip.

This is partly because of my occupation as a journalist but also because of my age, when names of towns and restaurants slip away with the ease of a French declension. Had it not been for my journal, I would not be able to tell you what words the nun spoke that left me agape under the dome of the Pantheon.

Joan Cook, the best traveling companion one could have, kept filling up reporter's notebooks with details like the poached pear I ordered for dessert in Florence. When we all got home, she would type the whole narrative up and make copies for the four of us. Traveling with her was like having an entourage of amanuenses to record one's every witticism. But this sort of thing really evades the issue. You need some notes of your own, plus the receipt from the toll on the autobahn, the bill from the Vietnamese restaurant in Marseilles, the postcard from the ski lodge that stayed open one more weekend to let you show your children how maple sugar is made. If you collect these things and do not collate them with some dates and notes, you just have a mess that you eventually throw out in exasperation.

It's simple. Buy one of those small (4 by 6 inches) spiral notebooks or the reporter's size, 5 by 7¾. Get a pencil that fits into the spiral on the side, and a miniature stapler. Staple the restaurant bill to one page, the postcard to the next. You can put a few notes on the opposite page to fill in any gaps: who was there, the weather, etc. The whole thing will fit into your pocket or purse. When friends ask you the name of the wonderful budget hotel in Arles, you will be able to give a good reply. Returning to Paris in 1992, I took out my notebook for 1988 to find the room number in the little hotel near Notre Dame so I could ask for the room again.

I recommend spiral binding rather than stitched because the whole thing does not disintegrate if you tear out a page to write down your address or give someone a piece of paper. I clip a small supply of my business cards inside the back cover to give to people when I want them to write or call me. Even out-of-date business cards that must be corrected are a help because they don't get crumpled up like paper.

My sister's journal is augmented by the copious numbers of color snapshots she takes. She gets double prints for a small amount extra and gives them to me, for which I am grateful. But even the sketchiest journal is better than gazing into the distance and trying to remember the name of the hotel in Mexico City with the indifferent food and the cheerful bar in the garden.

Children do not keep scrapbooks the way we did when young, but a pretty book with the child's name on the cover may encourage the child to write down a few things about a trip and save a postcard or other souvenir—a printed paper napkin, for example.

Jules and Jim and Thelma and Louise

Traveling with friends, not excluding friends who happen to be relatives, can be wonderful. It can also be a catastrophe. We have all heard of friendships wrecked upon the beaches of the Leeward Isles, at the Mall of America, in the cafés of New York or on the Appalachian Trail.

Here are some principles for those considering hooking up with old friends for a week or two of vacation. These are not goody-goody admonitions but the thorny underside, the extract of many friendships put through the pulper.

Numbers first:

Three on a trip is a mess. One person always ends up feeling left out, particularly when that person gets stuck with paying for the single room.

Four is about right. The group can always break into two equal parties and fits in two double rooms.

Five is workable. There can be parties of two and three, but, again, somebody may have to invest in the single. And five is the most that can fit in the ordinary rental car.

Six is the upper limit. It's hard to get any larger number to agree on what to do, and even harder to make them move in the agreed direction. Six is the dividing line in restaurants between an ordinary table and special handling.

Health: You must be nosy and even hard-hearted, because knowledge of health problems that can affect a trip is essential. Find out what you need to know even before you broach the subject of travel. If it is discovered belatedly that one member of the party has special demands because of, say, a recent cardiac event or broken foot, harmony is destroyed. The remaining two or three have an impossible choice—losing much of their vacation by doing only what the least able member can tolerate or striking out on their own and feeling like wretches. Candor is the watchword.

In one gathering of four friends I heard about, failure to make a realistic assessment about someone's health almost led to real tragedy. One person had undergone a severe emotional illness and the spouse, desperate to see other people and escape the house, was not candid about the degree of recovery, so the two couples set off on a sailing trip. Because this required four able bodies, eight hands and clear thinking in heavy weather, the spouse's overoptimism almost led to four deaths. We may sympathize with the ill traveler and the claustrophobic spouse, but demanding travel was not a rational treatment. Rather than easing the pain of the patient, it created stresses and suspicions. Even setting aside the expense, the experience mangled relationships and left everyone worse off.

The health issue may come up in less dramatic form—as when, for example, two couples of advancing age have retired to different areas and want to resume their friendship by traveling together. Best to run a test first: One couple can come to visit the other, perhaps staying in a hotel, to see if the old ties still bind. I don't know how to keep this venture from seeming like a job interview. Invent something. Compare it to no-fault divorce. Or blame me by citing this entry.

One remaining health problem: the heavy drinker. Those of us who have lived (barely) through ugly scenes in restaurants or bars at home or overseas will do almost anything to avoid another. View a friend's alcoholism as a disease that you cannot treat en route, and make your decision about traveling together accordingly. If you are a recovering alcoholic yourself and are not troubled if others in the party drink, you may volunteer to be the designated driver or guide. Otherwise, see **sober trips**.

As to the nature of the trip, there is always the question of where to go, what to see and how. If some in the group already know an area well the combination may not work out, although you could schedule separate side trips of one or more days. Yet such a situation can work beautifully. If any of my friends had decided to skip the Pantheon, I might have missed one of the marvelous moments of my life. As it was, the second-timers were inspired by an eloquent Protestant nun from Foyer Unitas who told us of the "direct contact with the universe" provided by this hole in the top of "the perfect pagan basilica." The real benefit of traveling with friends, I think, is that they can help you see new things or, even better, *see* things for the first time when you have been there before.

There is the matter of traveling style. If half a party consists of serendipists who like to discover things on their way to something else, and half are determinists who *know* what they want to see, the enterprise may suffer strain. Nor is it easy to keep harmony in a party of speeders and dawdlers. Make sure that you are either reasonably similar in approach or that you know how to strike a balance.

You know the theory that local beers do not travel well. Some people are like that: they wear better if they stay home. Take a look ahead of time at the intangibles—psychic stamina, good temper, sense of humor. They will need all of them to travel with you, and vice versa. Your level of fastidiousness should be comparable to theirs, as well as your attitudes on safety—speed limits, seat belts, hitchhikers—if you go by car. You can check on such things as promptness, stinginess, finickiness and allergies, for example, by doing a simple expedition to a local museum and restaurant. Beware if any participants insist on separate checks because they had only the tuna pie. This syndrome is one of the worst traveling personality disorders, less a matter of money than a lack of communality. Friends and I spent years treating a case from Maine, but failed; fortunately, we never had to have him as a traveling companion.

Finances, both the gross numbers and the level of expenditures, need advance attention. The party should have a consensus on hotel rates and eating out. Nobody should be made to feel like the Joads when they vote against a five-star hotel. On the road, set up a cash pool contributed to equally by all for such joint expenses as meals, taxis, parking, tolls and tour guides; the job of collecting and paying can rotate by the day or week. If you all have credit cards and are traveling in the industrialized world, you can divide a bill into two or even four equal portions on the separate cards—assuming, of course, that you have not included anybody with the tuna-pie syndrome. In any case, if you are traveling in Europe or the United States, there is no point in a discount for someone who does not drink wine or beer because soft drinks run up the tab just as fast. Not having a cocktail may merit a reduction. In our own foursome, we usually have the cocktail in the hotel room from our own bottles stock and thus the issue does not arise.

The larger movements of the trip will probably be planned well in advance, but it is useful to agree on a rough plan for the day at breakfast. A simple plan is diversity in the morning—tennis for the women, to the museum for the men—and then together in the afternoon—a ferryboat trip, dinner. Allow plenty of time to be separate even when you are visiting the same place, such as a museum: Meet at the water fountain in two hours.

The most intensive test of what sociologists used to call interpersonal relations takes place during a time when travelers are at close quarters 24 hours a day—on a rafting trip, a long hike, a chartered yacht, a tour. This is when personality deficiencies stick out at the elbows. Departing before the last sweep-up, leaving garbage in the pail for somebody else to take out, hair in the shower, dishes in the sink, too long in the toilet, forgetting things for others to fetch—not, in short, carrying one's own water. These shortcomings eviscerate enjoyment and eventually set travelers to grinding their teeth.

Be realistic about your own characteristics, and learn those of your companions before it's too late.

Kids Along

This topic has a library all its own, including books on the best hikes for children in various states. If you are in need of reference help here, I believe there are two items not likely to be soon matched.

Bubbles Fisher's *New York City with Kids* (Prentice-Hall) knocked my socks off when it first appeared as *The Candy Apple: New York City with Kids*, and I still think it is at the top of the heap. This book is oriented toward a grandparent who will entertain a grandchild as a guest in New York, something that speaks to my life. But it will give solid guidance to families traveling to New York. What other book do you know that critiques museum gift shops? Boat rides?

The other is Dorothy Jordon's long-lived newsletter, *Family Travel Times.* Ten times a year she issues her densely printed eight pages, reviewing everything she and her small staff can get to. Subscriptions are $55 a year: Travel With Your Children, 45 West 18th Street, 7th floor, New York, N.Y. 10011; 212-206-0688.

Lost Air Ticket

This is a pain in the neck, particularly if the ticket has been stolen. If it is a theft, report it first to the police so you get a case number, which you may need later. Theft or loss, report it quickly to the travel agent or airline. If the cost of the ticket was put on a credit card and you have not paid the bill yet, notify the credit card company immediately, giving all the information you can. If you have paid for it, the number of the ticket will be on the bill and this information may enable the airline to "blacklist" the ticket, that is, block its cashing or use by someone else. If the ticket is used or cashed you will almost never get a refund, although your property insurance might do something for you under the lost documents provision. The travel agent will have the ticket number and can notify the airline. Most travel agents have emergency numbers so you can call them from overseas, and if your homebound ticket is gone, this is the time to use that number.

You are more likely to get a refund on an overseas ticket because a user must present a passport in the same name. A domestic ticket is almost like money if it is stolen or found in the trash.

The instant problem is a new ticket. Airline policies vary on this, and even at the same airline they evolve. Some airlines say they owe you nothing because, in effect, you bought something and forgot it on the way home. Some legal beagles do not agree, pointing out that a ticket is a contract to provide carriage and the airline is not living up to its part even though you have paid your fee. But you don't want a lawyer's argument, you want a vacation. So fill out the lost ticket form. If the airline believes it has blocked use, cashing or transfer of the ticket, it may issue you a replacement ticket for a fee. A replacement ticket is most likely to be issued without difficulty on a return trip from a foreign country where the traveling companion or companions still hold tickets with sequential numbers and the boarding passes are for adjoining seats. More likely, you will have to buy a new ticket and pay the fare in effect at the time you buy it. Your refund should be for the more expensive ticket minus the service charge.

A few tips for avoiding theft. Have each member of a party

carry his or her own ticket. Store tickets in a safe-deposit box at the hotel if the place seems trustworthy. Carry a copy of the ticket, or the numbers on it, separately, with the photocopy of your main passport page. Never hide your ticket in the luggage under your bed.

Lost Documents

If you get mugged overseas and lose everything—your money, credit cards, passport, traveler's checks and identification—you are in a serious mess.

There may be reasons that your normal routes for assistance are not available. For instance, you may have your whole family with you. If this is so, here are various steps to pursue.

First, get yourself to the U.S. Consulate or Embassy, where you can start the essential process of getting a new passport. This is easier if you have extra photos, possibly safe at the hotel when you were mugged, and a photocopy of the front page of your vanished passport. At the embassy or consulate, you can also activate the Overseas Citizens Service of the State Department, which has a channel for getting emergency money for you. In 1991, 3,778 United States citizens used this emergency service.

Relatives or friends can send the money to Washington by credit card charge through Western Union, or in the form of a cashier's check or money order (by Western Union or by overnight mail) or bank wire transfer; personal checks are not accepted. Citizens overseas receive the amount, in local currency, often the next day.

The State Department charges $15 for the transmission, and various other charges for Western Union, banks and messages are involved.

The victim overseas usually starts the process by calling a friend or relative at home for help. If the call is placed at the embassy, the following steps can be explained by personnel on the spot. Otherwise, the relative at home, who now must carry the ball, can call the State Department emergency service at 202-647-5225 (there is no 800 number) between 8:15 A.M. and 10 P.M. Monday to Friday and 9 A.M. to 2 P.M. Saturday and learn the following details.

With a Visa or MasterCard credit card, Western Union may be used by phone, 800-325-6000 or 800-325-4176. Without either credit card, the process should be carried out in person at a Western Union office. Either way, the relative tells Western Union he or she wants to buy a money order for the desired amount plus the $15 charge. On the phone, Western Union has a format for the details. The money and message are addressed to Overseas Citizens Service, Department of State, Washington, D.C. 20520.

If a credit card is used, Western Union fees start at $21 for transmitting $50, $50 for $500 and $85 for $1,500. In person, using cash or a bank check, the fees are somewhat less: $13 for $50, $40 for $500 and so forth. There is also a charge for the message: $2 for the first 10 words, 20 cents a word after that.

If the bank can manage it, wire transmission is simpler since the money goes straight from the bank and not through the credit card with its interest charges. (You may not want your helper to wait if your call for help comes outside banking hours.) The bank should be asked to wire the desired amount, plus $40—the State Department's $15 plus a Washington bank charge of $25—to the American Security Bank, Branch 20, 2201 C Street, N.W., Washington, D.C. 20520. Include this designation: ABA 054000551. The phone number is

202-624-4750. The check is to be made payable to Department of State and the name and overseas city of the recipient specified. The local bank should be told that this money is not for deposit at American Security but simply being sent to a bank in the State Department building. Banks charge fees for wire transmissions; at my bank, it is $20.

The slowest route is to send by Express Mail or other overnight service a cashier's check or money order payable to the Department of State for the desired amount plus $15. A letter should give the sender's name, address and phone number, and the name and overseas city of the person in the emergency. The envelope should be addressed to Overseas Citizen Services, CA/OCS/EMR, Room 4800, Department of State, 2201 C Street, N.W., Washington, D.C. 20520.

Lost credit cards add another dimension to the problem. The credit card company needs to be notified as quickly as possible that the card has been stolen, and a new one needs to be obtained, probably without benefit of passport or other quick means of identification.

The companies all have their own methods and phone numbers to give this help. American Express, since it has 1,700 storefront offices worldwide, is probably in the local phone book. MasterCard gold and business cardholders are told to use 800-622-7747 worldwide, which users are supposed to memorize as 800-MCASSIST. Other MasterCard holders are told to turn to the nearest of the 1,600 Thomas Cook travel offices. Christoph Apt, a Visa vice president, says the company provides an emergency guide listing phone numbers, and if you packed it you are in luck. If you cannot find it, call the 800 number and ask for one.

Will the credit card company provide money to a cardholder who no longer has a card? If no local law prevents it,

American Express will cash a personal check for up to $200 once you are identified, probably through questions checked against your computer profile. If you have no checks with you, the company will provide a counter check. For the bank cards, you may have to wait for the delivery of a replacement card, although local affiliates of your home bank might help out. Both Visa and MasterCard say they can get a replacement card to you outside the United States within two days.

It makes life easier if you have recorded your credit card number—but not in the same place you keep the card. If your hotel took an imprint of your credit card when you checked in, your bill is one place where the number of the vanished card is recorded. Where a bank card was used, the hotel will sometimes add a cash advance to the bill, although once the report of the card's theft enters the computer, which is in a half an hour, the hotel will not be able to process the charge. However, Marianne Fulgenzi, a MasterCard spokeswoman, said that if the theft is reported directly to a Thomas Cook office a new number can be given there and a cash advance provided.

A few expedients: Do not carry all your eggs in one basket; keep a small amount of money in a leg or neck pouch. Take a copy of the information page of your passport, as well as the numbers on your credit cards and emergency access numbers, plus the record on any traveler's checks, and tape these into a plastic bag to leave in the hotel safe. Leave another copy with someone at home who can read it to you. Take along duplicate passport photos. My aunt's jaw was broken in a mugging and she had to endure a replacement passport photo with bruises and black eyes.

Lost Luggage

Among the most dismal of occurrences. You have arrived
ready for your vacation, but your bathing suit, beach towel,
flip-flops, nightclothes, underwear, book and vitamin pills are
somewhere else. Aaarrgghh.

Under **packing**, there is information about putting identification inside your luggage because of the vulnerability of
tags on the outside. It helps to put in a copy of your itinerary
as well. Without identification, if you are separated from your
luggage there is a good chance you'll never see it again.
There are also suggestions about packing a bag to carry on; if
two of you are traveling, it makes sense to carry on a bag
that contains the bare minimum both of you need. If carrying
everything on is possible and the matter is urgent, do it.

If you are traveling with a lot of stuff, or particularly valuable stuff, you would be smart to buy excess-value **luggage
insurance** from the airline when you check the luggage in:
Otherwise, if all your luggage is lost, the airline will pay each
passenger a maximum of $1,250 on a domestic flight, or $9 a
pound (remember, it was weighed) on an international flight.
I would be cautious about putting palmcorders and other
valuables in checked luggage in any case.

The next line of defense is to examine carefully the luggage
checks the airline gives you. If you don't know the airport
codes, ask. My husband and I, early arrivers both, sat for a
comfortable half an hour before flight time holding baggage
checks that showed our suitcases were going to take a nice
trip to San Diego while we were going to San Antonio. When
the agent at the podium suggested everyone look at their
baggage checks we discovered the error, but it was too late
to retrieve our clothes, although the airline assured us—
falsely—when we were aboard that it had gotten the bags
aboard, too. A friend renounced curbside check-in after a sky-

cap, lacking a printed check, wrote in "Portland" and the bag went to Oregon instead of Maine.

The government gets reports showing that the worst happens—luggage does not arrive with you, or arrives damaged or with some of its contents gone—6, 7 or 8 times for each 1,000 passengers, which is rather frequently. Only a small portion of this represents luggage that is lost forever, but if your bag doesn't show, here are the immediate steps to get you out of the losers' column:

Do not leave the airport without filing a report. This can be a ghastly undertaking if it is 2 A.M. or a van is waiting or the parade is stepping off. If you are unable to stay to file a report, or cannot have one of your party do it while you welcome the ambassador, you will seethe in frustration trying to learn the right phone number for the airline's lost luggage department at the airport and then trying to get that number to answer. It rings forever, or it is busy.

When you report your bags missing, you will be shown a set of pictures of suitcases and you will select which type yours was, and you will be asked to identify things inside and give your hotel, phone number and other information. As the traveling public filters out of the airport and mops begin to swing while you stand scribbling, tell the airline employee that you have no toilet articles and nothing to change into. Get a voucher or an agreement that you can be recompensed for these things if your suitcase doesn't beat you to the hotel. We were reimbursed $50 in the San Antonio trip, but even at a fire sale we could not buy a splendid wardrobe. Mercifully, the suitcase was returned to us the next night. Some airlines will not reimburse you for urgent needs until 24 hours have passed, so buy a bare minimum of things that will duplicate

what you own but don't have. Ask the hotel for a toothbrush.
A friend at the same hotel? Borrow if you can.

The rule of thumb is that if do not hear in three days that
your bag has been traced, it will probably not be identified.
The conventional estimate is that 95 percent of lost luggage
is recovered, but that still means a lot is gone. By the time
the search seems doomed, you should have prepared a detailed list of what you were carrying; your packing list is a
help. You file a claim with the airline, which by regulation
will yield you the $1,250 maximum or, under the Warsaw
Convention covering international flights, $9 a pound if you
did not insure for excess value. If you had luggage insurance
as part of trip cancellation insurance, you should file with
that company, too, although this luggage insurance is really
preposterous because $500 will buy the suitcase but not the
shoes. By the time you get to the level of your own insurance
company, you should have excavated whatever sales slips you
can, particularly if you lost anything with a lens—field
glasses or a camera—where age does not diminish the value.
The insurance company will deduct what you have already
received from the airline.

Some years ago, I visited the flea-market-style stores in
Alabama where lost luggage went to die, and a number of
people wrote in to say that if they could just get one peek at
the room where Airline Z stored its unidentified bags they
knew they could pick out their own. Trust me: This is impossible.

Start with the numbers. One month's "mishandled baggage" reports from the 10 big U.S. airlines totaled 264,286—
that is to say, more than a quarter of a million people complaining that month about at least one bag each. In this particular month, as an example, Delta received 53,646 luggage

complaints. Assuming that the 95 percent recovery figure is fair, and I believe it is a little gloomy, Delta was holding 2,682 unidentifiable bags by the end of that month. As the weeks pass, these bags are consolidated, moved from the room at the airport where they reached a dead end to a bigger storeroom, and eventually to something like an abandoned hangar in a desert. Three months' accumulation at this rate would be 8,000 bags. That is some storeroom.

At the end of three months—the amount of time the airline is required to keep on trying—an airline has settled with the disgruntled customer and is prepared to unload. Any contraband in the luggage—drugs, for example—is seized by the government. Money is claimed by the airline as is anything instantly convertible like uncut gems. As for the rest, the airlines have contracts with lost-luggage stores for everything else, without respect to weight, value or total numbers of bags. The dealers will not even hint at the amount of money they pay to the airlines for the leavings and I cannot guess.

After the picking over, the remaining contents are put back into the bag, which is taped shut, and the warehouse load is gathered up by a truck from Unclaimed Baggage in Scottsboro, Ala., or a similar company. I saw one of these long trailer trucks open up at the loading dock of a Scottsboro warehouse, and when the bags begin to cascade out I grasped why hope for a lost bag dies so quickly. Information on the inside is the only thing that will save it for you once you are separated from it.

A wistful note. At the counter in Scottsboro, I saw a salesperson pull out a thick gold charm bracelet. Each charm represented something different: a wedding, a rodeo, a grandchild, an anniversary. "I bet she cried a lot when she lost that one," the sales clerk said. Like me, she could not imagine putting such a thing into a suitcase and entrusting it to anyone. There is no insurance that will make up for such a loss.

Lost Passport

If it is only your passport that is gone, either genuinely lost or stolen, it can be replaced pretty promptly. (If all your documents and credit cards are gone, see **lost documents**.) If you have not left home yet but you have a ticket and now discover that you haven't got your passport, the nearest agency (see **passport inquiries**) will tell you how to go about replacing it promptly. The agency will probably want to see your ticket, not a travel agent's itinerary, to put you to the head of the line if the departure is soon. If you have data about your passport—a photocopy of the identification page, for example—things may go faster. You will have to pay the regular fees.

If you find your passport again, don't use it: It is now on the list of stolen passports the immigration people check when you come home.

If your passport is lost overseas or stolen there, the embassy or consulate can usually take care of a new one within a day. Again, things are sped by any documentation you can supply. Guard your passport. Often hotels like to keep them in their safe-deposit boxes to prevent your leaving the country with unpaid bills. The hotel cannot force you because you may need the passport during the day for purchases or other identification. Your judgment on the wisdom of turning your passport over must be based on what other travelers have said. Thailand, for example, is said to be a place never to part with your passport.

Luggage Insurance

When I get mired in mundanity by fixating on insurance, I remember a scene from my adolescence. A flamboyant friend of the family, sampling his birdbath of a martini, said that he had seen a ghastly sight that afternoon. "Your old friend Marvin," he said scornfully to my mother, "bought his wife a mink coat today. And there the two of them were, taking the 5:35 from Grand Central, and she was wearing it, and the insurance policy for the coat was sticking out of the pocket!" He was practically shouting. "So what?" I asked. "Listen," said the flamboyant one, whose living room was decorated with the splintered propeller of a Piper Cub he had crashed, "if you buy your wife a mink coat, you take wife and coat to dinner at 21 and then spend the night at the Plaza. You do not, egads, buy an insurance policy at the same time and ride the New York Central home. The man is a jerk."

So at the risk of sounding like a nerd, today's equivalent of a jerk, if you are planning a splendid long trip and are taking clothing and belongings to match, here are some words about insuring your luggage and its contents.

If you have homeowner's, condo-owner's or renter's insurance on the contents of your residence, there is some coverage for your luggage. But talk to your broker about whether you have a "standard" policy or an "all-risk" policy. Maria Lara, an insurance account executive at H. & R. Phillips in New York, says that a standard policy will cover lost luggage only if it is considered to have been stolen. An all-risk policy will cover it whatever happens to it. Similarly, a standard policy may pay a maximum of 10 percent of its face value for your luggage; a $30,000 policy on the contents of your home, for example, would allow only $3,000 for luggage. Find out how much more the premium would be for a better policy.

Since it covers you year-round, it may be a better deal than getting extra coverage from an airline.

If you consider inadequate the standard airline maximum payment of $1,250 for luggage lost on a domestic flight, and $9 a pound for luggage lost on an international flight, you can buy excess coverage direct from the airline. It's not cheap, usually $10 for each added $1,000 up to $5,000. You buy it at the counter when you check in. This is not often bought because once people get to luggage check-in, they want to get done with it and go someplace to sit down. But it is an option.

Travel insurance policies often have a little clause in case your luggage takes a trip without you, but the benefit is not very big, probably $500.

If you have all these policies, be aware that the last underwriter in line, usually your home insurance, is not going to duplicate any payments you have already received. If you reach the level of your own insurance and still have not received value on your luggage, be prepared with sales slips and other documents on what you lost. As usual, if it was cash forget it. You cannot insure cash.

Luxury Travel News

Andrew Harper's *Hideaway Report,* one of the better-known newsletters in the travel field, is written for cost-is-no-object people. The readership is said to have a median income in the area of $238,000.

Andrew Harper—the name is a nom de plume—describes his monthly eight-page letter as "a connoisseur's guide to peaceful and unspoiled places" in the United States and abroad. Harper travels anonymously to do his reporting and pays for everything at standard rates. He says that he limits his circulation to 15,000 to keep the places he visits from being overrun.

The places he reviews are high-priced—$320 a day, for instance, for one of seven Australian "country house hideaways"—and such prices are a limitation in themselves. For those not seeking the latest place, the newsletter still makes enjoyable reading. The writing is literate and pleasant though gushy. Sketch maps are included.

A valuable feature of the newsletter, "Hotel & Resort Watch," summarizes trends in reader reply cards. When many people point to a deterioration or improvement in a place, he includes it in this column using up, down and sideways arrows.

The December issues carry a list of "the most enchanting" small hotels reviewed in the year. They are divided by area: United States, Latin America, Europe and Asia/Pacific. Some examples: the Hotel Bel-Air in Los Angeles with double rooms starting at $295 a night; Invery House in Banchovy, Scotland, for $230 and up; and Tiger Tops in Nepal, $400 a night.

A sample copy of the *Hideaway Report* may be obtained free by writing to the editorial office, Box 50, Sun Valley, Idaho 83353. An initial subscription costs $85 a year. Renewals can be as low $49 if entered six months ahead. The subscription office is Box 300, Whitefish, Mont. 59937

Maps

The Pulitzer prizewinner Anthony Lewis, when head of the London Bureau of the *New York Times*, hated all London maps. "It doesn't matter where you buy it," he once said. "The top edge will be cut right through Islington, and since I live in Islington the map is useless."

A lifelong map nut, I was sure I could find one that did the job. I haunted map shops and bookstores in London and back at home for almost a year, but Tony Lewis was right. If the map had Islington, it was virtually a map of the British Isles, and if it showed central London in decent detail, no Islington.

A good map will save you every time, and a bad map should be left at home. How to determine which is which?

It's impossible to write a rule that will endure. The best way is to get a map from someone who lives there or who has visited and winnowed the selection. When my father was living in London in the mid-60s and none of us had traveled at all, he bought one that had good detail in the area of his flat on Eaton Mews and marked it up, including an X on his favorite local, the Duke of Wellington. He sent it to us in advance of our visit and we used it that summer and thereafter until it tore at the folds because we never found one better, even if it did not show Islington.

I finally found a good walking map of Boston in an airport shop (it's called Klein's Pictorial Souvenir Map of Boston), but I have never seen it elsewhere. My best map of Barbados is a freebie published by Banks Beer. The Manhattan bus map given away by the New York Transit Authority is the best thing you can offer a visitor because it's geographic, not schematic like the subway map, and it's no giveaway to un-furl a bus map since even residents do not understand bus routes.

A map that is good for walking is different from a driving map. We liked our Hallwag map of Paris, borrowed from a daughter-in-law, because it easily folded down to the area we were ambulating. Auto club maps tend to omit railroad lines; maps issued by individual states indicate that you drop off the edge of the earth when you leave the precincts that paid for the printing.

Still another sort of map is needed for hiking, or setting off cross-country. National and state parks sell or give away trail maps, but if you are into local trails that wind up hillsides you may want the government's topographical maps, prepared by the Geologic Survey. A good map store, like Hagstrom's on 43d Street in New York, will have a nationwide key map to show what is available. The supply is hard to maintain, Doug Rose says, but the one you want can be ordered once you know the series and number. In Britain, the much better known Ordnance Survey, also government published, is invaluable for detailed exploration. Stanfords (12-14 Long Acre, Covent Garden, London WC2E 9LP; 71-836-1321) has a good stock of these.

With the preposterous prices of maps in stores it is amazing that they aren't better, but the map publishing industry has still not fully settled on its role in the aftermath of the Arab oil boycott of 1972, which ended free oil company maps in the same stroke it ended free air for tires and cheap fuel.

For an automobile map, unless you are a collector, your most important concern will be to get a recent edition so you won't wonder where I-86 went (it became part of I-84). A copyright date may guide you, but it may not necessarily be the date that the map base was last revised but only the year it was reprinted. The 1994 road atlases, for example, were probably distributed in October 1993 and the latest information was added in July 1993. Just figure that every big date on a map book, like the date on a guidebook or a magazine, has been pushed one cycle into the future.

As an advocate of public transit, I could spend a whole book critiquing aspects of the American Automobile Association and its policies, but I do not argue with their driving information. Once you belong to a club, the maps are free, and if you tell your club where you want to go it will give you an up-to-date route map with detours and other kinks marked in detail, including driving time estimates with rest stops added in.

In my next life, I will know how to store maps. As a collector and user, I have too many and I refuse to let them go. Right now they are stored vertically in one of those three-tray kitchen caddy gadgets, shoved into a closet. Bookshelves do not work. However, I am a perfect map folder, unlike everyone else I travel with.

Mexico by Car

Mexico is the most popular foreign destination for U.S. visitors. Canada, of course, is number 2. One obvious reason is both have long borders with the U.S. and either can be reached by the American's favorite mode of travel: auto.

Driving into Mexico beyond the free-entry border zone, which includes Baja California, has been a problem of late because the government there wants to keep U.S. residents from driving in, illegally selling their autos—or stolen autos—and taking the profits out. Even clunkers sell for a lot.

The Mexican government has been working closely with the American Automobile Association to smooth out the procedures for driving in and to assure that drivers have all the documentation they need: proof of citizenship and a tourist card, a valid driver's license, the vehicle registration, documents for a car not your own and an international credit card issued outside Mexico—American Express, Diners Club, MasterCard or Visa. Those without a credit card must be prepared to buy a bond for the blue book value of the car, which will cost 1 to 2 percent of the value of the car.

If you are not an A.A.A. member, call the nearest Mexican consulate to get a detailed list of what is needed at the time of your trip.

A particular caution applies to children traveling into Mexico with only one parent or with grandparents or others. The adult must have, in duplicate, a notarized letter of consent for the trip from the other parent or the parents. This letter must have been authenticated at a Mexican consulate before arrival. A death certificate or guardianship papers, if appropriate, may be presented. This seems cumbersome, but a rise in kidnappings by parents without custody, or by grandparents, has made it important, and the U.S. government supports efforts to avoid messy extradition fights. Incidentally, the rules say that if a child holds a valid passport the other requirements are waived, but my guess is that with a very young child it would be wise to have the papers anyway.

Motel Chains

Motel chains provide free directories of their sites or, as they are flossily known in the business, their "properties." The advantage of a directory is that you get the direct number to call a specific place without having to pay for a call to directory assistance. Indeed, in all except the Motel 6 chain you can reserve toll-free through an 800 number, but if you want a specific type of room or want to know if the free breakfast includes cereal or the pool is open yet, pay the toll and call. For people using wheelchairs or needing a crib, there is really no other way to be sure your place will be ready for you.

A number of these directories have schematic maps to show where the motels are, since one could wander forever in the cloverleafs at interstate exits or airport access roads.

Here are numbers to call to get directories for most of the major chains. In these days of consolidation and chain purchases, sometimes one number links you to more than one chain. When the 800 numbers look goofy, it's because they are translated from some message—2-RAMADA, for instance. It's the sort of thing that can drive you mad on an all-numeral phone pad.

Budgetel: 800-428-3438

Choice chain: Comfort, Quality, Clarion and Sleep Inn,
    Rodeway, Econo Lodge and Friendship: 800-221-2222

Courtyard by Marriott: 800-321-2211

Days Inn: 800-325-2525

Embassy Suites: 800-362-2779

Fairfield Inn: 800-228-2800

Hampton Inn: 800-426-7866

Holiday Inn, Holiday Inn Express: 800-465-4329

Howard Johnson, HoJo Inn, Howard Johnson Suites: 800-446-
    4656

La Quinta: 800-531-5900

Marriott Residence Inn: 800-331-3131

Motel 6: 505-891-6161

Ramada, Ramada Limited: 800-272-6232

Red Roof Inns: 800-843-7663

Scottish Inns, Master Host, Red Carpet, Downtown and
  Passport: 800-251-1962
Super 8: 800-800-8000
Susse Chalet: 800-258-1980
TraveLodge: 800-255-3050

Museums

New York tourism officials, the ones who describe their job
as selling "seats and sheets"—tickets and hotel rooms—say
that every survey shows the same thing: Tourists come to
New York for its cultural excitement, for its museums, theater, bookstores, concerts and the like. The permanent part
of any city is the thing that draws us there.

Every guidebook virtually starts with the great museums,
the National Gallery, the British Museum. But there are
lesser-known collections that might be missed, so Nancy Frazier started a newsletter, *Museum Insights*, to cover the permanent collections in generally lesser known museums in the
United States and Canada.

Ms. Frazier does not include places to eat or stay or meth-
ods of getting there but concentrates on museums. A recent
issue led off with the American Advertising Museum in Port-
land, Oregon, with a photo of the famous Levy's ad showing a
Native American smiling over his bite of "real Jewish rye."
She has covered the American Kazoo Company Museum in
Eden, New York, as well as Ellis Island in New York and the
Isabella Stewart Gardner Museum in Boston.

This eight-page publication was begun in January 1989. The
writers are mostly colleagues of Ms. Frazier, a graduate student in art history and former newspaper reporter, although

sometimes subscribers submit articles. She says that the writers are not affiliated with the places they write about. "I pay a little or nothing," she says.

Ms. Frazier offers a personalized leaflet created to respond to a subscriber's interests and his or her itinerary on a forthcoming trip. Up to 10 museums may be included. A subscriber may receive one leaflet each year free. Ms. Frazier uses fresh research for the leaflets.

Museum Insights, Box 313, North Amherst, Mass. 01059; 413-548-9561. Six issues a year, $28; sample issue and index, $5.

National Parks Camping

The federal budget and the family budget have begun to create a crunch in popular camping places among the 100 national parks, monuments, wilderness areas, seashores and other places in the national system that provide camping. Most of the system is underused, and the government even publishes a list of these 170 "lesser-known areas" to try to level out the burden. (This 48-page booklet is publication 134Z of the Department of the Interior, available for $1.50 from R. Woods, Consumer Information Center, Pueblo, Colo. 81009.)

Reservations for the 14 most popular sites have been given to commercial contractors to handle. The current company is Mistix in San Diego, 800-365-2267, and it accepts reservations based on Visa, MasterCard and Discover cards and personal checks. The phone hours are longer in the spring and summer. Reservations are first come, first served, but are not normally accepted more than eight weeks in advance. To make a reservation by 800 number, you really need to know what you want and when the area opens for the season unless it is year-round. (*National Park Camping Guide*, publication 024-005-01080-7, $4 a copy from the Superintendent of Documents, Washington, D.C. 20402. This is reissued periodically and the number may change.)

These are the camping sites handled by Mistix. Some areas are open only to group camping.

Acadia in Maine: Blackwoods

Assateague Island Seashore in Maryland: Oceanside

Cape Hatteras Seashore in North Carolina: Ocracoke

Death Valley Monument in California: Furnace Creek

Grand Canyon in Arizona: North Rim and Mather

Great Smoky Mountains in North Carolina and Tennessee: Cades Cove, Elkmont and Smokemont

Joshua Tree Monument in California: Black Rock Canyon, Cottonwood Spring, Indian Cove and Sheep Pass

Ozark Scenic Riverways in Missouri: Big Spring, Akers, Pulltite, Round Spring, Two Rivers and Alley Spring

Rocky Mountain Park in Colorado: Glacier Basin and Moraine Park

Sequoia Park in California: Lodgepole

Shenandoah Park in Virginia: Big Meadows

Whiskeytown in California: Oak Bottom

Yellowstone in Wyoming: Bridge Bay

Yosemite Park in California: Lower River, Upper Pines, North Pines, Crane Flat, Hodgon Meadow and Tuolumme Meadows

900 Numbers

These are not toll-free; they have high per-minute charges. They have legitimate uses, including access to information from such organizations as the Better Business Bureau and call-ins to register political views. But they also have had a recent boom in the travel scam area: Postcards tell the recipient to call a certain number to see what they have won—a trip to Jamaica, perhaps, or an auto. Unless you give a credit-card number to claim a prize, you will not have won much, perhaps a dollar's worth of Mexican pesos. But you will have lost as much as $3.98 or $4.98 for each minute you stayed on the line, hearing questions repeated twice, slowly. This money, needless to say, is not a phone toll but goes to the company responding on the phone.

Late in 1992, Congress voted to direct the Federal Trade Commission to work out rules to regulate the pay-per-call industry, which comprises 900, 700 and 976 exchanges as well as others used locally, much as the credit card industry was regulated by the Truth in Lending Act. This, in the words of a Government official, will enable the pay-per-call system to realize its potential for providing information fast for a fee while protecting callers from being gouged.

Until the regulator comes, follow these guidelines for any call you make on such a number:

The first thing you should hear is how much the call will cost you per minute.

The second bit of information should be the average time it takes to complete a call.

Then the recording should say that you can hang up now and avoid all charges.

If the recording does anything else, hang up. Make a note in case you are charged anyway.

If you find that a teenager has gotten hooked into a "talk

line" or is enticed by an offer for a free gift or story, be aware that your telephone company cannot disconnect your phone for failure to pay. But tell everyone in the family to be ultra-cautious about 900 numbers.

The Federal Trade Commission has published a fact sheet on these numbers. To get it, write F.T.C. Office of Consumer Information, Sixth and Pennsylvania Avenue, N.W., Washington, D.C. 20580; 202-326-3650. Complaints should also go to the F.T.C., to aid in its enforcement efforts.

Nonsmoking Room

We always ask for nonsmoking rooms because they smell fresher, and where there is a nonsmoking floor in the hotel it usually means that convention groups will not congregate there at night. But one tiny problem arises: If you want to light a match to deodorize a bathroom—an ancient method—or to sterilize a needle for a splinter, you won't find any matches in a nonsmoking room. We have taken to packing a small box of the wooden matches you can pick up in fancy bars and restaurants. Used matches, incidentally, should be disposed of in the trash basket because they can clog the toilet.

Operator Rip-offs

The hesitant steps toward federation being taken by the European Community are having a beneficial effect on the travel industry. Regulations have been drawn up in at least two areas: Tour operators are required to give clients information about health requirements for visiting a country, and they also must give timely notification about major changes in a tour, with provision for refunds.

In the years I have been covering travel, both of these

areas have given rise to consumer problems in the United States, and lower-level court decisions have begun finding for the consumer, holding both tour operators and travel agents responsible for failing to inform clients. What happens next is unclear. Operators and agents can continue to give higher and higher settlements out of court. Or some form of regulation can develop, either through industry associations or through state legislation protecting consumers: Florida has moved in the direction of legislation requiring new agencies to post a bond.

In the meantime, consumer lawyers like Tom Dickerson in New York continue to act as gadflies. Dickerson brought a class action against the banks used by a failed charter operator, charging the company did not maintain hundreds of clients' charter deposits in escrow, and challenged another operator because a traveler was injured when thrown from a camel.

One thing seems clear to me from a recent complaint involving a couple's $7,000 investment in a wildlife tour of India. They said that since neither of the promised "noted" wildlife experts accompanied the group and they were not told about this in time to withdraw and book with another company, this constituted a "major change" and they should have received their money back despite cancellation deadlines. The brochure for the British division of the company provided such a recourse under European Community rules and British laws, which have been harmonized, but the American brochure did not. As long as such disparities persist, American branches of European-American companies will—and should—suffer, whatever the standing of the pound.

Travel is an essential element in European Community economies. Year after year, France receives more visitors than any other country in the world: 55.7 million in 1991, according to figures compiled by the World Tourism Organization in 1993, ahead of the United States by 13 million visitors. Spain, Italy, Austria, Britain and Germany are also in the top 10 host countries. But not much publicity has been given in the United States to E.C. efforts to regulate the industries that earn this important income. If the United States wants to keep its position as the top earner in travel —its income is double France's—it should start trying to measure up in consumer protection.

What to do meantime? Read the small type on any offering closely. For your health, find a **travel health clinic** or use the **immunization help by fax or phone** of the Centers for Disease Control and Prevention. For your enjoyment, be sure your travel agent gets you good details on the element of your trip that you consider the most important. If you want to hear a particular lecturer or visit a special city or port, be sure that the company knows you want to be informed in time about any change in this aspect of the trip: that you would rather postpone than miss this one thing. If you take the trip without having said in advance your primary reason for going was Petra, and you miss Petra, you will have a hard time demonstrating retrospectively that this was the only reason you went.

Be aware that cruises must frequently be rerouted, but if you start to miss more than you see, complain.

Outdoor Dramas

In the summertime, the woods are full of 'em. In 1993, there were 90 theatrical troupes performing in 33 states, some with full professional casts, some only partly pro. Usually, they depict the history of the area or of its people, but some places present musicals like *The Wizard of Oz*. The grandfather of all these is Paul Green's *Unto These Hills*, which has been running in North Carolina since Lassie was a pup. If you are going to an area that ties into a child's school project, look for one of these dramas. They stick with you.

An association of these production companies publishes a guide each year that is available for $5, usually in April. The Institute for Outdoor Drama, C.B. 3240, NationsBank Plaza, Chapel Hill, N.C. 27599.

Oxygen

Users of supplemental oxygen face barriers when they fly. No U.S. airline allows the passenger to use a personal tank while aboard, but most do provide oxygen, which must be ordered in advance and for which there is a charge, usually $50. The passenger's own empty tank may be checked as luggage, but this varies by airline. Separate provision must be made for oxygen during an plane change or stop, and upon arrival at the destination airport.

A volunteer working for the American Lung Association, Gail Livingstone, in 1992 pulled together a useful leaflet on airline rules, which do change frequently, and other advice for oxygen-users. The current version of the leaflet "Airline Travel with Oxygen" may be obtained from a local branch of the lung association. If no listing can be found, a call may be made to 800-586-4872. In any case, be aware that you or your travel agent must talk to the airline in advance.

Packing

My sister and I share a common travel disorder: packer's block. It's like writer's block, minus the cachet. An episode begins when the suitcase is opened preparatory to travel and

the traveler suddenly feels an urge to alphabetize the medicine cabinet or wax the kitchen floor. A therapist friend, diagnosing this folie à deux, linked it to separation anxieties
stemming from our father's occupation as a traveling salesman.

The cause is simpler. We both travel a lot and both take
pride in our Mary Poppins roles as providers of Band-Aids,
vodka, headache remedies and other things everyone else has
forgotten. But we both have had our luggage sent to wrong
places and passionately want to cram everything into carry-
on bags, which creates a conflict. Underwear or vodka?
Detective novel or travel alarm? Better to alphabetize the
medicine chest.

The best hope, but a pale one, is to get a good packing list
prepared in advance. You prop this against the suitcase and
just work by rote, allowing no diversion for arranging your
books by color. Try not to pack on the bed, which is the
wrong height for your back—it will start to hurt after the
second editing of the pile. A table is better.

This list is built on the inverted pyramid theory: the further down you go, the less essential the item. Always remember David Niven as Phileas Fogg preparing to girdle the
world in 80 days—he just threw money into a valise. A rotten solution, but a solution: Take money and buy what you
cannot carry.

First, tape or pin your name and home address and a copy
of your itinerary to the inside of the suitcase and the shoulder bag or purse you will carry. If you lose a bag you want it
to find you, not wend its way back home or to lost-bag
heaven in Alabama. If you do not have a luggage tag on the
outside of your bag, the airline will make you write one out.

Use an office address if you do not want to disclose where your home is.

Items at the top of the list should be carried on your person.

Tickets and itinerary. Photocopy of your tickets, to be carried in another pocket or purse. Copy of confirmation of hotel reservations.

Passport. Take a photocopy of the identification page with you, leave one with someone staying home and, if you can, leave one with your office or travel agent. Extra passport pictures if you want the weekly ticket on the Paris Metro or other sorts of cut-rate transit passes. You may need one for an unexpected visa requirement, and you will be glad to have them if your passport gets lost.

Cash. Some in your wallet, some elsewhere. A modest sum in the currency of the country where you are going. If you are like me, you previously brought home 10-franc coins, which at the current $2 rate of exchange were worth too much for an airport charity jug. If you are going back to a place whose currency you saved, dig the money out and take it.

Credit cards and automatic teller machine card (see **A.T.M.**). If you are going to rent an auto, you may want to take two credit cards in case a freeze is put on one after an accident. Carry a copy of the credit card numbers separately. Leave a copy of the numbers at home with the passport information.

Traveler's checks. The slip for making a claim carried separately.

Bank checks.

Glasses. An extra pair. Ditto contact lenses. A copy of the prescription. Sunglasses. Eyeglass repair kit.

Prescription and nonprescription medicines. Do not put these in a suitcase that will be checked because you cannot get it out if you need it in flight, or later if the luggage has been sent to the wrong city. Copies of the prescriptions. Take medicines in small, well-labeled containers. Don't get smart and repack them in, say, film containers or unlabeled bottles. This drives Customs people whacky.

Comb and toothbrush, toothpaste.

Address book. Tiny notebook. Pencils and pens.

Tissues. Packs of moistened towelettes.

Camera and film. A friend suggests protecting the camera by wrapping it in underwear in your carry-on bag, so you at least have a change in the event of an unplanned overnight at an airport. Take a small transparent kitchen bag with a closure to bring home your exposed film: When you pass it around the **X-ray** device at airports, it will reveal its harmless contents.

Reduce your key ring to what you absolutely need, probably the front door key, and leave the rest behind. Unless, that is, you parked the car at the airport.

And now the stuff for the suitcase proper:

Hairbrush, shaving kit, other toiletries.

Tissues. April in Paris can be a mess if you have a runny nose. December at Snowmass likewise. The pocket packs that most manufacturers sell are the neatest way to do it although not the cheapest. If you always have a pack in your pocket, the grimmest filling station toilet can be endured. I leave five or six in the bottom of my suitcase.

Changes of underwear.

Shampoo, liquid laundry soap and skin gops. Use plastic bottles and put them into a leakproof container.

Sunscreen and insect repellent for the right places and sea-

sons. Essentials for first aid; if you are going to a beach, read
beach first aid.

Bathing suits. If swimming is important, pack one in your
shoulder bag or purse. Suits sold in hotel lobbies are all size
5 and cost a fortune.

Changes of outer clothes. A sweater. Gloves in all sea-
sons but summer in the tropics. Socks and stockings. Neck-
ties.

Battery radio or personal tape player plus earphones.
Extra batteries. In any power failure, these will save your
sanity.

Raincoat. Even if you don't need it for the weather, it can
serve as a bathrobe in pinch. A plastic poncho won't do that
duty, but it saves space.

A second pair of shoes. Wear the bulkier pair and pack the
smaller. Neither should be new.

Nightclothes. Slippers, the airline giveaway kind or the cuf-
fless socks usually worn with tennis shoes. Flip-flops will
serve.

Cap, hat or scarf.

Needle and thread. Pocket mirror. Good tweezers. A few
Band-Aids of the right size for blisters. Sticky tape.

Folding canvas bag to use for getting gifts home. A fanny
pack or other small bag for carrying your essentials on a
walk.

A pair of good children's snub-nosed scissors, which do not
create alarming X rays at the security barrier.

Now comes the category you will want to ignore if you
often find yourself running for a plane or train. They make
your baggage feel so heavy you think you are doing body-
building on the way to Gate 103.

Pepto-Bismol, for the diarrhea belt. Liquor, or anything else liquid in a glass bottle.

Cassette tapes.

One-cup coffeemaker. Plug adapter. Coffee. (But see **electric current.**)

Can opener. Corkscrew. Swiss Army knife.

Compact two-language dictionary.

Map. Guidebook.

The packing list.

(If this list does not seem onerous enough, see **gadgets.**)

Passport Inquiries

Here are information phone numbers for 13 regional passport agencies. These lines play recorded messages and allow you to select the information you want through pressing Touch-Tone telephone buttons. If your nearest number will be a toll call anyway, use the line at night or on the weekend when it is cheaper. Have pencil and paper ready.

Boston: 617-565-6998

Chicago: 312-353-7155

Honolulu: 808-541-1919

Houston: 713-653-3153

Los Angeles: 310-575-7070

Miami: 305-536-4681

New Orleans: 504-589-6728

New York: 212-399-5290

Philadelphia: 215-597-7480

San Francisco: 415-744-4444

Seattle: 206-220-7777

Stamford, Conn.: 203-325-4401

Washington: 202-647-0518

Information from these numbers tells how to get a first passport, where to get forms and apply and so forth. If you are planning a first trip overseas, make the passport agency call an early priority, particularly if you plan to travel in the spring or summer when activity picks up.

Renewing a passport by mail became faster in 1993 when the government opened a huge new facility in Portsmouth, New Hampshire, served by a post office box in Pittsburgh. To be able to renew by mail, you must meet these qualifications:

1. You must be living in the United States.

2. You must be able to submit your most recent passport, which must have been issued after you turned 18 years of age and the passport must be not more than 12 years old.

3. You must have filled out application form DSP-82. Information about getting this form may be obtained through the phone numbers above. It is available for asking at designated post offices and county clerks' offices.

4. The passport, form DSP-82, two identical passport photos and a check or money order for $55 made out the Passport Services should be mailed to:

    Passport Lockbox
    Box 371971
    Pittsburgh, Pa. 15250

Passports are now valid for 10 years. The first 10-year passports began to expire in 1993 and this began a bulge of renewal applications that is likely to continue for several years, paralleling the rise in foreign travel. On New Year's Day of the year your passport expires, you should start steps to renew it because January and February are slack times for renewals and you can get your new passport back in two weeks or less. By April, things are jamming up. If you are planning a trip during the year, take out your passport and be sure it will be valid for long enough. Many airlines will not let you aboard a plane bound overseas if your passport has less than six weeks to run because of the possibility of accidents or other circumstances that might delay your return.

After you get your passport, make photocopies of the page with your identification and picture and store them. If you lose your passport, it will make it faster to get a new one.

Passport Pictures

Take along some extras, particularly if your passport is new and you have a surplus. They take up no space and certain foreign transit passes require them. If you lose your passport, having two extra pictures will make it faster to get a replacement. Keep them with the receipt for your traveler's checks and the photocopy of the important pages in your passport.

Passports in the Carribbean

Not so long ago, most places in the Caribbean or Bahamas did not require a passport for entry. This has changed, and even if a travel agent or tourism spokesperson says that only "proof of citizenship" is required take a passport and avoid time-consuming and embarrassing disputes. The same precaution applies to all of Mexico below the border zone.

Phones Overseas

For those of us who grew up with the world's finest phone system with human beings to respond to our questions, grappling with phones overseas is sometimes trying. The American long-distance phone companies have, however, given us a way to cope: USADirect is a service of A.T.&T. that permits its credit card holders to dial an operator in the United States from 110 points overseas, and the two other major long-distance providers, Sprint and MCI, now have similar services. With them, you can call home without having to work through an operator speaking a language you may not be secure in. A.T.&T.'s World Connect service uses the USADirect operator and permits calls to 48 other foreign countries from wherever you are. A folding plastic card with the access numbers is available to credit card holders. To receive this A.T.&T. directory or for information: 800-331-1140.

MCI has a similar service, Call USA, that operates from 40 countries to the United States, and a service parallel to World Connect, which is called World Reach, that works from these places to some other foreign countries. For information: 800-444-3333.

Sprint's number for its Sprint Express, which operates in 68 places overseas, is 800-877-7746.

Nonetheless, in some countries it still takes a token or a coin of minimal value to get access to any part of the system, even the call-home services. A bystander in the Mexico City airport thrust on me a handful of coins to enable me to call collect, and I learned that the whole handful was probably worth 3 cents. If the guidebook says you will need them, get them. To learn another way to make phone calls without valuable coins, see **debit phone card**.

Phone Surcharges

The hotel amenity that makes everyone mad is the telephone. From the minute you pick it up it seems to eat money, starting with surcharges for calls to "free" 800 numbers all the way down to charges for calls you try to make but go unanswered. In many cases, letting a child into the minibar would be cheaper.

The worst situation appears to be dialing a long-distance call from your room, with the toll to be charged to your room bill. Even when you dial every digit yourself, it will probably be billed at the higher operator-assisted rate, and there will be a surcharge beyond that; the not very high priced Courtyard by Marriott levies a surcharge of 50 percent of the cost of the call.

Using a credit card linked to your regular phone company either to charge the call or to call collect will get you around the worst problem. But the hotel may not let you get away with this without dinging you for the call you must make to reach your phone company: 75 cents is common.

An important new Federal Communications Commission regulation took further steps against the technology that blocked your ability to reach your regular long-distance company to place a credit card or collect call. This says that any room phone that could be modified at a cost of $15 or less must be adjusted to allow guests to reach the long-distance companies they want by dialing that company's 10-XXX code: 10-ATT for A.T.&T.; 10-333 for Sprint and 10-222 for MCI.

Another part of the F.C.C. rules specifies that while the hotel may impose a surcharge for 10-XXX calls, the surcharges must be applied equally to all the access numbers. If it costs 75 cents to reach Sprint, it must cost 75 cents to reach the other companies, too.

Depending on the type of instrument in the hotel room, it

is sometimes possible to avoid paying the 75-cent hotel charge for each call in a sequence of calls by not hanging up between but by pressing the # sign between calls. That, of course, does not avoid the phone company's per-call charge for credit card calls.

Some hotels that apply the access-call surcharge do not do so for 800 number calls. If this is the case, use the phone company's alternate route to credit card service: MCI, 800-950-1022; A.T.& T., 800-321-0288, and Sprint, 800-877-8000.

Some hotels are getting wise to this avoidance of their surcharge, however, and exact surcharges on 800 numbers that are used for access to credit card calls even if they do not levy surcharges on other 800 calls. Whether they catch up with all the **debit phone card** numbers is another question.

Kurt Schroeder at the enforcement division of the F.C.C. said the equal-cost ruling did not seem to be violated by allowing free calls to all the carriers by the 800-number route, but, in any case, he said the issue had not come before the commission.

From the standpoint of making sensible decisions, including whether to go in your pajamas to the pay phone in the lobby, the most important part of the F.C.C. Telephone Operator Services Act is the requirement that all telephones for consumer use in hotels, hospitals and universities post information that rates are available on request, the identity of the carrier used by the hotel, a notice that another carrier may be used by dialing the access code, and the address of the F.C.C. complaint department. Normally, hotels eliminate the need to respond to requests for rates by posting the rates and surcharges, too. In some states, this is mandated.

The law is indifferent to the size of surcharges, but not if they are unequal in application or if information about them is not clear in advance. Complaints should be sent to the F.C.C., 2025 M Street, N.W., Suite 6202, Washington, D.C. 20554. The state consumer protection agency is also probably interested; these are listed by state name under **consumer assistance**.

Pillows, Airline

On the inquiry of a reader, I researched the cleanliness of airline pillows and headsets. Wow! My friends are phlegmatic to indifferent to the horrors I routinely disclose but after this one, I couldn't go out for weeks without being besieged. I think the reason is that we all operate on the assumption that things offered to us—forks, motel beds, towels, airline pillows—are fresh. Sometimes, they are not. In the case of airline pillows, definitely not.

In the airline profit squeeze that followed deregulation, the lines changed pillows during the nightly servicing on layover instead of doing it after every flight leg or flight. The little plastic earmuffs on the headsets may not have been replaced either, and from the standpoint of one medical researcher this is the more serious problem.

If you want to sleep, take your own pillow. One traveler simply stuffs a full-sized pillow into her carry-on bag, but there are inflatable models and one beanbaggy collar-contour model, called a Bucky, filled with buckwheat seeds, that is wonderfully comfortable and probably deserves a space on the packing list if you like to sleep aboard. These are about $25 each. Information: Bucky Products, Box 31970, Seattle, Wash. 98103; 206-545-8790 or 800-692-8259.

If you have an infection or any pain in your ear, you may want to skip the headset entirely.

Radar Detectors

These are illegal in only a few states, but Canada, believing
that their use creates accidents, goes all out after them. All
the provinces and territories have been known to seize them
and to fine offenders for their use. So if you have one, put it
in the trunk when you drive across the border.

Red-Eye Express

Unlike the grand old newspaper term "lobster shift," for
which no one has any reliable etymology, the red-eye express, which punches in for roughly the same hours as the
lobster shift, requires no explanation to anyone who has ever
ridden it.

An eastbound flight across the United States will eat up an
entire day because what the air trip does not consume the
three lost hours on the clock will steal. Answer: Do it at
night, when the lost time matters less except to your metabo-
lism. Presto, the red-eye express. This off-hours flight en-
ables the airline to get its equipment to the East for the first
day flight, which is popular because it leaves early and, by
the clock, arrives in a couple of hours.

To take some of the red out of the red-eye and enjoy some
sleep, all rules are turned upside down. If it's a wide-body
plane and underpopulated, book a seat in the center of the
wide center row. If the flight is not sold out and the usual
pattern follows, you can have a whole row to stretch out in.
Wear loose, worthless clothes, because no one is likely to
meet you at the hour you arrive. You have time for a good
dinner with West Coast friends, but try to eat lightly and not
drink a lot before you board. Carry a water bottle and an
eyeshade and your own pillow. Turn down the drinks and
meal. Take off your shoes and wear socks or airline slippers.
If you use a blanket, buckle the seat belt outside it so the

flight attendant need not ask if you are buckled. The eyeshade serves as a DO NOT DISTURB sign. Practice nothingness. Think sleep.

Of course, the most common flights to Europe are really red-eye night flights, but little about them can be whipped because you leave earlier and cross more time zones. **Jet lag** is the result rather than just red eyes.

Retreats

Monastic guesthouses, religious centers. Some of these places offer rooms for the night as a service or a way of supporting the religious community. Others provide periods of retreat to groups or individuals. Judging by letters and phone calls, opportunities to get away from the hurly-burly and perhaps even meditate are increasingly popular. Sometimes, I suspect that the callers are looking for B & Bs where they don't have to make conversation with the owner, and this is surely the route.

Producing lists and guidebooks to such places is a cottage industry for their devotees. Some are works of charity, some self-published; others have commercial or religious backing. Some are revised regularly and may be ordered; the books may go out of print, but try the local library before you give up.

A group called Retreats International publishes a yearly list of 600 Christian retreat centers in the United States, mostly Catholic. *Directory of Retreat Centers* costs $15 from Retreats International, Box 1067, Notre Dame, Ind. 46556; 219-631-5320.

A list of 150 Protestant retreat houses in the United States and Canada is issued by the North American Retreat Directors Association. The association asks for $2 for handling and mailing. N.A.R.D.A, Stony Point Center, 17 Cricketown Road, Stony Point, N.Y. 10980; 914-786-5674, fax 914-786-5919.

Victoria D. and James J. Hughes got interested in religious houses that offered short stays without religious implications. After visiting a few, they began researching by mail to create a list and then published *Overnight or Short Stay at Religious Houses Around the World*. It has been growing steadily since 1989, and the 1993 edition is to have a few pages of pictures although the book is essentially still a list. It is available for $17.95 postage paid from Hugen Press, Box 2286, Bloomfield, N.J. 07003; 201-743-9285.

A Guide to Monastic Guest Houses by J. Robert Beagle was published by Morehouse, a religious publishing house, in 1989. Its 132 pages cover 129 guesthouses, mostly Roman Catholic and Episcopal. It has sketches and descriptions, much in the manner of a B & B guide. This costs $11.95 in regular bookstores. Inquiries: Morehouse Publishing, 78 Danbury Road, Wilton, Conn. 06897.

Catholic America, Self-Renewal Centers and Retreats by Patricia Christian-Meyer was published in 1989 by John Muir, Box 613, Santa Fe, N.Mex. 87504. Muir says it sold the rights to this but does not know who has them now.

Traveler's Guide to Healing Centers and Retreats in North America by Martine Rundee and Jonathan Blease, was also published in 1989 by John Muir, Box 613, Santa Fe, N.Mex. 87504.

The Good Retreat Guide by Stafford Whiteaker, a list of 200 places in Britain, Ireland and France, was published in 1992 by Rider, distributed by Trafalgar Square, North Pomfret, Vt. 05053; $22.95.

Sanctuaries: A Guide to Lodgings in Monasteries, Abbeys

and Retreats of the United States by Jack and Marcia Kelly
was published in a Northeast edition by Bell Tower, part of
Harmony Books, in 1991; $13. The volume for the West Coast
and Southwest was published in the same format in 1993 for
$15.

Guide to Retreat Center Guest Houses by John and Mary
Jensen was reissued by their C.T.S. Publications in 1992. It
gives details on 225 places in the United States, Canada and
overseas and gives bare-bones listings on 170 others. Available for $14.50 from C.T.S., Box 5486, Fullerton, Calif. 92635.

Some of these guides include Buddhist and other non-
Christian centers, but they are rare.

Room Service

My father was a salesman on the road through most of the
Depression, when service was cheap and plentiful, and many
of his tales concerned hotel life in towns I heard of again only
in crossword puzzles. One of my favorites was a hot day
when he and his fellow worker Zack were in some poor place
in Olean, New York. Zack called the desk to order a pitcher
of ice water. "But, sir, the middle faucet in the basin provides
ice water," the desk clerk replied. "But I want to hear the ice
cubes clinking down the hall" was the response, and they got
their pitcher of water.

That is why I love room service—being grown up and able
to ask for fulfillment of a fantasy of clinking ice cubes, a
thermos jug of steaming coffee, a tiny jar of jam, the creak-
ing of the rolling table.

I thought it was an embarrassing secret all my own until I
learned that Mimi Sheraton, my idol as an eater, food expert
and iconoclast, had a similar private taste. There comes a
time when you have been on the road for a week or so when

you need a night by yourself, to sew on a button, she wrote, or to wash your hair, prop your feet up and turn on the television set. She confessed to her million-odd readers that her favorite order was a chicken sandwich. And then, because Mimi wastes nothing, she reviewed a bunch of chicken sandwiches she had ordered over the years. Not chicken salad, you understand, but sliced real chicken off a chicken carcass. By the time I finished reading the comparisons of boiled and roast chicken, of white bread and whole wheat, I would have died for a chicken sandwich delivered to my door, watercress extending from underneath the bread, homemade mayonnaise on the side, with a sturdy pepper mill and a sweaty bottle of premium beer.

Room service is labor-intensive, and it is found these days only in higher priced hotels, where I usually stay only for a conference or convention, and in motels with real restaurants. These days the minibar substitutes for the delivered tray with a glass, dish of ice, drink and plate of snacks. At some no-restaurant motels, the desk will provide you with a menu for an order-and-deliver place in the area, but this is going to arrive with plastic plates and utensils, which takes the zest out of it for me.

There is also a double reverse. The popularity of pizza as a eat-in item, particularly with families, has led many places to provide it as a room service item while pretending it comes from an outside place with a pizza oven. These hotels even provide a separate phone number and disguise the hotel waiter in a special uniform. One waiter described having to deliver the pizza as an employee of Tony Il Fako or whatever the name was, then having to reappear with the beer as the regular room service waiter.

When I get a wonderful room, like one I once got in La

Posada de Albuquerque overlooking the Sandia Mountains, I dive for the room service menu. I want to know what I can order, and how late I can order, so I can sit at my table and enjoy my view.

I put my room service charges on the room bill, but I always tip in cash because I have no idea how long the waiter has to wait to get the tip otherwise. At a hotel that includes a service charge with the room service bill, I still tip the waiter a dollar or two in whatever currency. Of course, if it is a la-di-da meal where the fish must be boned or the banana flambéed, I fling money in all directions, but this is not a frequent occasion. Like Mimi, I want to hunker down with my chicken sandwich.

Russia

If you plan to go to Moscow and St. Petersburg, or to Kiev, Ukraine, be aware that diphtheria has been resurgent in these places and current immunization is recommended by the Centers for Disease Control and Prevention. If all you need is a booster, you should get this shot at least two weeks before your visit to allow antibodies time to build up. (Recommended has an optional sound, but taking action is *urgent* for your own safety. See **immunization help by fax or phone**.) If you did not get the basic diphtheria-tetanus combination in childhood, you may need to start seven months ahead of time.

A combination of causes brings this 19th-century problem to the fore again. A drop in child immunizations is the main one, U.S. researchers believe. Vaccine was short, and Russian physicians often decided against giving shots to weaker children on the grounds it would further jeopardize their health.

In 1992, there were 774 cases in Moscow, with 24 deaths—nearly double the number two years before.

A booster is needed for adults who have not had a diphtheria shot in the last 10 years. It is usually administered in combination with a tetanus shot, which is the most basic protective shot for American children and adults. Frequently, however, according to Rosamond Dewart, who edits the Centers for Disease Control annual, *Health Information for International Travel*, people involved in an accident get a tetanus toxoid (Tt) shot and not the tetanus-diphtheria combo (Td) because physicians are reluctant to give unnecessary vaccines. So prospective travelers to Russia and Ukraine should check their medical records, and if you call the physician on the phone ask to have the full name given because "Tt" and "Td" sound so much alike.

Safety in the Air

If you dress for comfort rather than style on an airplane, you can dress for safety at the same time. Wear layers of nonconstricting clothes of natural fibers and flat shoes; avoid nylon socks or stockings and hair spray because they are so flammable. When you are aboard, spot the two exits nearest to your seat and then take a walk to memorize the number of seat backs between your seat and the exits so you could find them in the dark.

If you feel confident of your own ability to handle an emergency exit door, you can go take a vacant seat in the exit row after the door is shut. You take a responsibility in doing this, but do it if you consider yourself a good choice for it. Do not do it if you are likely to meet an embarrassing challenge from a flight attendant about your capacity for the job.

There is virtually no chance that you will be involved in an air crash. If you got to the airport okay, the worst part is over. If you want to chew on some statistics, here they are: Each year, 450 million people in the United States take an airplane trip. Ninety to 100 people a year have been killed in plane crashes over the last 10 years, but 107 people *a day* were killed in auto accidents in 1992—and that represented a drop of 5.5 percent from the year before.

To refine it somewhat, takeoff and landing are the times of maximum hazard and fire is the real danger then, so if you must worry, worry about finding the exit in the smoky dark. The number of over-water ditchings in recent years is one, so do not expend your precious worrying time contemplating the mysteries of the flotation cushion. Think about making your feet comfortable in a pair of socks instead of shoes so you can walk back and forth and count seat backs. The exercise will do you good.

Safety Overseas

If you think you have reason to worry about revolution, up-heaval, guerrillas, street crime and the like in the place you plan to go, do some reliable research. The best information will come from a friend or friend of a friend who has just visited the area that interests you. Depending on the volatil-ity of the situation, I would disregard information more than four weeks old. I would not accept assurances from a travel agent or tour operator unless this expert actually went there and you can get answers to your questions: Did you leave the hotel in the evening? Were you afraid about mugging? Is transport functioning?

Second best but still pretty good is information available to the public from the State Department, formerly by phone and recently by fax. For more than 15 years, the State Depart-

ment has been issuing bulletins about areas of danger overseas. These came in various degrees of urgency: "Warning,"
"Caution" and "Notice." They evolved ad hoc, and there were
no benchmarks for the levels.

In December 1992, the system was overhauled and simpli-
fied. For each of 194 countries, there is now a "Consular Information Sheet" that provides all sorts of important
information: the address and phone number of the American
Embassy or Consulate, entry requirements, drug penalties,
driving restrictions, the quality of medical care and the likelihood that the hospital will want cash or a credit card in advance of treatment. These sheets also contain sections labeled
"areas of instability" and "crime information."

If you are going anyplace but the most visited overseas
tourist centers, you should get a copy of the pertinent Consular Information Sheet. Many brochures and guidebooks reprint the latest available version of this uncopyrighted
information, but the State Department is constantly revising
and reissuing its own sheets, so it's cheaper and better to tap
the government.

In addition, under the newer system the State Department
now issues a warning when conditions in a country are so
dangerous or unstable that they constitute a threat to American travelers and the United States is not able to help a
traveler in an emergency. After the shift to the two-tiered
system of consular information sheets and warnings, 13 warnings were in force, and the number has risen as high as 19.
Before the shift, when warnings, cautions and notices were
issued, 53 of them were in force at the various levels, almost
a third of the 194 countries where the State Department
keeps tabs. The new system gives travelers a more rational
basis for deciding to skip a place.

One other question comes up here: Does the State Department know things about traveler safety it is not telling? Since the airliner explosion over Lockerbie, Scotland, in December 1988, when the department was accused of having withheld news of a telephone threat, it has not been allowed to apply a double standard. So the answer is no.

How to get hold of the warnings and consular information sheets?

The fastest way is fax: Dial 202-647-3000 on the phone attached to your fax machine and order an index. A voice will prompt you to press certain keys on the fax, and then you follow the instructions to confirm your order and start the fax machine. With the index, you can order any publication you like. To get the latest information on a country, you do not need an index: just press the first four letters of the country; instructions are given for numbers to use instead of the missing "Q" and "X." Be prepared, though, if the keys on your fax phone are all numbers, as some are: You need to have a regular phone or a diagram in front of you to do it right.

A number of regular publications of the State Department, "Your Trip Abroad" and the like, are available by the fax route, too. It's not a nice stapled booklet with a color cover, and the print fades pretty quickly, but it's fast and legible.

Unlike the fax information system used by the Centers for Disease Control and Prevention in Atlanta, you pay for these faxes because you initiated the call, switching on the fax machine when instructed. However, call can be made in the middle of the night or on holidays, when the rates are lower.

To hear the same material—for a maximum of three countries per call—call 202-647-5225 on a Touch-Tone phone and follow the instructions to the material you want. Like the fax number, this operates 24 hours a day so you can call when the tolls are lowest.

Another route to get warnings or consular information sheets is through any of the 13 regional **passport** agencies in the United States, and at field offices of the Department of Commerce, which are listed in the blue pages of the phone book. Copies of the sheets and warnings are also available at embassies and consulates abroad. They may be obtained by mail. Send a request listing the countries and enclosing a self-addressed envelope and enough postage to pay for one sheet for each country you have requested, to Bureau of Consular Affairs, Room 4811 N.S., Department of State, Washington, D.C. 20520.

Because State Department information is fed into the computers used by travel agents for making plane reservations, it is also available from them but you probably have to ask for it. It also flows through the Official Airline Guide electronic edition, which is available on these computer services, among others: Compuserve, Dow Jones News/Retrieval and Genie. On the main O.A.G. menu, it can be called under 5, Worldwide Travel Facts.

Scams by Postcard

I optimistically assume that people who have bought this book are aware of the travel scams that lie behind the computer-imprinted postcards you get offering trips to Hawaii for $49 and other improbable deals. But an editor at the *Times* once called me for help when a household member was suckered by one of these, so I'll squander an entry to warn anyone who has not learned about these operators.

Time pressure, expiration dates, call-right-aways and other efforts to hustle you are just that: efforts to hustle you out of your money. Any legitimate offer made by a postcard to your home can be explored at leisure through examining brochures and other information you request. You can do all the comparison shopping you want. Do not be rushed into a deal. Do not give your credit or charge card number to anyone who calls you with such an offer nor to anyone whom you call in response to such a postcard offer. Do not respond to any assertion that an offer will expire in a few days and never be made again. Confidence artists are trained and they know our weak spots—the fear we may miss out on something—and they play on this.

These schemes, usually operated out of rooms with rows of phones and trained operators with confiding voices and scripts, are fiendishly designed. You must seal your ears against them, as Odysseus against the sirens. Typically, there is at least one operator who will tell the victim, coaxingly: "This time period has really expired, but let me ask Ms. Zilch if we can get one more in . . . Oh, I am sorry, we can't, but would you be interested in . . ." A naive New York couple approved a charge of $590 on their card for a trip and month after month passed and it could not be scheduled. They were on their way to a further charge that would have brought the total to $1,238 when they wrote the *Times*, enclosing letters recounting a familiar course of events and a series of attacks upon their credit cards.

When I researched this case, I found that the state of Florida had a mound of complaints against the company. When the article appeared, the company nonetheless threatened legal action. It said that the couple were not really angry, quoting one letter from them to the "good guy" phone salesperson saying: "We know you really tried hard for us. God bless you for your caring."

It may be hard for you to believe that people pretend to be helpful and kind solely because they are confidence artists. But believe it. The stock-in-trade of the confidence artist is a nice manner, one that gives you "confidence."

Should you get trapped in such a mess, notify your charge card or credit card company as soon as the light dawns. Tell the company you have not received the services you were charged for. It has now been established that the Visa and MasterCard 120-day time limit for registering a "charge-back," as it is called, begins to tick when you realize you are never going to get your purchase, not when the charge is placed against your account. Some responsibility has now been laid upon credit card companies and banks to stop accepting charges put through by companies with sky-high charge-back levels. In one case, the company was told it was barred from receiving money through the credit card network, so the scam operator persuaded a shoe store to process charges for it in return for a percentage. And while the money flowed in, the credit card company just could not figure out for months and months why the tiny shoe store was experiencing such a boom. But the credit card company was forced to swallow some of the losses, protecting the customers, because a simple investigation at any point would have showed the shoe store was simply laundering the charges for the scam artist.

State agencies (see **consumer assistance**) may be able to bring pressure. If you are really jobbed, be sure to send documentation on each step to the agency and the local Better Business Bureau because at least you can help someone else avoid the same operators. If you can get through to consumer affairs officers in your town or state, they will be able to recite virtually the whole scam script back to you. Humiliating as it may be, it's better to get even this way than steam in anger and silence.

At one point, there were all sorts of offers connected with free weekend visits to resorts offering time-shares or condominium rentals. These have apparently slacked off with the recession and efforts by that part of the real-estate industry to police its act, because I have not heard complaints lately. But when the gemstones racket gives out and there are no more takers for $49 weekends in Hawaii, these other offers may revive. Beware.

Seat Pitch

This is responsible for making the coach section of the plane so miserable. It is not the floor distance between seats but the distance from a particular spot on one seat to the same spot on the seat in the next row. At 29 inches, I am immobilized. At 30 inches, the same. After that, I can move my legs slightly.

One way for the airlines to meet recently enacted rules for access to the emergency exits is to widen the space between the rows of seats adjoining the exit, which may give 34 inches or more in pitch. But there is no way of predicting how your plane will be configured, and some airlines for safety reasons will not assign seats in the exit row before all the passengers have checked in. If you are on a plane that is not full and the exit row has space, as soon as the door is shut you can go sit in the exit row unless you are likely to be challenged on your ability to cope with the exit door in an emergency. A long struggle was eventually resolved over whether it was discriminatory to require that people in the exit row be able to see, and the requirements for seating in that row require this and other capacities, so read them be-

fore you sit. If you have someone else to care for—a child or
an older person—you may not sit there.

If you are crammed in, put your health first and get up and
down a lot and walk around. Drink water. Use the toilet.
Pick over the magazines. Do not worry about making seat-
mates stand; it's good for them, too. Do not cross your legs
or do anything that will impede your circulation. (See **economy class syndrome**.) My need to get up and down is why I
like an aisle seat, although if it is not a jumbo jet, the window seat makes more comfortable sleeping.

Second Driver

Some auto rental companies levy an extra daily fee if someone other than the renter will drive the car. A reader asked
me if this fee wasn't crazy, and I agree that it is. The second
driver must be as qualified to drive as the first, and the
rental company is not suffering double exposure to a potential accident, as rental companies contend, but reduced exposure because the second driver will spell the first driver
when fatigue sets in.

My cogent arguments have not persuaded anyone yet. But
however preposterous it is, pay the two bucks, because if
there is an accident that brings police attention and an un-
listed driver is at the wheel, the rental company will throw
the whole financial burden in your lap on the grounds that
you have violated the rental contract.

Senior Airline Vouchers

Most older people who make domestic trips regularly—to a
seasonal home, for instance, or to see grandchildren—prefer
to buy books of airline coupons, which are worth it if they
are making at least two round-trips in the one-year period of

validity. Each coupon is good for a one-way ticket, although some airlines require two coupons for Hawaii or summer trips because there are potentially more full fares to be sold. The buyer must be 62 or older. Over the years, I have not received many questions about coupon books because the people who need them—that is, those of us who travel in long-familiar ruts most of the time—pretty quickly find their way to them.

Basically, while prices change, lines that compete with each other between certain cities tend to offer the same prices. Early in 1992, Trans World Airlines, just emerging from bankruptcy, was charging $496 for a book of four coupons and $620 for a companion book for someone not 62, sold at the same time. The senior coupon book at the time came with a bonus certificate for 20 percent off any ticket to Europe. At the same time, America West was selling four for $430, eight for $720; Continental, $549 for four, $949 for eight and was also offering Freedom Passports for more trips at a higher price. American, USAir, Northwest, United and Delta had books of four coupons for $568, eight for $984.

Clearly, before buying a coupon book the buyers should price out their rates and be sure the periodic fare wars do not undercut the coupon price. Or, alternatively, if the coupons are bought for impulse trips, that the buyers plan really long trips. Using coupons for a New York to Boston run would be folly.

Flights using coupons must be confirmed 14 days ahead of time, although a coupon user can fly standby at any time. USAir allows children aged 2 to 11 to use a coupon, but only when making a trip with the coupon purchaser. Many lines have days when coupons may not be used.

Occasionally, coupon users hit some of the disadvantages of

the plan. One couple found seats allowed for coupon holders
on the flight she wanted had sold out 11 months and 30 days
in advance, the earliest date one can reserve an airline seat.
The particular Delta flight they wanted came up from Florida
to New York in time to connect with European flights from
Kennedy Airport; tour operators booked those seats at the
first moment and the couple waited a few hours to call, until
they got out of bed at 6 A.M., and they lost out.

When a Delta spokesman was asked how many seats of the
180-odd on the narrow-body 757 were set aside for coupon
holders, he said not many, although he would not put a number on it. Is it possible that no seats are set aside for coupon
holders? "Never," he said. "Although I never say never." He
explained what should be clear to all users of discount tickets: Treatment is not equal. He said the number of seats
assigned for coupon users, frequent fliers and other low-
revenue travelers was determined by how easily the line
could sell the other seats for a more profitable price. Popular
flight, few cheap seats. "We make every effort to fill the
plane at full fare," he said. "We'd be foolish not to."

Senior Organizations

Many play an important role in travel. The major one, the
one everyone knows, is A.A.R.P., or American Association of
Retired Persons.

With 33 million members in 1993, this organization, founded
in 1958, is the largest for older people in the United States,
and its glossy publication, *Modern Maturity*, which comes
free to members every two months, is the biggest circulation
magazine in the country. A "nonprofit, nonpartisan" organization, it authorizes all sorts of things for sale under its name,
from investment plans (Scudder right now), credit cards and

insurance (Prudential, Hartford and Foremost at this writing) to auto clubs (Amoco) and travel (American Express). These corporations, you may be sure, work for a profit, and as the scandals that have attached to big "nonprofit" health insurance companies attest, nonprofit does not mean a lack of big bucks.

People may join A.A.R.P. at the age of 50, and membership is provided to spouses regardless of age. Membership information is available from Box 199, Long Beach, Calif. 90801. Membership is cheap: currently, $8 a year. You get the membership cost back about the second time you get a senior citizen discount, usually $5, at a motel. Membership is particularly valuable for youthful-looking 50-year-olds or even younger spouses who may travel by themselves. People like my Aunt Rebecca, who is a constant traveler in her mid-80s, don't need an A.A.R.P. card, because, as she says ruefully of the senior discount at motels, "They don't ask, they just give it to me automatically."

This organization negotiates contracts with travel agencies to offer escorted tours and the like under the A.A.R.P. banner. It came to a parting with its first travel bureau, which spun off into Grand Circle Travel. At this writing, American Express is the chosen agency; earlier it was Olson TravelWorld. Olson was a high roller for some time; it was also chosen for a previous cycle of Olympic Games tickets but nonetheless later defaulted before being bought up by another company. American Express was doing some "re-engineering" early in its time as the A.A.R.P.-authorized travel agency, but it remains the largest travel agency in the United States. It seems to be delivering for A.A.R.P. better than Olson.

Several people who watch the senior market, including

Gene and Adele Malott, publishers of *Mature Traveler* newsletter, and Arthur Frommer, say that the Olson A.A.R.P.
tours were more expensive than offerings not restricted to
seniors. Gene Malott said early in 1993 that he thought that
American Express had brought the price for an A.A.R.P.
tour down from the Olson level. (Look at the material on
Saga and Grand Circle under **single strategies** for alternatives).

   To me, A.A.R.P. is not a lovable organization; its soul
seems elusive at best. I have never heard anyone say how
many friends they made on an A.A.R.P. trip as I hear about
Windjammer or Grand Circle trips every time the subject is
broached. And because every branch except the A.A.R.P. ad-
ministrative-lobbying office in Washington seems to be
housed apart from headquarters, the organization is hard to
get a handle on. For example, I heard an A.A.R.P. speaker
give a vigorous talk about the problems of the single-room
supplement, a favorite topic of mine, but no one in the
Washington office had ever heard of her and I could not track
her down to interview her.

   One coda: A.A.R.P. provides an excellent, cheap ($10 each
time I took it), volunteer-taught refresher course in driving in
all 50 states. I think this may be the organization's best contribution to America's older people. It creates safer drivers and it
can lower liability premiums in about half the states and may
also reduce any accident points on a license. It taught me things
I needed but had not heard before. The "55 Alive/Mature Driving" course—the number refers to speed, not age—is based on
long research into causes of the accidents of older people:
poorer eyesight, slower reactions, diminished hearing, failure of
depth perception. Information: 55 Alive, 601 E Street, N.W.,

Washington, D.C. 20049. For other courses, see **driving classes**.

Two other nonreligious organizations for seniors have an ideology and more sharply defined goals:

The A.F.L.-C.I.O. has always urged union members to join the National Council of Senior Citizens—1331 F Street, N.W., Washington, D.C. 20004, 202-347-8800—in preference to A.A.R.P. It was formed in 1961 to lobby for Medicare and now has five million members. Membership costs $12 a year for a couple, with no minimum age although you must be 65 to buy the Medicare supplement. If all you want is a card for a motel discount, this organization's card works perfectly well and you will not be swamped with ads and magazines but only an occasional newsprint publication.

The National Association of Retired Credit Union People, established in 1978, has a minimum age of 50 and membership dues are also $12 a year. Members must be active or former credit union members. It, too, offers motel discounts as well as insurance and travel services provided by an outside agency. The membership card enables one to cash a check for up to $100 at a participating credit union in the United States. Information: Box 391, 5910 Mineral Point Road, Madison, Wis. 53701; 608-238-4286 or 800-937-2644, ext. 3760.

Senior Resources

The older population is galloping along in size and almost every travel-related company is offering some enticement to get part of this market: figure 10 percent off as a starting point on tickets and hotels. Other entries in this book offer guidance but I cannot list everything, it's moving too fast.

Among the books you may want to look at is the deliberately overtitled *Unbelievably Good Deals and Great Adventures That You Absolutely Can't Get Unless You're Over 50*, by my old friend Joan Rattner Heilman, published for $7.95 by Contemporary Books, 180 North Michigan Avenue, Chicago, Ill. 60601. It is in its fifth edition at this writing and may go on forever because such material must constantly be brought up to date. She talks about hotel discounts, brand name by brand name, ski discounts and so on.

The *Mature Traveler* monthly newsletter has a harum-scarum look that probably derives from its homemade design. Gene and Adele Malott publish this themselves in Reno and they get most of their material from press handouts, although they use freelance articles and write about their own trips. The Malotts accept discounts and free trips and thus can make no overwhelming claim to objectivity. But they have a fearless quality when they report on advertised senior discounts that cost more than the regular offerings, and several years ago they fingered big guys: Olson TravelWorld's offerings for A.A.R.P. A.A.R.P. has since changed its travel supplier and Olson TravelWorld has defaulted and been purchased by another company, but the Malotts had the courage when it was riding high. The Malotts have published a book, *Get Up and Go* (Gateway Books, San Francisco, $10.95), but a newsletter is more valuable in following a moving target. A subscription, 12 issues, costs $24.50 and a sample copy will be sent for $2. Mature Traveler, Box 50820, Reno, Nev. 89513.

Showering

If you have been warned not to drink the water, keep your mouth shut when you wash. (see **ice**)

Single Strategies

The infernal penalty for traveling alone is called the "single supplement" by tour operators, which makes it sound like something you really want. You don't. It's the extra charge that the tour operator or cruise line hits you with if you are not traveling with a companion and must buy a room by yourself.

Are there ways to beat it? A few. They may not be your thing but you might as well learn about them if you detest being soaked for going it alone. With the number of people taking tours solo rising steadily—most are older—some marketing genius should find a way to capitalize on it. In fact, that is part of the success of Club Med, which has a variation on the freshman roommate draw at many of its villages. Everyone pays the same fee, and if you are by yourself the Club Med people will match you with someone they hope will be compatible.

The dreaded single supplement turns the sock inside out on the motel sign that reads: Single $32, Double $38. If you are driving along alone, it does not bother you that for only $6 more you could have brought along a buddy. But when the tour operator offers a price of "$19 a person in double occupancy" and you have to pay $32 because you are alone, then it bothers. A lot.

Some tour operators will try to match you up with someone else who is compatible on smoking, snoring and other important points of contention so you can get that bed for $19. Some entrepreneurs and clubs carry want-ad newsletters that give you a chance to try your own matchup, and such projects finally segue into personals: "Friend wanted for travel" and such.

If this is all distasteful to you, be aware that the hotel with nothing but double rooms prefers to have two people in there to eat in the dining room, drink in the bar and tip the maids, and if you are going to occupy that room with your one mouth, one pair of bendable elbows and one wallet the hotel wants to recover something, which is understandable if not lovable. Not acceptable, in my mind, is the tour operator who not only passes along the single supplement it must pay in your behalf but adds profit for itself on top. Check it out before you buy.

Sometimes, in Europe, there are true single rooms—tiny things with single beds—even in modern hotels. I had one for a conference in Zurich that had a window facing a huge clock tower, and I loved it despite its hospital-like look. If the tour operator uses such hotels and you can get such a room, the single supplement should be sharply diminished because you are not forcing the hotel to give up revenue. Some tour operators warn that single rooms in old hotels in Europe are likely to be small, dark and inside the building—yes, European hotels have interior rooms with fake windows—and if this is the case you'll just have to figure you don't want to spend a lot of time in there anyway.

Calculate what it is costing you per night to get a single room before you start looking for a roommate. On a tour, there is no reason for you to pay more for your plane, bus or train seat, your lunch or your luggage transfer, so the supplement figure that is listed—probably 15 percent or more of the lodging cost—applies only to the room. Divide that by the number of nights you will spend in hotels and see what you are paying.

Grand Circle in Boston is a company that sells overseas escorted tours, longer stays abroad and cruises, all by marketing directly to people over 50. It began life as the travel arm of the American Association for Retired Persons but went independent and is very successful. You can get invited to one of the selling parties they hold around the country. The one I attended, in a big New York hotel, struck me as a combination Tupperware party/camp reunion. The clients are hugely loyal and get a boot out of being recognized for the number of trips they have taken. Grand Circle will try to find a same-sex roommate for you and says that it will reduce the single supplement by 50 percent if that fails. For some long-stay trips, there is no single supplement. Grand Circle Travel, 347 Congress Street, Boston, Mass. 02210; 617-350-7500, 800-248-3737. Grand Circle does not give commissions to travel agents so you will have to do this one yourself unless your travel agent is your sister-in-law.

Saga Holidays offers bus tours, both in the United States and overseas, long stays and cruises to people over 60, and will seek same-sex roommates on request. At one point, it reported a 70 percent success rate, which may be because the older you get the more likely you are to be traveling alone. Saga Holidays, 120 Boylston Street, Boston, Mass. 02116; 617-262-2262, 800-343-0273.

There are two long-established idiosyncratic newsletters that find travel companions. With both, the editor is the message. Jens Jurgen swamps me with mail, scribbles all over everything about his recent coups and could hardly be less suave: Feel free to reprint my tips on how to thwart a pickpocket, he says. He attacks the task of supplying potential travel companions with the same enthusiasm. His newsletter subscription rates vary depending on whether you want to window-shop or put yourself in the window for consideration, too. Jens Jurgen's Travel Companion Exchange, Box 833, Amityville, N.Y. 11701; 516-454-0880.

Miriam E. Tobolowsky in Los Angeles likewise reminds me

of an aerobics instructor I once had at Grossinger's—corny but so full of life she is irresistible. Her subscription rate for six newsletters a year is $40. Partners in Travel, Box 491145, Los Angeles, Calif. 90049; 213-476-4869.

I recently saw a listing for a new one of these organizations designed for people over 50, but the price is high and because it's new I have no reports from would-be matchers on whether it gives good value or not. For $120, it acts as a clearinghouse, providing a monthly listing of short profiles. Partners for Travel, Box 560337, Miami, Fla. 33256; 800-866-5565.

One newsletter, *Going Solo*, is in marked contrast to these organizations; it is well-designed, with stylish graphics and occasional photographs. It does not do matchups but looks into places and ways for single travelers to enjoy everything. (See **solo travelers**.)

Sober Trips

Vacations for recovering alcoholics and others are a new idea for those in 12-step programs to get over substance abuse. Cruises and other trips can incorporate meetings and other events the group needs to support its efforts because, as one organizer said, people in recovery programs often consider vacations threatening or places where it is easier to make a slip. In addition, the participants assist each other in more subtle ways. "We have to learn to face social situations that we formerly met with a drink in hand," Steve Abrams, an organizer, said. "In a sober vacation group, there's a lot of support and identification to make it easier."

Some recovering addicts do not like the idea of creating a segregated world insulated from the normal stresses that recovering people must learn to cope with, but as one said, "Listen, if it works . . ."

Such groups welcome family and friends. Here are some organizations that offer sober vacations, but if you have a group of possibly 10 people who want to plan something of your own, tour operators will probably do it for you. At the level of 10 participants, you should be allowed to take along one person free and this may be ideal if your group has a leader.

Celebrate Life Tours, Box 8201, Buckland Station, Manchester, Conn. 06040; 203-246-1614, 800-825-4782. Trips into New England, cruises. Jack Wilbur, organizer and leader.

Idaho Afloat, Box 542, Grangeville, Idaho 83530; 208-983-2414. Sobriety Adventures was established in 1988 by Scott Fasken, a recovering alcoholic who heads the rafting company Idaho Afloat. Regular trips are limited to 25 people, including one counselor, but it can be doubled with enough notice. Meetings are held nightly at campsites along the Snake River.

Serenity Trips, 199 Neponset Avenue, Dorchester, Mass. 02122; 617-825-8532. Lodge weekends, trips to Cancún, cruises.

Sober Vacations International, 26560 Agoura Road, Suite 106, Calabasas, Calif. 91302; 800-762-3738 or 818-878-0008. Club Med trips a specialty, skiing, river rafting, cruises. Popular with New Yorkers.

Solo Travelers

Going Solo, "the newsletter for people traveling alone," has for five years looked stylish and has been full of fresh information. Unlike most publications for single travelers, this does no pairing-up work nor does it focus on the few known strategies to avoid hotels' hated penalty rates for single travelers. (See **single strategies**.)

Jane Doerfer, the proprietor, in well-edited first-person articles by staff members, freelancers and nonprofessional writers, concentrates on places and occasions to be enjoyed alone, on groups one can join without being entombed in a bus and on restaurants with communal tables or other nonisolating eating arrangements for those with no dining partner.

In its six eight-page issues a year, *Going Solo* has touched on hiking with the Wayfarers in Scotland, budget ryokans—or inns—in Japan, using a rail pass to tour the United States, joining an Outward Bound wilderness challenge, eating alone in Paris, and evaluating hotel safety. There are regular features on weekend excursions and travel tips. Prices and addresses for more information or reservations are included.

Ms. Doerfer has also sought hotels that welcome single travelers, lately including two in San Francisco. Single power!

Considering that most solo travelers are women, making it easy to fall into stereotypes, Ms. Doerfer includes a welcome number of male writers and topics that interest both sexes, for example—boardsailing and Europe on a motorcycle.

Going Solo, Box 123, Apalachicola, Fla. 32329; 904-653-8848. One year, six issues, $29. A sample copy is $5 plus $1 postage; the price can be applied to a subscription. Back issues are available at $5 each plus $1.

Sports Equipment

All airlines know how to deal with golf bags, even those the size of howitzers. And all airlines that serve popular ski areas know how to handle skis, although judging by what I have seen for sale at the **lost luggage** depots in Alabama handling them does not necessarily involve delivering them to you at the other end. (If you are taking new skis of a popular brand, it's probably smart to use an electric scriber to etch your name on the top of each ski.)

Getting other sports equipment to where you're going is dicier. Kayaks, bicycles, surfboards, sailboards, vaulting poles —all long objects that do not fold or telescope—may present problems. If you are entering a sports event and want to have your own kayak rather than renting one, call the airline before you book a flight and find out if there is a flight you can take that uses a plane with a luggage compartment that can handle your boat. Don't forget that if you are connecting, you may end up on a light plane where there is no prayer of getting the boat aboard and you may have to pay to store or ship your boat home again as freight.

If you get a glib answer from the airline, don't trust it. Norman Sims, a member of the board of the Appalachian Mountain Club, was told that his kayak would be just fine going from Hartford to Colorado, but when he got to the airport the baggage handler told him the luggage was containerized and the boat would not go in except as freight. As freight, the kayak would cost $300 to ship one way, and since the kayak cost $600 Sims did without and rented.

Bicycles, packed in cartons, normally go as luggage with a modest surcharge. When we did this a lot, we bought a carton and used it, pasting new labels for each direction, until it became a wreck. Some airlines more than others require that the bikes be broken down, so ask in advance about pedals. Wear your bicycle helmet if it does not fit in your luggage.

If you have a weird long object that you have been told will go aboard the plane you are taking, get to the airport early when the cargo compartment is first being packed so you have your best shot at it. Sometimes, it is not the size of the cargo space but the maneuvering space through the door that causes the problem.

When tennis camp breaks, you see kids stow seven and eight rackets in the overhead, but one tennis player in our family got stopped once carrying on his racket. He opened his suitcase and put it in and that was the end of that, but don't count on rationality at security gates when a metal object puts magnetic fields in flux.

A warning: Airlines sometimes change equipment at the last minute, and what fitted on the jumbo may not fit on the DC-10. So the person who is seeing you and your kayak off should remain at the airport until the door shuts and the plane pushes back lest you have to send the boat home again. Once the airplane pushes back, if there is then a change for the worse in equipment the airline can be expected to take responsibility for your boat, delivering it on the next flight, or sending it back to your home if necessary.

State Tourist Offices

Here is a list of addresses and phone numbers for requesting tourist information from the 50 states, the District of Columbia and the 12 Canadian provinces and territories. Postcards are best for mail requests; 800 numbers used to respond to requests for material are sometimes answered in other states, so calls to toll numbers may get better answers to questions.

Every two years, the Practical Traveler column tests the responses to mail requests for information. An answer usually takes five weeks, so allow that. If you have complex and detailed questions, use a toll number so you are sure to speak to someone who is actually in the state. A couple of states have assigned their phone information lines to state prisons, but our cursory experience with inmate "information specialists" shows that they are well informed and can get you what you need.

United States

Alabama Bureau of Tourism and Travel, Post Office Box 4309, Montgomery, Ala. 36103; 800-252-2262 or 205-242-4169

Alaska Division of Tourism, Post Office Box 110801, Juneau, Alaska 99811; 907-465-2010

Arizona Office of Tourism, 1100 West Washington Street, Phoenix, Ariz. 85007; 800-842-8257 or 602-542-8687

Arkansas Tourism Office, 1 Capitol Mall, Little Rock, Ark. 72201; 800-628-8725 or 501-682-7777

California Office of Tourism, Post Office Box 9278, Van Nuys, Calif. 91409; 800-862-2543 or 916-322-2881.

Colorado Tourism Board, Post Office Box 38700, Denver, Colo. 80238; 800-265-6723 or 303-592-5510

Connecticut Department of Economic Development, 865 Brook Street, Rocky Hill, Conn. 06067; 800-282-6863 or 203-258-4355

Delaware Tourism Office, 99 Kings Highway, Box 1401, Dover, Del. 19903; 800-441-8846 or 302-739-4271

District of Columbia Convention and Visitors Association, 1212 New York Avenue, N.W., Washington 20005; 202-789-7000

Florida Division of Tourism, 126 West Van Buren Street, Tallahassee, Fla. 32399; 904-487-1462

Georgia Department of Industry and Trade, Box 1776, Atlanta, Ga. 30301; 800-847-4842 or 404-656-3590

Hawaii Department of Tourism, 2270 Kalakaua Avenue, Suite 801, Honolulu, Hawaii 96815; 808-923-1811

Idaho Department of Commerce, 700 West State Street, Boise, Idaho 83720; 800-635-7820 or 208-334-2470

Illinois Bureau of Tourism, 100 West Randolph, Suite 3-400, Chicago, Ill. 60601; 800-223-0121 or 312-814-4732

Indiana Division of Tourism, 1 North Capitol, Suite 700, Indianapolis, Ind. 46204; 800-289-6646 or 317-232-8860

Iowa Department of Tourism, 200 East Grand, Des Moines, Iowa 50309; 800-345-4692 or 515-242-4705

Kansas Travel and Tourism Division, 400 Southwest Eighth Street, 5th floor, Topeka, Kans. 66603; 800-252-6727 or 913-296-2009

Kentucky Department of Travel Development, 2200 Capital Plaza Tower, Frankfort, Ky. 40601; 800-225-8747 or 502-564-4930

Louisiana Office of Tourism, Post Office Box 94291, L.O.T., Baton Rouge, La. 70804; 800-334-8626 or 504-342-8119

Maine Office of Tourism, 189 State House Station 59, Augusta, Maine 04333; 800-533-9595 or 207-287-5710

Maryland Office of Tourism Development, 217 East Redwood Street, Baltimore, Md. 21202; 800-543-1036 or 410-333-6611

Massachusetts Office of Travel and Tourism, 100 Cambridge Street, 13th floor, Boston, Mass. 02202; 800-447-6277 or 617-727-3201

Michigan Travel Bureau, Post Office Box 30226, Lansing, Mich. 48909; 800-543-2937 or 517-373-0670

Minnesota Office of Tourism, 375 Jackson Street, 250 Skyway Level, St. Paul, Minn. 55101; 800-657-3700 or 612-296-5029

Mississippi Department of Tourism, Post Office Box 22825, Jackson, Miss. 39205; 800-647-2290 or 601-359-3297

Missouri Division of Tourism, Post Office Box 1055, Jefferson City, Mo. 65102; 800-877-1234 or 314-751-4133

Montana Travel Montana, Room 259, Deer Lodge, Mont. 59722; 800-541-1447 or 406-444-2654

Nebraska Division of Travel and Tourism, 301 Centennial Mall South, Room 88937, Lincoln, Nebr. 68509; 800-228-4307 or 402-471-3796

Nevada Commission on Tourism, Carson City, Nev. 89710; 800-638-2328 or 702-687-4322.

New Hampshire Office of Travel and Tourist Development, Post Office Box 856, Concord, N.H. 03301; 603-271-2343

New Jersey Division of Travel and Tourism, 20 West State Street, C.N. 826, Trenton, N.J. 08625; 800-537-7397 or 609-292-2470

New Mexico Tourism and Travel Division, Post Office Box 20003, Santa Fe, N.Mex. 87503; 800-545-2040

New York State Department of Economic Development, 1 Commerce Plaza, Albany, N.Y. 12245; 800-225-5697 or 518-474-4116

North Carolina Division of Travel and Tourism, 430 North Salisbury Street, Raleigh, N.C. 27603; 800-847-4862 or 919-733-4171

North Dakota Parks and Tourism Department, Capitol Grounds, Bismarck, N.Dak. 58505; 800-435-5663 or 701-224-2525

Ohio Division of Travel and Tourism, Post Office Box 1001, Columbus, Ohio 43266; 800-282-5393 or 614-466-8844

Oklahoma Tourism and Recreation Department, 500 Will Rogers Building, Oklahoma City, Okla. 73105; 800-652-6552 or 405-521-3981

Oregon Tourism Division, 775 Summer Street N.E., Salem, Oreg. 97310; 800-547-7842 or 503-373-1270

Pennsylvania Office of Travel Marketing, Post Office Box 61, Warrendale, Pa. 15086; 800-847-4872 or 717-787-5453

Rhode Island Tourism Division, 7 Jackson Walkway, Providence, R.I. 02903; 800-556-2484 or 401-277-2601

South Carolina Division of Tourism, Post Office Box 71, Room 902, Columbia, S.C. 29202; 800-346-3634 or 803-734-0122

South Dakota Department of Tourism, 711 East Wells Avenue, Pierre S.Dak. 57501; 800-732-5682 or 605-773-3301

Tennessee Department of Tourism Development, Post Office Box 23170, Nashville, Tenn. 37202; 615-741-2158

Texas Department of Commerce, Tourism Division, Post Office Box 12728, Austin, Tex. 78711; 800-888-8839 or 512-462-9191

Utah Travel Council, Council Hall, Capitol Hill, Salt Lake City, Utah 84114; 801-538-1030

Vermont Travel Division, 134 State Street, Montpelier, Vt. 05602; 800-528-4554 or 802-828-3236

Virginia Division of Tourism, 1021 East Cary Street, Richmond, Va. 23219; 800-847-4882 or 804-786-4484

Washington State Tourism, Post Office Box 42513, Olympia, Wash. 98504; 800-544-1800, 206-586-2088

West Virginia Division of Tourism and Parks, 1900 Washington Street East, Building 6, Charleston, W.Va. 25305; 800-225-5982 or 304-558-2200

Wisconsin Division of Tourism Development, Post Office Box 7606, Madison, Wis. 53707; 800-432-8747, 800-372-2737 or 608-266-2161

Wyoming Division of Tourism, I-25 at College Drive, Cheyenne, Wyo. 82002; 800-225-5996 or 307-777-7777

Canada

Travel Alberta, 3rd floor, City Center, 10155 102d Street, Edmonton, Alberta, Canada T5J 4L6; 800-661-8888 or 403-427-4321

Tourism British Columbia, 1117 Wharf Street, Victoria, British Columbia, Canada V8W 2X2; 800-663-6000

Travel Manitoba, Department 20, 7th floor, 155 Carlton Street, Winnipeg, Manitoba, Canada R3C 3H8; 800-665-0040 or 204-945-3777

Tourism New Brunswick, Post Office Box 12345, Fredericton, New Brunswick, Canada E3B 5C3; 800-561-0123

Newfoundland and Labrador Tourism Branch, Post Office Box 8730, St. John's, Newfoundland, Canada A1B 4K2; 800-563-6353 or 709-729-2830

Northwest Territories, Travel-Arctic, Post Office Box 1320, Yellowknife, Northwest Territories, Canada X1A 2L9; 800-661-0788

Nova Scotia Department of Tourism and Culture, Post Office Box 130, Halifax, Nova Scotia, Canada B3J 2M7; 800-341-6096

Ontario Travel, Queen's Park, Toronto, Ontario, Canada M7A 2E5; 800-668-2746 or 416-314-0944

Prince Edward Island Department of Tourism and Parks, Post Office Box 940, Charlottetown, Prince Edward Island, Canada C1A 7M5; 800-565-0267 or 902-368-4444

Tourisme Quebec, C.P. 979, Montreal, Quebec, Canada H3C 2W3; 800-363-7777

Tourism Saskatchewan, 1919 Saskatchewan Drive, Regina, Saskatchewan, Canada S4P 3V7; 800-667-7191 or 306-787-2300

Tourism Yukon, Post Office Box 2703, Whitehorse, Yukon, Canada Y1A 2C6; 403-667-5340

Stepping Lightly

Tourism with a light impact on the environment, or "eco-tourism," is finally coming to the fore, a reflection of a real concern for the condition of forests, beaches, dunes, clean water. Two high-country chalets in Glacier National Park built by the Great Northern Railway, Sperry and Granite Park, have been closed because without plumbing and a treatment facility untreated human wastes were being dumped back into the wilderness, where they attracted bears and polluted the water.

Everyone remembers Ray Bradbury's science fiction story where a trip into the past is conducted with the strict proviso that no one may walk off the designated path. Someone steps on a butterfly nonetheless and when the protagonists return to their own era, everything is utterly changed. When I see boardwalks in the Muir Woods, the netting holding the side of Mount Rainier, the snow fences buried in the Cape Cod dunes, I feel the same way. The constrictions are awful, the unusability of Glacier Park chalets is a pity, but to have none of this survive for our grandchildren would be worse.

Which brings me to a practical project conducted by a woman I admire, Kay Showker, a travel writer. Ms. Showker, in bravely undertaking to write *The 100 Best Resorts of the Caribbean* (Globe Pequot Press, 1993), prepared a questionnaire for the resorts to learn how certain environmental matters were handled. She acknowledges that no international standards exist and that she is no expert, but she asked the resorts to respond to questions about recycling gray water, use of plastic cups, water-saving showerheads, aerosols with fluorocarbons, avoiding air-conditioning where sea breezes were available and similar questions. Seventy-five resorts responded. Ms. Showker awarded "green leaves" to 20 as a starting point. "Without exception," Ms. Showker said, her respondents welcomed the questionnaire. Some resorts said the questionnaire itself alerted them to other things to be done.

She said that she would send copies of the questionnaire to readers of her book who requested it and would welcome suggestions. Caribbean tourism depends totally on beautiful beaches and clear water and this sort of work can improve awareness all around.

Environmentally aware tourists know what they are looking for, but as one of the organizers of the Clearwater project to clean up the Hudson River said, you have to engage in a dialogue before you start complaining about your new supporter's plastic straws. Or, to phrase it another way, before you object to the helium balloons that will be let loose at your neighbor's party have a solution in mind: Be sure they are tied down, and at the conclusion of the party give everyone a pin and let them puncture the balloons and collect the waste.

Stuck at the Airport

No airline guarantees its schedule. The airlines say it, and the government says it. I could have embroidered a pillow with that caveat on it in the hours I have spent stuck in airports.

What this means is that if you miss that big contract, or that overseas flight, the wedding or the funeral because the plane is late, whatever the airline's problem the airline is not going to make it good to you. If there is an utterly essential engagement at your destination, do not cut your schedule so tight that any delay will throw it off. Take an extra day. If you are traveling on an emergency basis, the stranding will make the emergency worse, but the airline will not settle money on you on that account.

If you are stranded at your home airport because a flight is canceled late in the evening, the airline expects you to go back home and return for your next scheduled shot at getting where you are going. If your home airport is a long way away, and the trip back impossible, the airline is not concerned. However, you can ask the airline to recommend an airport hotel; they all have hotel rooms on tap. Mind you, you will have to pay for your room, but you might get a nicer room if the airline reservation clerk is willing to book it for you.

If you are stranded midtrip by weather or safety problems, as many on the East Coast were by a blizzard in 1993, the airline may or may not take care of you. Officers of American Airlines, which was not in bankruptcy, described to the *Times* the care the line lavished on its stranded travelers in that storm, only to be hit with a blast of chapter-and-verse letters about neglect, rudeness, lack of housing and food. American apologized. So an airline's policy and the behavior of its personnel may be two different things. If you are stuck and no one offers any help, ask the airline what it can do for you. At a minimum, ask for a phone call to the people who are meeting you and a voucher for a meal. If another airline has a flight to your destination, ask to be transferred. If you face a night at the airport and the line offers only a blanket of uncertain provenance, you have little recourse.

Delta has a reputation for holding connecting flights when the feeder flight is late (its flight delay reports from the Department of Transportation reflect this), but I was stranded in Dallas–Fort Worth once for a narrow miss when I had allowed 45 minutes for the connection. Sometimes, I was told, flights have to meet an airport noise curfew and late-night flights may be less likely to wait for straggling feeder flights. Delta gave me and all the rest of the continuing passengers an overnight kit and a hotel room with breakfast, a free phone call and a jitney ride to and from the hotel. I did not consider that bad treatment, particularly when I got a corner room for showing my membership card in the hotel chain's frequent stay program. Of course, I was only 15 minutes late for my talk the next day, so my attitude was softened.

Sometimes, a cancellation will bring a rebooking on the first available flight and you may get to travel first class as a consolation. And, rarely, you will get a bonus of a flight coupon to be used later.

Mostly, though, it is just a wretched situation. Your best hope is that the personnel will be courteous and sympathetic and try to do something within the line's policy rules, but working for airlines these days does not appear to create invariably amiable agents.

Student Fares

Student fares come in two essential varieties. Simplest are the tickets sold by airlines three days before departure to travelers under age 26. Often these fares are the same as the fare-war fares but without the requirement for advance purchase.

The other type is sold by agencies that specialize in student travel, of which the two biggest are Council Travel, which has more than 40 offices nationally, and S.T.A.—the initials no longer stand for student travel agency—which has 10 offices in the United States and 110 overseas. These student fares are a result of negotiations between the agency and the airlines; airline sales people usually have no idea what the fares are or where they may be obtained. To keep business travelers from latching on to the cheap tickets, the airlines specify the maximum age of a traveler to whom a student ticket may be sold and ask that age and status be verified. Some contracts permit sales for spouses beyond the allowable student age, some allow teachers and school administrators to get the reduced fares.

Status is verified through the Student Identity Card, which is issued in many countries to young people from 12 up. This card costs $15 and is sold by most agencies that deal in student travel; it is based on a bursar's receipt or registrar's declaration or other document and is valid for a year. For young people who are not students, there is an International Youth Card, and there is also an International Teacher Identity Card. They all provide sickness and injury insurance.

Council and S.T.A., which are also **consolidators**, sell cheap charter flights and air-land packages where no age limits are specified. In the spring break travel period, they move stadiumloads of students to Daytona Beach, Cancún, Negril, Jamaica and wherever else it is happening. Both issue brochures, and Council, which is the business subsidiary of the nonprofit Council on International Educational Exchange, issues a catalogue of its books, ID cards and other programs. Council: outside New York, 800-743-1823; in New York, 212-661-1450. S.T.A.: outside New York, 800-777-0112; in New York, 212-477-7166.

Suite Hotels

About 1986, when motels were still being built hand over fist rather than being bought from other chains and renamed, the all-suite motel looked like the hottest thing going. When the recession began, they suffered the same squeeze that the rest of the hotel industry suffered. But if you are going to travel with a passel of kids, they are worth looking at.

When you consider that the average hotel-motel room is 300 square feet—that is, 15 by 20 feet—and probably contains two queen-sized beds, you know you are going to get a night of togetherness, particularly when you see those beady eyes at the edge of the covers peeking at the late-night TV along with you.

A suite may provide a better way, particularly since they often have two television sets and a refrigerator as opposed to a mini-bar. The suite may not be two rooms but two areas divided by a waist-high planter, so ask before you try. The biggest chain, Embassy Suites, which appealed to me because it took a leading role in training employees for the Americans With Disabilities Act, also undertook to make one floor child-safe—bumpers on coffee-table corners, inflated covers for the hot-water taps, a supply of peanut butter and bread in the refrigerator—but the plan does not seem to have expanded beyond the first year. If an Embassy Suite is your choice, ask if it has a childproofed room.

Other big chains in the field catering to families on vacation, as opposed to people making an extended stay, are Radisson Hotels, Guest Quarters Suites, Crown Sterling Suites, Comfort Suites, Lexington Suites and Marriott Suites. The average daily rates are higher than regular motels, but, then, they have been busier than regular motels.

Some hotels and motels that do not consist entirely of suites have "summer programs" that rent a second, adjoining room for half the price of the first room. This provides the same benefits as a suite. A price comparison is worthwhile, particularly if you sense that the hotel might lower its price to get your business.

In any case, if you are traveling with family it never hurts to ask a hotel or motel if it has a suite available and what it would cost.

Sun

"The most prevalent health hazard in the Caribbean," the State Department says tartly in "Tips for Travelers in the Caribbean," is one you can avoid: overexposure to the sun. It does not delve deeply into the matter except to recommend a shirt over the bathing suit for snorkeling, which I have certainly found to be essential. I will go a couple of steps further.

The Caribbean is not the only place where the problem is prevalent; tennis courts and swimming pools in gritty cities will give you the same problems of overexposure if you do not prepare, and with anxiety about the ozone layer the problem has intensified. Sunburn and sun poisoning are only overtures to basal cell carcinomas and worse. Almost everyone in my family has a little something taken off the face regularly, and we now worship the sun with far more deference than in our youth.

One more item: The number on the sunscreen signifies how much additional time you can stay in the sun if you use the screen. If you could endure the sun without burning one minute with no anointing, you can stand it for 15 minutes wearing No. 15.

Well, one more: Wear a wide-brimmed hat if you treasure your hair.

Survival Overseas

This issue should be put sharply into perspective, although people resist it. Most American leisure travelers who die overseas die of what they would have died of at home: heart disease, upper respiratory infections and chronic diseases, like diabetes, that are not being controlled. But a solid 25 percent of the deaths of travelers overseas are caused by injuries, 27 percent of these deriving from traffic accidents.

People resist these facts. Dr. Larry W. Rumans, a specialist in internal and tropical medicine in Topeka, Kansas, and three colleagues did a survey of what people thought was going to get them on a trip. They used as subjects 100 clients of a travel clinic in San Diego who were at least 60 years old and who planned trips to Europe, Africa and Asia. They were given a questionnaire listing six choices as the "greatest threats to life during international travel." An airplane crash ranked first, picked by 45 travelers. Then a road or auto accident, with 19; malaria, 18; AIDS, 12; and diarrhea or dysentery, 6. The Rumans study pointed to a need to prepare travelers more thoroughly for the hazards they are likely to meet.

The death rate from injuries is higher than at home because foreign roads and traffic rules are different, people drive faster, there may be lax law enforcement. In addition, perhaps in pursuit of adventure—or renewed youth—people take more chances on vacations: They rent cars without seatbelts, or they act like fools and race off on a motorcycle or moped for the first time, and without a helmet. Years ago, a classmate of mine died in a motorcycle accident on his tour of duty for the State Department in Africa, and for a long time I believed that this was a terrible fluke that snuffed out a brilliant career; it turns out that in one of the few groups of overseas Americans whose mortality rates and causes of death are studied, Peace Corps workers, the death rate in motorcycle accidents is quite high. Too tired, too late, too lonely, they speed off on Saturday nights and die in the effort.

The meager research on death overseas among American travelers and expatriates produces statistics that show that avoiding accidents—now described, intelligently, I think, as "preventing injuries"—is the first line of defense for the traveler overseas. It is also the second line, because the injections and blood transfusions that often follow injuries present a hazard of their own.

Dr. Stephen W. Hargarten of the Medical College of Wisconsin in Milwaukee and two other physicians conducted a study in 1992 of American civilian deaths overseas and it is one of the few windows into this obscure area. The National Center for Health Statistics does not record or analyze these data, so Hargarten and his colleagues went into the correspondence files of the Passport Office, where consular offices overseas report the deaths of Americans that are reported to them—and not all are. They analyzed two years, 1975 and 1984, the most recent year then available. There were 10,000 deaths reported in the two years, 5,453 in 1975 and 4,677 in 1984.

"Deaths from infectious disease were expected to be a major category of mortality, particularly in the less-developed countries of the world where Americans lived or traveled," the researchers wrote in Public Health Reports for March-April 1992. "However, there were only 169 deaths in the . . . classification. . . . (less than 2 percent of all deaths for both years.)"

They reported finding only five deaths from malaria, typhoid fever and leptospirosis—that is, infection from sewage or bad water. Three people contracted malaria overseas and died at home.

On the other hand, injury death rates, principally from auto accidents and drownings, were greater than anticipated. The injury death rate for American men traveling or living in developing countries was 130 to 175 per 100,000, depending on age, but higher in all cases than at home, where it ranged around 100 per 100,000. However, in developed countries, travelers and expatriates showed an accidental death rate of less than 100 per 100,000. One factor in this variation is the impact of adventure travel and the rougher forms of transport generally found in the third world. The researchers also said that the lower rate for travelers in Europe was parallel to the lower accidental death rate found at home among people with money and status. One might extrapolate from this that richer travelers to Europe probably hire a driver or stay over at the chateau if they plan to swill too much champagne.

Cancer death rates were markedly lower overseas than at home, which does not mean that travel will save you but only that terribly sick people are less likely to travel. However, for those with a taste for the wry there is one semihidden aspect of cruise travel: People who are dying sometimes decide that they would prefer to die at sea, away from home concerns and while being pampered by an attentive staff. Cunard learned too late of this fact, and at one travel health conference it was reported that the four-place mortuary of the *QE2* was not always adequate to the vessel's need. Freighters that take a few passengers also sometimes carry the dying on their last voyages, because the itineraries are long and leisurely and the absence of a physician aboard does not trouble people who have made this choice. Some people find this grim, but as I get older it sounds like a rather affirmative choice if the money is available.

At the end of their research into how people die overseas,

Dr. Hargarten and his colleagues said: "Travelers should avoid motorcycles; small, less protective motor vehicles; and small, nonscheduled aircraft. They should use seat belts and should not swim in unfamiliar waters." Although tropical diseases "are not an important cause of death," they pointed out that although you might not die of malaria you can certainly get very sick from it, and many do, and proper precautions should be taken in advance.

Dr. Hans Lobel, a malaria expert at the Centers for Disease Control and Prevention, who is an officer and founder of the recently formed Association for International Travel Medicine, was asked to compress a lifetime of knowledge into a single piece of advice for health while overseas and his conclusions were roughly the same. "Buckle your seat belt and take your condoms," he said.

The comparative dangers of getting AIDS in medical treatment and through sexual contact, by the way, are illustrated by 1992 figures from Britain: 429 travelers returned home infected with HIV after heterosexual sexual contacts aboard; 25 HIV infections and 5 AIDS cases in returned travelers were attributed to blood transfusions.

Translate Lobel's pithy advice however you like but the underlying message of a man whose field is malaria is that most travelers can avoid the mortal threats in travel by commonsense steps. The rest is scare advertising.

Swimming

Salt water should not be a threat to your health except for overdeveloped shores on the Mediterranean. But if you are overseas and considering entering fresh water you have not met before—pond, lake or stream—the water is likely to be what one medical expert described as "thinned sewage," and should be avoided. If a hotel's other standards seem good, the pool is probably okay. One doctor said she felt safe if she could smell the chlorine. Because you are not likely to put your face into a whirlpool bath you probably need not worry so much, but if your skin is broken someplace you may want to skip it. For either the pool or the whirlpool, wash off before and afterward.

Symbols

Below is a selection of graphic symbols used internationally in public places and highways to identify the sites of toilets, to indicate wheelchair accessibility, to show the way to hospitals and a new one, to indicate an automatic teller machine, or A.T.M. They are here as a last resort; if you can't make yourself understood, point to the sign and see if that helps.

Telephone	Currency Exchange	First Aid
Lost and Found	Baggage Locker	Elevator
Toilets	Information	Hotel Information

Taxi

Bus

Rail Transportation

Air Transportation

Car Rental

Restaurant

Baggage Check-in

Baggage Claim

Customs

Immigration

Smoking

Parking

Handicapped

Gas Station

Picnic Area

Hospital

**Hearing Impaired
Services**

Amplified Telephones

**Telecommunication
Devices for the Deaf
(TDDs)**

Services for the Blind

**Automatic Teller
Machine
(A.T.M.)**

Alan Stillman, an enterprising entrepreneur, has created a folding color-printed card called Quickpoint, with a variety of more complex graphic designs: film developing, fried or boiled food, haircuts, and the like. To aid vegetarians, he has a picture of a raw steak with a bar line across it. He uses the same device with a saltcellar and a sugar spoon for those dietary preferences. Stillman said he devised the card after a bicycle trip of two and a half years during which he carried five pounds of dictionaries. It fits into a business envelope and is sold by mail order for $5 by Gaia Communications, Box 239, Alexandria, Va. 22313; for information, 703-548-8794.

For another means of inching your way across the communications gap, see **cabs in a strange language**.

Tetanus

The Centers for Disease Control and Prevention note that 117 cases of tetanus were reported in the United States in 1989 and 90, of which 24 percent were fatal. Just another statistic, except for a couple of facts: The risk for tetanus is greater for people over 60 who lack protective levels of anti-toxin; and the initial tetanus toxoid shot or booster protects for 10 years. Immunization is easy; the disease is dreadful. So if you are preparing for travel, most particularly adventure travel overseas where tetanus may be prevalent, get a booster.

People going on safari or into other places where scratches and wounds are common should particularly heed this warning; a splinter can do it. Because animal wastes may contain tetanus toxins, if your travel takes you into woods and meadows that have been used as pasture, tetanus toxoid is important. The shot is usually given with a diphtheria toxoid, which is not such a bad idea either, particularly if you are traveling to the former Soviet Union where diphtheria has had a resurgence. (See **Russia.**)

Third World Duty-Free Goods

Most people do not know that a large number of items made in the developing world may be brought home free of United States duty beyond the provisions of the $400 exemption or whatever level may apply. Baskets made of rattan or willow from Senegal, unset jade from Taiwan, toys from Israel, records and tapes from Trinidad and Tobago, coral jewelry from Barbados—all are on the list. If you are visiting in the developing world and something locally made appeals to you strongly, you may be in luck.

These come in duty-free under a rule called the Generalized System of Preferences, established in 1978, intended to encourage commercial importers to buy 2,800 specified products from more than 100 developing nations.

To learn if you are visiting a country that qualifies and which products from that country are on the list, you need a leaflet called "G.S.P. and the Traveler." This, along with a booklet called "Know Before You Go, Customs Hints for Returning Residents," a booklet on trademarked goods and a third one on mail imports is in a "travel pack" that the Customs Service will send on request. Write to your local Customs or regional office. Information is given under **Customs**.

The G.S.P. leaflet explains that the goods must also meet other Customs and Fish and Wildlife Service requirements. As you suspected, items made of ivory, skin, fur, tortoiseshell or whalebone are dubious. Unless you have confirmed in advance that they are legal, you will lose a fight with the Fish and Wildlife people at the Customs barrier. There are other items that are off the list, period: shoes, clothing and other products made of textiles, watches, some electronic devices and certain glass and steel products.

Other than that, the general idea is that the item was "grown, manufactured or produced" in the developing country and that it was bought there. Some countries are so poor that they must import their raw materials, but if the item is "substantially transformed" in the process and derives at least 35 percent of its value from this transformation, in the view of a legal expert for the Customs Service, it will qualify. Be aware that food items have their own series of limitations, controlled by the Department of Agriculture, and this is not a matter of duty but a matter of entry.

Toothbrushing

If the water's no good to drink, it's no good for toothbrushing either. If you do not have a jug of mouthwash, get bottled mineral water, or ask for a pitcher of boiled water for your room. I have brushed my teeth with beer, but you do not feel like a toothpaste commercial afterward.

Tour-ese

Hotel arcana (see **advertising, how to translate**) are nothing to the nuances in a brochure for a conducted tour, especially one where you are bused from place to place. I am grateful to Trafalgar Tours of New York and its amazing boss, Nigel Osborne, for a lot of this revealing material. Trafalgar, which is huge, generates a proportionate amount of angry customer mail, but Osborne is mercifully direct in answering it. We fouled up, he says. Or, we didn't realize what kind of pressure on European hotels would be created by a season with the World Cup, the Oberammergau passion play and the Van Gogh exhibition.

His company published a leaflet in which the veils of obscurity were lifted on the differences between the terms *visit*, *view* and *see* and he gave this information away to clients and anyone else who asked. Why? He said his salespeople were wasting too much time on the phone explaining to prospective customers what to expect. I believe him.

Motorcoach.

One glossary (not Trafalgar's) called this a "huge highway passenger vehicle used to perform any travel service other than scheduled transportation for individually ticketed passengers." Folks, it's a bus. It probably carries 40 to 50 people. Does it have a toilet, or euphemistically, a lavatory? Ask.

Tour means you will get out and get a walk around Notre-Dame, for example, with a guide, or possibly that the bus will cover Antietam, probably with an informed commentator, rather than speed past or through it. I think a tour of a big museum show with a docent or art historian adds immeasurably to the experience, and I still feel gratitude to the Protestant nuns from the Foyer Unitas in Rome who in half an hour turned me into a lifetime devotee of the Pantheon. I guess I am a tour-ist.

Visit, on the other hand, means that your bus will stop a sufficient time for you to see the attraction, but that may be it.

View, on still another hand, probably means you will get a chance to take a picture or make a brief stop. It will not be a pit stop, you may be sure.

See means you will if you don't blink your eyes. The bus will pass this place. Glimpse might be more precise. "Yes, I saw the Opera House in Vienna." You are not lying, technically.

Why not see or perhaps enjoy. These locutions mean that the item is not on the paid-for itinerary. Trafalgar Tours codified these two, siblings of available. They all mean that you can get a tour or a visit on your own, or for an extra payment. My belief is that if a brochure contains a color photo of a place for which the caption is "Why not see the Pyramids" or "Perhaps you will want to enjoy a bateau mouche," you are probably in for disappointment all around. But you are warned, at any rate.

Tour Operator Default

This mouthful means that you paid for a package trip, including airfare, hotels, meals, bus transportation—the works— and the operator has ceased to operate: is gone, kaput, defaulted, bankrupt, history. This can happen before you ever get your trip, as it did in the spring of 1993 to the student clients of Milestone Educational Institute of Massachusetts, where millions of dollars saved from baby-sitting and car washes disappeared. Or it can happen while you are on the trip, as it did to many clients of Hemphill Harris Travel of Encino, California, when it turned off the faucet in October 1989, abandoning tour groups in Australia, New Zealand, Japan and India.

Each case has its own intricacies, and attorneys general and lawyers have pounded away on these details. But in the preventive department, the lines are pretty simple.

When you or your travel agent selects a tour company, ask if it is a member of the U.S. Tour Operators Association. The travel industries are full of trade associations, most of which I have found are not very helpful to the consumer. But this group has value because it requires its members to maintain a protection fund to make refunds to travel agents and travelers if the member company defaults. This organization does not have many members and they are all big companies. In fact, Hemphill Harris was a member although the membership was on the brink of ending because the company had changed hands and the rules require a certain number of years under the same ownership. If there is any doubt in your mind, call U.S.T.O.A., 211 East 51st Street, New York, N.Y. 10022; 212-944-5727 and ask. When the organization was maintaining a $5 million pooled fund, it was drained a couple of times by big defaults but then replenished each year by premium payments from member companies. The system now requires each company to provide its own fund, not touchable except by those who need refunds after a collapse.

If your travel agent has been hearing rumbles about your tour operator, you may want to reconsider if it is not a member of U.S.T.O.A., or in the case of a bus tour a member of the National Tour Association, which maintains a smaller fund to pay up to $100,000 to clients of one of its members in the event of default (National Tour Association, 546 East Main Street, Lexington, Ky. 40596; 606-253-1036). If the operator responds that it uses an escrow account to hold your money until you get your trip and you or the agent is still dubious, call the escrow bank and check it out.

Whatever you buy, pay with a credit card if you can. If the company goes away before you have paid for your trip, don't pay. If you have paid, call the credit card company and ask for a charge-back. This may work or may not.

Buy a **cancellation insurance** policy or **emergency evacuation** policy that also covers for default or bankruptcy. You have to read the small type to learn about this, and it is not a universal feature. Do not buy the policy from the tour company you are going to use because this will void the default coverage. Most specifically, do not buy a **waiver** or some similarly titled offering from the tour operator. Hemphill Harris, at the time of its default, had been selling cancellation "protection plans" to clients for $50 each and this money went down the tubes with the rest of the company.

Travel Agents—Whose?

A really nice question, in the legal sense: Whom does the travel agent represent, the traveler or the airline? Historically, the travel agent is the authorized representative of the airline, cruise line or railroad. But the agent has also been ruled liable for not acting in behalf of the traveler—by with-holding information, for example. I will skip the legal deci-sions in this area because there are a lot more to come, particularly in instances when a tour operator defaults and agents have been selling bookings over the sounds of the death rattles in the backroom.

The questions I get asked are: Should I use a travel agent, and who is *your* travel agent?

I think it's silly not to use a travel agent. A travel agent will put the trip together for you, allowing enough time for airport connections, finding good fares, cheap auto rental rates and remembering to specify you want a nonsmoking room overlooking the pool. If you use the same agent, these preferences will be in the computer along with your frequent flier numbers and your credit card numbers, so the whole thing can be wrapped up quickly.

One of the things I most value is the computer printout of the itinerary, which gives flight numbers, ticket numbers, reservation confirmation numbers, hotel phone numbers and addresses and all other pertinent details. If I leave a copy with my relatives, they can reach me in an emergency. Most of these services are free because the airline commissions and, optimistically, the hotel commissions pay the travel agent. A travel agent can put together an independent tour for you or can shop for a package tour that will come close to your needs.

A travel agent may have enough influence with an airline to rewrite your ticket to the new sale price without having you pay the fee for changing that eats up the saving.

Everytime I report a story about student groups stranded in Madrid or defrauded of their car wash money, I wonder why the teacher who arranged the trip did not call in local agents, present their needs and pick one to do the job. A local company must continue to operate in town and face parents and teachers, and for its 10 percent or so commission on the total cost the agent can do research about the stability of the tour company and its escrow accounts as well as the quality of the hotels. The arrangement of having one teacher travel free for each 10 students is not precluded when an agent does the work; the agent can negotiate this, too.

But if you want to have a friend at the agency, be a friend. Suburban agents have told me they have researched a cruise right down to the cholesterol in the hors d'oeuvre only to have the client place the order with an agency with a bigger discount. If you avoid this sort of unfair behavior, you can have an agent who will bail you out in an emergency or put together a complicated trip with many meshing pieces. In any case, if you are determined to use a call-'em-up-and-order-the-ticket agent do the research yourself, don't use the time of your regular agent and then buy elsewhere. (Yes, I believe in R.S.V.P.s for dinner invitations, too.)

Big agency or small? Find out who wants your business. I would go in in person and test the water. The number of agency offices has grown explosively since computer reservation systems, or C.R.S.s, came to the business in 1976, and corporations began to rely on agencies to book business travel. So you may get a local office of a big company, or a small company that belongs to a big co-op network, to take advantage of its discounts. American Express is the biggest in the country at this writing, followed by Carlson, Rosenbluth and Thomas Cook. If you find a local office of one of these, with an agent who lives in your neighborhood or whose child baby-sits for you, you have an obvious place to start. The small agency with a computer reservation system can give you everything the big one can except probably for deep cruise discounts, so there is another choice. Agencies that do not book airlines but only bus and train trips may not have computers.

Who's my agent? Over the years, I have had three, not counting the people at the *Times* who formerly made bookings for me on trips when I was not traveling anonymously. All were recommended by friends or relatives who continued to use them. I trust my current agent implicitly and we exchange a lot of professional information on the phone. No, my requests are not handled by the head of the office and I get no special favors. Friends who travel even more than I do likewise view their agents as friends and essential resources, so I have no reason to press the case of my agent over theirs. I do know from interviewing a lot of my friends' agents that tastes and personality are important in a good match.

What are the characteristics of my agent? The office is near mine so I can get there on my lunch hour. There is a fax so I can send complex requests in writing. When I say I want a written confirmation of a hotel reservation, I receive a fax copy promptly. I get the usual two copies of my itinerary. When my agent is on vacation, someone else in the office knows what to do and where the ticket has been filed. The agency has emergency 800 numbers that can be reached from all over the world. He is also not too proud to take a good suggestion from an amateur.

If you want an agent, you probably want one like this. Ask a friend.

Travel Health Clinic

When this book was planned, it was to include a national list of travel health clinics that were qualified to help you prepare for a trip, particularly to the tropics or other places in the third world. Never mind. There are 500-odd in operation now and I eventually realized that a whole book could be consumed with such a list.

To find a good clinic, call a nearby medical center or teaching hospital and ask. If this doesn't work, call a tropical medicine specialist—most travel clinics must be able to cope with malaria and yellow fever—and ask someone at that office. You can ask your primary care doctor but, as one correspondent said, you must be ready to fend off assertions that Doc knows how to cope quite well with your needs or can simply look in a reference book. No reference book, even one published annually, is going to be up-to-date on recent epidemics overseas and phone calls to the right places are necessary for fresh information.

Of course, there are clinics and there are clinics. When you call a recommended clinic, ask when it was established and how many patients it sees in a year. Long Island Jewish Hospital's Travel Immunization Center in New Hyde Park, New York, was seeing up to 4,000 clients yearly in the early nineties; the Travel Well Clinic at Emory University in Atlanta, which has close ties to the federal Centers for Disease Control and Prevention, 1,200. Areas with fewer people who travel are not going to show anything like these numbers, of course. Bigger numbers should indicate greater expertise and also probably a greater diversity of vaccines on hand.

Your next question should be the cost of an initial visit and the cost of a basic shot. You can pick any one you like, but tetanus is probably the easiest if you want to compare costs of various clinics: It can range from $10 up. The new vaccine for Japanese encephalitis is probably going to cost $50 a shot, and three are given over 30 days. This is a case, however, where a clinic with a bigger practice will be able to charge a lot less; the vaccine, Je-Vax, can be bought cheaper in bulk but has a short life once the pack is opened. This is not a shot for everyone going to Asia, only people who will be in rural areas, or are staying for a long time.

In any case, be smart. A cost of $3,500 a person for a wild-life tour of India or a long trip to China is not unreasonable these days. Is it really wise to scrimp on the $300 or so it will cost to get good medical preparation for the trip? If you want to look at it that way, some of these shots are probably valuable for you whether you travel or not. See **tetanus** to learn what I mean.

As the optimal 30-day span for giving encephalitis vaccine and the optimal two-week period for diphtheria antibodies to build up indicate, you should schedule your first clinic visit well before your departure. Some shots can be given together, but some mask the value of others and must be given in sequence. Be sure you have your exact itinerary because some nations require or do not require yellow fever immunization depending on which countries you have recently visited. A good clinic will give you a good interview and some sheets or pamphlets of advice. A really top-notch clinic will see you on your return and ask about everything, both for your protection and for the clinic's guidance in assisting others. (See **health overseas**.)

If you are having no luck finding a clinic near you, Dr. Leonard Marcus, a leading member of the International Society of Travel Medicine and an official of the tropical medicine society, has prepared a list of 100 clinics in the U.S. and overseas. The tropical medicine society, the professional orga-

nization of most travel clinic directors, does not have a certification for travel medicine specialist, so a list like Dr.
Marcus's carries no one's imprimatur at the moment. Dr.
Marcus urges that prospective patients do their own checking, too. Are people in the clinic experienced in diagnosing
and treating tropical diseases? After all, he says, even someone who is taking malaria prophylaxis can still get malaria
and correct diagnosis is essential to recovery. Have people in
the clinic lived and worked overseas?

The typed list gives an alphabetical directory of physicians
and their clinics, and a listing alphabetized by state and town.
Authorization to give yellow fever shots is noted. To receive
the list, send a self-addressed 9-by-11-inch envelope with 98
cents postage to: Dr. Leonard C. Marcus, Travelers Health
and Immunization Service, 148 Highland Avenue, Newton,
Mass. 02115.

Twilight Time

When I was a nubile maiden, this was a wonderful song
played by a music group called the Three Suns "from the
lounge of the Piccadilly Hotel in Times Square." More than
one thing has changed. To me, twilight now means a dangerous time to drive an auto. Not so dangerous as night but still
fraught. Put on your headlights promptly. My husband is a
consensus person and puts them on when he sees 10 oncoming cars with lights on, but I am self-assertive and like to be
one of those 10.

Little by little, research is beginning to persuade U.S.
safety and legislative experts that the use of "day running
lights," or headlights in broad daylight, is a safety plus. Two
studies in Canada showing reductions in head-on crashes pro-

duced legislation requiring that all autos models from 1990 on automatically turn on the lights with the ignition.

In the United States, a number of states now specify that lights must be turned on if windshield wipers are needed or if a storm without rain turns the sky dark. In 1993, the National Highway Traffic Safety Administration issued a ruling that permitted automakers to offer new cars with a feature like the Canadians'. In addition, a device may now be bought and professionally installed to turn the headlights on with the ignition or with the windshield wipers. It illuminates the beams at a lesser, lower level than regular night headlights, saving fuel and bulbs as well as reducing the impact on the environment.

Dr. Frank Kennel, the former director of traffic safety for the A.A.A. who wired his car this way early on, said the only disadvantage of having lights on in daytime is now he is no longer able to be sure that the oncoming car that blinks its lights at him is giving the traditional highway warning of a police speed trap ahead. However, he said, since he does not speed it is not a real problem.

Since the Canadian legislation went into effect, those of us who drive in areas that attract a lot of Canadian cars have realized that headlights in daytime may not be solely a result of absentmindedness. It may be "lights on for safety."

Two-Second Rule

Driving experts say safety requires you keep two seconds of decision-making time between you and the auto in front of you. When that car passes a signpost, start counting and you should be able to count one thousand one, one thousand two before you pass the same post. Teachers point out that it take two seconds for you to absorb the information, for instance, that the front car has gone into a skid, make a decision and act on it. This has to do with time, not speed. If you are over 50 years old, give yourself three seconds. The synapses are slowing down.

Ukraine

If you plan a trip to Kiev, Ukraine, see entry on **Russia** for health information.

Visas

 Do not assume you know a country's visa requirement; these come and go. For a long time, most Caribbean countries required no visa and sun-hungry tourists took off from airports in the Northeast virtually on impulse. This is no longer so, and you can get surprised by being turned back before you leave or, worse, at the tropical airport on arrival.

Ask the travel agent specifically if you will need a visa; if you do not use a travel agent, call the State Department fax information line, 202-647-3000, on the phone attached to your fax and order "foreign entry requirements." Or you can call 202-647-5225 on a Touch-Tone phone and follow the instructions to hear about the requirements for the countries you are going to visit. You can learn about three countries per call. Or you can call the embassy or consulate of the country involved; the information on visas is usually reliable because they issue the visas. Do not, however, place any confidence in the information on inoculation requirements you receive from an embassy or consulate; see **immunization help by fax or phone** on this.

For business travelers with long itineraries, a stapled booklet Foreign Entry Requirements may be ordered for 50 cents from the Consumer Information Center, Pueblo, Colo. 81009.

This publication is revised frequently; don't use an old one. It is State Department publication 10046, and in Pueblo it is labeled Dept. 456Z.

If you are tight for time and cannot stand in a visa line, there are services that will do it for you for a fee. In New York, the yellow pages list 10 "passport and visa services." Travel Agenda, one of these, specializes in toughies like Eastern Europe, where extra fees now grease the wheels in a classic manifestation of capitalist economics, or is it capitalist politics?

One warning that cannot be repeated too often concerns travel to Mexico, and this material will also be found under the entry **Mexico by car**. If you are taking with you a child who does not carry a passport and the other parent is not going along, or if you are a grandparent, you must have a notarized letter of consent for the trip from the parent or parents. You may slide through 10 times, as one reader had, and get stopped the 11th time, causing loss of reservations, tickets and the works.

Some cruise lines, with their eyes on the legal difficulties of extradition, now require this certification. It is exasperating, but if you are involved in any custody dispute consider the alternative.

Waiver

Or penalty waivers. This term, sometimes printed in the "small type" page of a tour or cruise brochure, should itself be a warning since the overpriced collision damage waiver sold with auto rentals has become a cause célèbre. But someone bites every day.

At this writing, brochures from companies as prominent as Tauck Tours and Holland America Line include a bold-faced entry, "Waiver" or "Penalty Waiver" or some similar phrase of art. For a certain fee, the company selling you the tour or cruise agrees to forgo—waive—its own penalties if you cancel your reservation within a specified period.

However prettily embossed, this is not real insurance for several reasons:

One obvious reason is that no insurance pool is created with the charges, as in insurance. The operator is simply charging a fee to forgo collecting a possible penalty. Therefore, the payment of the waiver fee is no help if the company ceases operating, as the luxury operator Hemphill Harris did in 1989 in a noted recent case. The money paid for the waivers disappears along with everything else and there is nothing to refund to the customer. Many freestanding cancellation policies cover for the bankruptcy of the operator, providing you don't buy it from the operator.

Second, waivers also cease their effect before the trip begins, sometimes as much as three days ahead. This means they are worthless in the event of a last-minute cancellation where you are probably going to lose the whole payment for the trip.

Third, it probably has clauses that put holes in your protection. Two women traveling together bought their company's penalty waiver. One fell ill within the coverage period and was unable to make the trip; she lost only a modest administrative charge. The other woman decided to take the trip anyway but discovered that she now had to pay the single supplement rate for a single room, and the waiver, as is customary, offered no help on meeting this added expense.

Understand what a waiver is before you buy it. Sometimes, a brochure says only "ask about our penalty waiver," in which case get some real information quickly. If a waiver fits your needs, buy it, but I bet it won't. So leave yourself time to buy **cancellation insurance**.

Walked

This disagreeable piece of "hospitality industry" jargon means that the guest with a reservation—that's you and me —is sent to another, presumably comparable hotel because the original hotel has overbooked its rooms. It is also remotely possible that the hotel has messed up your reservation or has guests who did not leave when they told the hotel they would. I have heard hotel owners say that the computer program did not show a whole bunch of reservations but I have *my* reservations about that.

This has happened to me more than once, including one spring at a very pleasant place in Paris, the Hôtel des Saints Pères in the Latin Quarter, which friends had recommended highly. I was disappointed as well as humiliated.

What to do? On the spot, if you have a guaranteed reservation backed by a Visa, American Express, MasterCard or Diners Club card, your first night at the new hotel is going to be free. Your taxi, van or whatever to the new hotel should also be free. Tell the clerk that you know that a free first night is the policy, but even if you forget in your consternation you can write later and lodge your claim with the card company.

But you may not have a reservation number or a slip, nothing to establish your claim, which was my case in Paris, even though the *Times* had made the reservation and the clerk's disdainful remarks about my travel agent fell on unreceptive ears. Unless the city is full up, the hotel will probably pay for your trip to a sister hotel anyway, or to one nearby. You may want to delay deciding whether to come back to the original

hotel until you see the new one. In my Paris experience, the
hotel where I was sent, the Parc St.-Séverin, had a wonderful
view over a church garden that I would not have given up
and the prospect of facing the clerk again made me angry
anyway. The next time we had to stay in Paris, we returned
there and enjoyed it a lot.

The advent of the fax machine means that your travel
agent or you can probably get a confirmed reservation
quickly, which will keep the hotel clerk from trashing your
travel agent. Get paper if you possibly can.

If the hotel or the chain does not give a reservation number when you call to reserve a room, get the name of the
person you talked to. Once our kids were walked by a Days
Inn after a midnight arrival in Denver. When I called the
Days Inn in the morning to tell them we were setting out on
the 60-mile drive to pick them up, no one at the motel had
ever heard their name nor could find any record of the reservation I had made nor wished to hear my tale of woe from a
roadside pay phone: You must have the wrong place, they
said. I was fit to be tied, with my children and grandchildren
lost, facing calling every motel in that huge city. The only
thing that saved me was having noted the name of the
woman who had taken my reservation. That established that
I had the right motel and created enough credibility for
someone to go into the office, find a paper record of the ex-
punged reservation and the name of the motel where the
tired band of four had been dispatched at 1 A.M. In my private capacity, I wrote Days Inn and that letter got "lost,"
too, but eventually I got the money back for their motel
night and their breakfast together with an apology.

So write down a name if you do not get a number. For
some reason, big sections of the hospitality industry proceed

on the notion that the customer is usually wrong and is trying to cheat the hotel to boot.

Water

Few things make one feel more like an obnoxious American
than asking, in words or by demeanor, "Is the water safe?"
And safe is a relative term at best. As Rachel Carson taught
us, plenty of families who grew up in what is romantically
designated "the heartland of America" drank water that was
loaded with chemical runoff from the heavily fertilized and
treated fields. National efforts have been made to assure
pure water, but for years we were unaware of the human
price that might be paid for abundant crops.

However, the traveler's question does not comprehend
these now political issues but is directed to the possibility
that sewage and drinking water may be mixed and that travelers' **diarrhea** or worse may be the result.

If you are traveling in a part of the world where you have
doubts about the safety of the water supply but are staying
in a big elaborate hotel, you probably need not worry because
the hotel survives by caring for others like you who have not
built up an immunity to the local bugs. Take a bottle of hotel
water with you on your day trips if you like. If water in the
hotel is not working for periods of time, it is probably suspect. Ask for a pitcher of boiled or treated water for drinking
and toothbrushing.

If the whole matter is in doubt, find a way to boil your
water. You may find local people accustomed to this proce-
dure; a Chinese friend brought us a gift from his home in
Hangzhou, a giant-sized porcelain container contoured like a
tiny-spouted teapot that is used for cooling drinking water
that has been boiled. Get the water up to a vigorous boil and

let it cool, but don't add ice. If it is cloudy, boil it for five minutes. When it's cool, you can do something about the flat taste by pouring it from container to container or adding a pinch of salt.

If boiling is impossible, you can add iodine. Tablets with various trade names are available from sporting goods suppliers. Otherwise, add five drops of 2 percent tincture of iodine to each quart or liter of clear water; 10 drops if the water is cloudy. Let the water stand for 30 minutes. If the water is very cold, let it stand for several hours so the iodine works.

If none of this is possible, water that comes from the tap too hot to touch will probably be safer than cold water. Let it cool, of course.

One of the places not to drink the tap water is aboard an airplane, either in the bathroom or from those bulkhead dispensers. Airlines top off their tanks wherever it is convenient and inexpensive, and the mathematical possibilities of what you are drinking stagger the mind. Bring along bottled water to counteract that dry air, or request mineral water frequently.

Another place not to drink the water is from a stream. It goes against the American grain not to take a cooling drink from those sparkling waters, and it is further confusing to realize that the famous Sierra Club cup, built shallow and wide to dish up a drink from a stream without disturbing the sludge, is an encouragement to an unwise act. The parasite **giardia** lives in those waters, product of the animal life in the wilds, and giardiasis is nothing you want.

Everytime I have written in the column about water safety, I get bundles of literature from manufacturers of water filters, some of them pretty formidable instruments. The Centers for Disease Control and Prevention in Atlanta, and

Dr. Richard Dawood's authoritative book, *Travelers' Health: How to Stay Healthy All Over the World*, concur that no maker of a portable filter has reported on tests proving these gadgets make water safe to drink. The water may taste better and have fewer bits floating in it but it must still be boiled or otherwise treated. These two authoritative views enable a medical amateur like me to bypass discussion of filters with a clear conscience.

Weather Radio

The television weather channel is a popular feature of cable service, and often enough, when I check into a hotel, that's where the selector is set. Someone heading out wants to know what to look forward to.

Whatever the reasons, the National Oceanic and Atmospheric Administration radio broadcasts are less well known, although you can pick them up from a battery-powered weather radio even when the power has failed in a storm. This government agency has almost the perfect acronym, NOAA: You can almost see Noah himself, dispatching a dove to see if the storm has abated.

The inexpensive weather radio is a prominent item on our packing list for the beach. The broadcast from the nearest station of the agency comes in at 162.4 megahertz or thereabouts, but not on a car radio unless some rare local station is picking it up and rebroadcasting in a dead period. On the wall of my office, we have a barometer with a built-in weather radio, and when the going gets rough, someone turns it on to see if subway flooding is likely and then romantically continues on to hear about things in the Hudson Canyon and Watch Hill, Rhode Island. I ungrudgingly buy it

9-volt batteries just to hear that reassuring voice from the eye of the storm at Rockefeller Center.

Weather radios can cost as little as $15. If you are on the fringe of a broadcast radius, be sure you can return the device if it does not pick up where you plan to use it. A more expensive set may do the job. Swimmers, divers, dinghy sailors and others without costly equipment should carry a weather radio. Throw it in the suitcase if you are making an auto trip.

What's My Hotel?

Everyone—well, almost everyone who travels a lot—has had the experience of forgetting where they are staying. The harder you think, the more elusive the name. Sometimes, you remember a name and when you get there that is not the hotel at all. It may be the difference between the Parc St. Séverin and the St.-Séverin, or it may be the difference between Lambs Street and Lambs Conduit Street or Water Street and River Street. But you are lost and you feel like a character in a spooky movie.

The usual problem in finding your way back is that you left the hotel on one fork of a Y-shaped street and walked on down the main stem. Now you are returning on the sidewalk on the other side of the main stem and are being led out on the other fork. If the memory block is really bad, work backward in time until you come to a name or place you know will have a record. Your office. Call it. Your travel agent: Call collect to the emergency number you have.

This can be prevented. If you have a printed itinerary, keep a copy in your wallet or ask for a business card or postcard from the front desk and put it in your pocket when you leave. This will also give you the phone number. If you

are an all-day walker and museum visitor, let this become a
habit, like being sure you have the key in your hand before
you latch the front door.

Wheelchair Users

Two important laws are improving the ability of disabled to
participate more widely in travel: the Air Carrier Access Act
of 1986 and the Americans With Disabilities Act of 1990.

The A.D.A. is a broad civil rights act for all people who
have some impairment of a major life function, and it affects
employment, access to public buildings, hotel facilities and a
wide variety of transportation facilities. The hotel industry,
after fighting the whole idea, finally pitched in and has made
an effort to adapt its facilities and to train its employees. (My
favorite is a training film in which the waitress turns to the
person seated next to the wheelchair customer and says,
"What will he have?" and the wheelchair customer says, "I'll
tell you myself. It's my legs that don't work, not my mouth.")
Amtrak is chugging ahead. The bus industry got the longest
lead time for getting buses with lifts, presenting Congress
with cost arguments that the advocates for the disabled at-
tacked repeatedly. I consider this unfortunate because bus
travel is vital to many disabled people. But in a few years
from this writing, the piper must be paid.

The A.D.A. covers cruise ships that fly the U.S. flag, but
there are only two such at the moment, both in Hawaii. It is
unclear which agency will take the burden of requiring enforcement from the foreign-registered vessels that derive the
majority of their trade from U.S. travelers embarking at U.S.
ports.

The Air Carrier Access Act prohibited discrimination
against people with disabilities aboard U.S. airlines and in

facilities owned, leased or operated by those airlines. There is some overlap because Title II of A.D.A. covers public airports.

Here are some publications that are useful in understanding the laws and making them work for you:

"Air Carrier Access," published by the Eastern Paralyzed Veterans Association, is available free from the association, 75-20 Astoria Boulevard, Jackson Heights, N.Y. 11370, or regional offices in Buffalo and Philadelphia. This 32-page booklet, revised in 1993, goes step-by-step through the airport and getting aboard. Black-and-white pictures illustrate important points such as crossing your arms while riding in the boarding chair.

"Access Travel: Airports, a Guide to Accessibility of Terminals," published by the Airport Operators Council, is a big booklet of tables showing the facilities of 553 airports around the world. Parking, door widths, visual paging services, toilets, telecommunications phones and other important features are annotated. Single copies are available free from Consumer Information Center, Department 578Z, Pueblo, Colo. 81009.

"New Horizons for the Air Traveler With a Disability," published by the Department of Transportation, to some extent duplicates the Eastern Paralyzed Veterans booklet but it does not have pictures and does not use the easy-to-follow, question-and-answer format. It also costs money: 50 cents from the Consumer Information Center, Department 484Z, Pueblo, Colo. 81009.

An increasing number of travel agencies specialize in booking wheelchair users. For cruises, this is particularly important because cruise lines that say certain ships or cabins are accessible to wheelchairs are often stretching a point. For example, a ramp may be installed to get a chair over a ledge between the cabin and the toilet, but once the chair gets inside it may not be able to turn around. I have talked to wheelchair users at shipboard receptions and they have pointed to elevators that do not open onto decks containing major public areas. This sort of thing makes them cross, and I am on their side.

One specializing agency is Nautilus Tours, 5435 Donna Avenue, Tarzana, Calif. 91356. It publishes a newsletter called *Tide's In* (Travel Industry and Disabled Exchange) and will send a sample copy in return for a stamped, self-addressed business envelope.

Frances S. Rubiner at USTravel Systems, 2903 East Grant Avenue, Tucson, Ariz. 85716, is one of the most knowledgeable people I have talked to in this area. Like many such expert agents, she started in the field before computers and knows how to talk special cases through with the airline. Her advice is sound and she is one of the two or three leaders in opening up this area of travel. In mid-1993, she said that the possibilities for the disabled were now such that "we have progressed to walking from a crawling stage," and she is one who can judge.

Betty Hoffman of Evergreen Travel in Washington and her partner and son, Jack, do not take anyone's word for it but try out all sorts of "accessible" facilities, particularly cruise ships. Evergreen Travel, 4114 198th Street S.W., Lynnwood, Wash. 98036; 800-435-2288.

In a way I am reluctant to identify these pioneers because I fear that many people will call them to pick their brains and then reserve the trip directly. Try to be fair. They are not publicly financed, they live on commissions.

A longer list of agents specializing in travel for the disabled is maintained by Helen Hecker, a nurse and self-publisher. It is available for $19.95 plus $2 for shipping from Twin Peaks Press, Box 129, Vancouver, Wash. 98666; 800-637-2256.

W.P.A. Guides

When World War II was over and it was again possible to pack for auto trips, our mother went to the public library and checked out the pertinent volumes of the American Guide Series, the books on states and cities created by the unemployed authors and photographers who joined the Federal Writers Project of the 1930s. She believed in the New Deal as she believed in bourbon and she never ventured into the unknown or known without a reliable guidebook. To her, the word reliable meant that Franklin D. Roosevelt did it.

She owned a decent number of the Federal Writers Project volumes, crucially *U.S. One, Maine to Florida* and *South Carolina: A Guide to the Palmetto State*, which she bought on publication in 1941 because her family's home was in the South Carolina guide. She wrapped the ones she borrowed in covers fashioned from grocery bags, we packed nighties and toothbrushes and were ready.

The three of us, she, my sister and I, riding south in a 1937 Packard with an "A" ration sticker still on the windshield, saw things that the rest of the world sped past. One drove, one navigated and one read:

"At 1.9 miles on the main side road is a dirt road; right here 0.4 miles to Hampton Plantation." No matter that "the main side road" had been straightened, the "scenic" or "old" road could be traced and, in this case, the home of Archibald Rutledge, poet laureate of South Carolina, could be found. The poet was away from the "Home by the River" he wrote about, but his son, whom the guidebook would probably have characterized as "colorful," was at home, alone, and glad of company other than the snakeskins and bottles he was collecting in his outbuilding.

We tottered through armpit-high weeds to the riverbank and I narrowly avoided stepping on a snake, which our host said he planned to shoot. He took us through the plantation house, which he told us had been built to its full dimensions, starting in 1757, by "Daniel U-gee O-ree." From the book, we understood that these two famous Low Country names were "Huger" and Horry," although at other moments our comprehension of our host's spoken word was nip and tuck and nip.

That July day, restoration of Hampton had halted and the air from the sluggish Santee River barely kept the great vacant upstairs rooms, which had been repapered in a design of blue squares, from being an oven. In the ballroom, vast and empty, we stood and inhaled the stillness as the younger Rutledge reiterated what the book had told us, that President Washington, on a visit, had been so charmed with Eliza Lucas Pinckney, the mother of Mrs. Daniel Horry 2d, that he had later asked to serve as her pallbearer.

I am a fan of the movie *Gone With the Wind*, but every time I see it I suspect I am the only one present who is able to smell as well as see Tara's empty, musty rooms.

Growing up with guidebooks educated my taste and made me hunger for Indian burial grounds, sites of hangings, historic houses, writer's homes, places connected with John Brown, stations on the Underground Railroad, places named Ong's Hat and Cowpens and Popham. My grandmother would travel outside Spartanburg, South Carolina, to buy the best peaches, at Posey Belcher's Peach Shed, but it was years before I heard this name as laughable: The Federal Writers had conditioned me to expect and treasure the exotic, the

gritty and neglected, the uncertainty of local lore, the un-
traceability of crucial etymologies.

When our kids climbed out of strollers and into the back
seat of the auto, we headed south to pay homage at ancestral
tombs and visit Florida on roughly the same tour I took as a
young person. We packed up a rainbow of American Guide
volumes and I was stunned to find that in some cases we
were the first borrowers of the books from the Columbia
University libraries.

This time there was a chain across the ruts leading to
Hampton, so we chose instead the route to Harrietta Plantation. Finding this place involved getting to a junction at a
filling station and following a dirt road for 1.6 miles. The
children, skeptical of their elders and their old-time guidebooks and finding it all not a little spooky, were amazed when
we conjured forth a white house with a double portico
amongst the Spanish moss. "A two-story frame house, built
in 1797 by the second Mrs. Daniel Huger Horry for her
daughter Harriot," I read. We talked about the black men
and women who built and maintained these huge establishments and some about the Civil War and about the civil
rights movement, which the kids already understood. Except
for the sounds of the summer creatures, the silence was bot-
tomless, as if no one was alive for miles around.

We walked around to the front of Harrietta, to the vast
lawn and specimen trees leading to the river. "Isn't it funny,"
one son said, "it doesn't face anyplace, neighbors or anything."

We tucked the remark away in the belief that such insights
are not available at Colonial Williamsburg or Disney World.

I inherited *U.S. One* and *New York Panorama* and a couple
of others in the American Guide Series, but I bought others

wherever I encountered them. The best prices come when you find New Hampshire for $1 at an Iowa farm auction, but when the goal of owning an entire set overtook me I found myself buying *New Orleans* in the Vieux Carre for too much and barely whimpering. Like all book collectors, I prefer dust jackets and maps in the pockets, but I buy worn ones, too.

In time historians got interested in the series, and when I read *The Dream and the Deal* by Jerre Mangione, my plan suffered a setback. The output of the Federal Writers did not cover a mere 48 states and a few cities but consisted of something like 300 books, regional guides, almanacs, multistate guides and even county histories. I trimmed my goal.

The creation of the guides is itself a story terrible and wonderful. Alexander L. Crosby, a pioneer member of my union, the Newspaper Guild, on strike by himself at the *Staten Island Advance*, supervised the New Jersey guide and wrote six of the 46 tours in the book because he enjoyed them so. Vardis Fisher threw letters from Washington into the fire to keep the Idaho book from being delayed by politics. Josef Berger became Jeremiah Digges to write *Cape Cod Pilot*, a unique project (none of the other guides had an identified author) that the W.P.A. embraced and that many people think is the best written of all. The Massachusetts guide came under sharp criticism for the space it gave to Sacco and Vanzetti.

Some of the guides have been republished, sometimes with their progressive attitude retouched, sometimes with new photographs. But if you are looking for roadside history, any edition will work. Interstates may obliterate sections of state roads, but that tangential sign "Old Route 1" is usually findable. And the Indian burial ground? Keep looking.

X Ray and Film

This is one of those arguments that go on and on: Does the security X ray at the airport fog your film? The security people will tell you no, unless you are using film faster than 1000 speed, which most of us amateurs do not use. However, a number of caveats apply. First, those machines are sometimes giving out more juice than they should, unknown to their operators. Professional photographers who visited the Soviet Union in its Soviet days said that they had problems with fog unless they passed the film outside the X-ray machine, which sometimes agitated the security officers. Second, passing through a number of machines may have a cumulative effect on the film that one pass does not. Third, I do not have a lot of confidence in those film protectors that film stores offer for sale.

I use the unpatented Mahoney technique, developed by Ursula Mahoney, picture editor of the *Times* Travel Section. Label each exposed cartridge and store them in a clear plastic bag. Hand the bag, whose contents are obvious, to the security guard before you pass through. Unexposed film, still sealed in its cartons, can likewise be passed around in a plastic bag.

One last thing. Whatever you decide to do, do not forget there may still be exposed film in your camera and it needs the same treatment as the film with your precious pictures.

Notes

Notes

Notes

Notes

Notes

Notes